ἐστὶν καινὸν καὶ παλαιόν

τὸ τοῦ πάσχα μυστήριον

THE LAMB'S HIGH FEAST

SUPPLEMENTS TO

VIGILIAE CHRISTIANAE

Formerly Philosophia Patrum

TEXTS AND STUDIES OF EARLY CHRISTIAN LIFE
AND LANGUAGE

EDITORS

J. DEN BOEFT — R. VAN DEN BROEK — W.L. PETERSEN
D.T. RUNIA — J.C.M. VAN WINDEN

VOLUME XLII

THE LAMB'S HIGH FEAST

MELITO, *PERI PASCHA* AND
THE QUARTODECIMAN PASCHAL LITURGY
AT SARDIS

BY

ALISTAIR STEWART-SYKES

BRILL
LEIDEN · BOSTON · KÖLN
1998

This book is printed on acid-free paper.

Library of Congress Cataloging-in-Publication Data

Stewart-Sykes, Alistair.
    The lamb's high feast : Melito, Peri Pascha, and the Quartodeciman
paschal liturgy at Sardis / by Alistair Stewart-Sykes.
        p.   cm. — (Supplements to Vigiliae Christianae, ISSN
0920–623X ; v. 42)
    Includes index.
    ISBN 9004112367 (alk. paper)
    1. Melito, Saint, Bishop of Sardis, 2nd cent.   Homily on the
Passion.   2. Quartodecimans.   3. Liturgies, Early Christian.
I. Title.   II. Series.
BR65.M453H653   1998
263' .93—dc21   98-27580
                                                                                    CIP

Die Deutsche Bibliothek – CIP-Einheitsaufnahme

[Vigiliae Christianae / Supplements]
    Supplements to Vigiliae Christianae : formerly Philosophia Patrum ;
texts and studies of early Christian life and language. – Leiden ;
Boston ; Köln : Brill
        Früher Schriftenreihe
        ISSN 0920-623X
Stewart-Sykes, Alistair:
    The lamb's high feast : Melito, Peri Pascha and the quartodeciman
Paschal liturgy at Sardis / by Alistair Stewart-Sykes. – Leiden ;
Boston ; Köln : Brill, 1998
        (Supplements to Vigiliae Christianae ; Vol. 42)
        ISBN 90–04–11236–7

ISSN   0920-623X
ISBN   90 04 11236 7

PRINTED IN THE NETHERLANDS

MATRI MEAE ALICIAE EDITHAE STEWART
IN PIAM MEMORIAM

CONTENTS

PREFACE

In his article "The Quartodeciman Passover and the Jewish Pesach" Professor Rouwhorst expresses a certain defensiveness about devoting an entire article to the paschal liturgy of the Quartodecimans. Perhaps an even greater defensiveness should be expressed about the presentation of an entire book on the subject. However this is the first complete study since that of Lohse in 1953, since when significant textual discoveries in *Peri Pascha* mean that much greater weight can be given to that text in understanding the Quartodecimans. This is also the first attempt to understand *Peri Pascha* in the light of the forms of argumentation employed by Graeco-Roman rhetoricians, which in turn impacts on the place which might be assigned to *Peri Pascha* in the Quartodeciman liturgy.

This book began life in an undergraduate seminar at Birmingham University in 1987 conducted by Professor Frances Young, in which I first encountered Melito and *Peri Pascha* and first formulated the thesis which is presented here. The idea grew, and became in time a doctoral dissertation, presented at Birmingham University in 1992 under the direction of Professor Young and examined by Dr Iain Torrance and Professor S.G. Hall. The bulk of the work was undertaken in Cambridge University Library when I was assistant priest in the Parish of Saint Andrew and Saint George in Stevenage, England. In that time the Rector, Fr Melvyn Barnsley and the people showed great patience with their curate, and an anonymous benefactor assisted with funding the research when the Church of England expressed a lack of interest. After Dr David Parker encouraged me to seek publication years were spent in revision, during which time I was privileged to teach and learn at Codrington College in Barbados. Extensive new research was undertaken to advance the thesis and the original manuscript was completely rewritten. Professor G.A.M. Rouwhorst then read the manuscript very thoroughly on behalf of the editors of Vigiliae Christianae and made a great many suggestions for the improvement of the work. To all of those mentioned, and to many others, I am deeply indebted. The greatest debt of all however is expressed in the dedication.

Low Sunday 1998   *Birches Head Vicarage,*

Stoke-on-Trent

INTRODUCTION

The purpose of this work is to determine the place of Melito's *Peri Pascha* in the paschal liturgy of the Quartodecimans at Sardis. Its conclusion is that *Peri Pascha* constitutes the two parts of the Quartodeciman liturgy. The first part of the work is a liturgical homily on Exodus 12 which was delivered on the eve of Pascha, and the second half is the text of a commemorative ritual which constituted the celebration of Pascha itself. This conclusion is based on a formal examination of the text in the contexts of Graeco-Roman rhetoric and of Jewish and Christian paschal liturgy. On the basis of this classification it is possible to reconstruct the entire Quartodeciman paschal liturgy.

The first chapter has two objects. Firstly it deals of necessity with a number of introductory topics such as the date and authenticity of *Peri Pascha* (1.1.2) and the person of Melito himself. Melito is shown to be bishop and a Christian of Jewish descent (1.1.1). Some attention is also paid to the city in which he worked (1.1.3). These sections update the existing introductions of Hall and Perler in areas apart from the overall argument which is to follow in the book. Beyond this general introduction a contribution is made to the overall argument of the study through determining the evidentiary base which may be employed in reconstructing the rite of the Quartodecimans (1.2.2) and in attempting to place Melito in his cultural and theological context as a Johannine Christian who kept Pascha in accordance with that tradition (1.2.1). This is a necessary preliminary to the substance of the book which is to be found in the latter two chapters since it is necessary to see the Christian tradition from which the Quartodeciman tradition derived.

The second chapter is likewise a necessary prolegomenon to the main substance of the argument. Before seeking to show that *Peri Pascha* has a place in the paschal ritual of the Quartodecimans it needs to be shown that Jews at the time before the parting of the ways kept Pesah with a domestic seder (2.1.2), that part of that seder was the recitation of the haggadah (2.1.1; 2.1.4), and that these liturgical traditions might be passed on to Melito through the Christian tradition (2.1.3). This being demonstrated it is also argued that the essential point of this ritual was commemoration of the events of the Egyptian Passover (2.2). This in turn provides a rationale for the Quartodeciman liturgy celebrated by Melito.

The third chapter is a form-critical examination of *Peri Pascha*, in the life-setting both of the Hellenistic world and the (ultimately Palestinian) Jewish tradition which was passed to Melito through his Johannine heritage. This reveals the work to be a complex of forms. The first half is seen as being simultaneously a targumic midrash (3.1.7-9) and a Hellenistic rhetorical history (3.1.5) with a methodological post-script (3.1.6). The customary classification of *Peri Pascha* as a homily is thus shown to be wanting (3.1.1). The second half is shown to be simultaneously an epideictic prose-hymn (3.1.4) and a Passover haggadah (3.1.2); this latter insight builds on the seminal work of Hall, though significant doubt is thrown upon Hall's division of the text in two and his explanation of the purpose of the first half (3.2.2). Most significantly all these forms may be claimed as liturgical (3.2.3). The function of *Peri Pascha* is shown on this basis to be commemorative and so liturgical. It is intended to make present the exalted Christ to the worshipping community through the remembrance of the Egyptian Passover and of the Passover at which the crucifixion took place. It should thus be described not as a homily but as a commemoration.

In the light of these findings there follows a new look at the Quartodeciman paschal liturgy. Not only the content of the liturgy but also its background and setting are studied and all existing evidence reviewed. The subject of commemoration is shown to be the death of the Lord at the Passover (4.1.1), and it is suggested that this commemoration occurs around midnight of the 14th/15th Nisan in accordance with Johannine chronology (4.1.2). The celebration proper is preceded by a vigil which was marked by fasting (4.1.4). The existence of some controversy among Quartodecimans about the point at which the fast is to be broken is uncovered (4.1.3), but Melito is shown to be a "mainstream" Quartodeciman who breaks the paschal fast at midnight (4.1.5). The vigil is celebrated with a reading of Exodus and a typological commemoration of the Egyptian Passover (4.2.1), but without the practice of baptism (4.2.2). We suggest that the text of this commemoration is to be found in the first half of *Peri Pascha*. This is followed by a joyful celebration in the presence of the Lord (4.2.4). The second half of *Peri Pascha* is shown to be the liturgical text lying behind this celebration, as Christ is held to be present not only in proclamation but through the quasi-sacramental actions of the Quartodeciman seder, in the context of which *Peri Pascha* is delivered and as a result of which delivery Christ is held to be present (4.2.5). The effect of this is to realise the eschatological hopes of the Quartodecimans (4.2.3). The conclusion is thus that *Peri Pascha* is the oldest Christian liturgy extant in its entirety. The conclusion is reached primarily on internal grounds, but external evidence of the paschal liturgy is employed in support of this conclusion as it is shown that the conclusion reached fits neatly with the other evidence for Quartodeciman Pascha such as that contained in the *Epistula Aposto-lorum*. To conclude, some suggestions are made concerning the *Nach-leben* of the Quartodeciman liturgy in the liturgies of the later and wider church (4.2.6)

CHAPTER ONE

MELITO, SARDIS AND THE QUARTODECIMANS

The centre of this work is an analysis of *Peri Pascha* into its constituent genres and forms, in order that its place in the rite of the Quartodecimans may be established. There have been previous analyses of *Peri Pascha*, but insufficient attention has been paid to the religious and cultural background of the work and none to the rhetorical shape, as opposed to the style, of the work. We intend to make good this omission in order that the formal analysis of *Peri Pascha* may be based on a clear understanding of the religious and cultural setting of the work. This is essential in view of our central argument, that *Peri Pascha* functions simultaneously as a haggadah and a prose-hymn in the Quartodeciman Pascha, in that we must show that Melito might have access both to Jewish paschal traditions and to the rhetorical practice of the Hellenistic world. We also intend to show that Melito was a Christian schooled in the Johannine tradition, and that this tradition was essential for his understanding of pascha. So this first chapter aims to supply a general introduction to Melito of Sardis and to his work *Peri Pascha*. Beyond this general introduction it aims to contribute to the overall argument of the book by clarifying the thought-world, or combination of thought-worlds, from which *Peri Pascha* derives.

1.1 General Introduction

1.1.1 *Melito of Sardis and the Quartodecimans*

Until quite recently little was known of Melito except what is recorded of him by Eusebius.[1] Eusebius is writing of the dispute late in the second century between the churches of Rome and Asia concerning the correct time at which to celebrate the paschal mystery, whether on Sunday only or in accordance with the Jewish Passover regardless of the day of the week. He records a letter by Polycrates, the Bishop of Ephesus, recording notable figures who had kept Pascha on the fourteenth of Nisan, among whom is mentioned "Melito the eunuch

---

[1] Eusebius *HE* 5.24: 4.26.

whose whole career was in the Holy Spirit, who lies at Sardis..." Elsewhere Eusebius gives a list of Melito's works and quotes from his *Apology* to the Emperor Marcus Aurelius and from his *Eklogai*, or selections from the Old Testament, in which Melito gives us his Old Testament canon and tells of a visit to Palestine. Apart from this there are but a few inconclusive references in other ancient writers, which themselves are chiefly gathered from hints left by Eusebius.[2]

We may deduce a number of significant points from the letter of Polycrates. Firstly we may deduce that Melito had but recently died at the time in which Polycrates wrote, compared to the other authorities whom Polycrates cites, such as Philip and John the apostles. If this is the case we may date his death to ca 190. Hall dates Melito's *Apology* fairly precisely between 169 and 177, and, on the basis of the notice in Eusebius mentioned above, he dates *Peri Pascha* uncontroversially between 160 and 170.[3] A birth date can only be guessed at.

More significantly we may deduce that Melito was a member of one of those groups of Christians who became known as Quartodecimans, those who kept Pascha on the fourteenth of Nisan[4], in accordance with the custom that had been handed down from Judaism. This evidence has not, however, gone undisputed. Huber suggests that Polycrates is motivated apologetically rather than purely historically, and that this therefore makes his evidence untrustworthy.[5] He goes on to argue that Melito was not a Quartodeciman. The argument is complex, and would better be dealt with in a wider discussion concerning Quartodeciman practice in all its aspects. In essence he argues since Clement defends the Johannine chronology in his work on the Pascha which, according to one possible interpretation of Eusebius, concerned chronology and was written against Melito, then Melito must favour the synoptic chronology. Since the Quartodecimans were wedded to the Johannine chronology, then Melito could not be a Quartodeciman. Finally he notes that an eager eschatologi-

---

[2] For details see Hall *Melito of Sardis* xii

[3] Hall *Melito of Sardis* xii. Even this uncontroversial dating of *Peri Pascha* is by no means certain. See 4.1.3 below.

[4] Lohse *Passafest* 9 suggests that Quartadecimans is in fact more correct, meaning those who kept the quarta decima of the month. Huber *Passa und Ostern* 5 takes issue with this and claims Quartodeciman as correct. Since the term is in any case a translation of the Greek τεσσαρεσκαιδεκατίτες this is something of a *logomachia*. We use Quartodeciman here throughout not because we are convinced by Huber's arguments but simply because it is more common! We question whether the word really describes keeping the fourteenth of Nisan at 4.1.4 below.

[5] Huber *Passa und Ostern* 33-37

cal expectation was an essential part of the Quartodeciman practice, and that this is not displayed in *Peri Pascha*.

It is clear that there are a number of unproven premises in this argument and to deal with them all in this introduction would be to presuppose the findings of the completed work. It may be stated here, however, that the argument concerning chronology is based on a notice in Eusebius[6] whose historical value is at least as dubious as the evidence of Polycrates, and the interpretation of which is far from clear. The idea that immediate eschatological expectation is an essential part of Quartodeciman belief is derived from the *Epistula Apostolorum*, a work which derives from a Quartodeciman milieu.[7] However, the Quartodeciman provenance of any work does not dictate that everything contained therein should therefore be true of every Quartodeciman community at every time. Quartodecimans were not a denomination like Lutherans but simply a group of localised Christian communities who had in common a date and manner of celebration of the paschal mystery which distinguished them from other groups in the Church; thus even if eschatological expectation does play a central role in the pascha of *Epistula Apostolorum*, which is itself far from certain, that does not necessarily mean that the same emphasis should be found in Melito's setting.[8]

Every point in Huber's argument is highly questionable and his theory has been accepted by none.[9] Although we may hope to deal thoroughly with every point in his argument in due course, this must wait on a study both of Melito's writing and its context, and will take place in the context of a broader treatment of the issues surrounding the Quartodecimans and their practice. It remains reasonable to proceed on the working hypothesis that Melito was indeed a Quartodeciman.

Apart from the fact that Melito was a Quartodeciman, Stewart-Sykes is also able to deduce from Polycrates' statements here that Melito was Jewish by birth.[10] Polycrates lists the στοιχεῖα of Asia who were Quartodecimans and Bauckham draws attention to the artistry

---

[6] *HE* 4.26. See 3.2.2, 4.1.5 for further discussion of this notice.

[7] On *Epistula Apostolorum* as a Quartodeciman document see Stewart-Sykes "Asian Origin"

[8] On the eschatology of *Epistula Apostolorum* see Stewart-Sykes "Asian Origin"; on Melito's eschatology see 4.2.3 below.

[9] See especially Cantalamessa "Questioni Melitoniane" for an extensive critique of Huber

[10] Stewart-Sykes "Melito's Anti-Judaism" 275-279

with which Polycrates writes.[11] So he points out that the number of witnesses to Quartodeciman practice number seven, and that this indicates the completeness of their evidence, and that Polycrates therefore makes himself appear as a "supernumerary eighth." The particular luminaries enumerated by Polycrates have been chosen for some reason and Bauckham suggests that they are named because Polycrates is claiming that he is himself related to all of these in some way. He mentions that these are all his συγγενεῖς. Stewart-Sykes points out that normal classical usage employs the term συγγενής and its cognates to mean relationships within an extended family or within a nation, and to refer to relationships between families claiming a connection or states claiming a common origin. This is, he suggests, the probable sense in which Polycrates employs the term. After a consideration of the possibilities he concludes that the only possible συγγενεία to which Polycrates may be referring is Jewish. Melito was Jewish by birth, an attribute which he shares with a number of significant leaders of the Asian Christians.

We may also deduce from Polycrates' writing that Melito was Bishop of Sardis. Hall notes that whereas Polycrates names some as bishops Melito is not given this distinction, and suggests that the identification of Melito as bishop is the work of Eusebius.[12] He is able to note in this context that Ignatius of Antioch writes no letter to the Church at Sardis. The two reasons given for Ignatius' failure to write a letter to the church in Sardis are that there was no bishop, or that the extent of Judaistic practice at Sardis made Ignatius inimical to this Christian community.[13] The second reason is the more probable; we shall note below extensive ties between the Christianity of Sardis and its Jewish roots; but even if the first explanation is the correct one, and there was no bishop at the time of Ignatius, this is hardly relevant for the time of Melito, perhaps some fifty years later.

We may agree with Hall that the fact that Eusebius makes him bishop is certainly beside the point; however those described as bishops in Polycrates' list are also martyrs, and it may be this double qualification that causes him to employ the term at this point. Hall is not the first to deny that Melito was Bishop. Nautin had argued that Melito was not bishop, because he is said by Polycrates to be awaiting the ἐπισκοπή from Heaven in the resurrection.[14] According to Nautin

---

[11] Bauckham "Papias and Polycrates" 29-30
[12] Hall *Melito of Sardis* xii with reference to Polycrates, quoted by Eusebius at *HE* 5.24
[13] So Johnson "Christianity in Sardis"
[14] Nautin *Lettres et Écrivains* 71

this means that Melito *deserved* to be bishop, but was not on the grounds of his being an eunuch, a state of affairs that would be put right in the world to come! This is firmly rejected by Mohrmann;[15] the word ἐπισκοπή refers to the return of Christ.[16]

In fact Polycrates does state, elsewhere in his letter, that Melito was bishop. After his mention of the seven luminaries of Asia (the last of whom is Melito) who kept the fourteenth Polycrates goes on to say that ἑπτὰ μὲν ἦσαν συγγενεῖς μοῦ ἐπίσκοποι. We have already suggested that this is a reference to the preceding list.[17] Melito, according to Polycrates, would thus appear to have been Bishop. Moreover Polycrates refers to Melito as governing when he states that ἐν ἁγίῳ πνεύματι πάντα πολιτευσάμενον. Lawlor and Oulton translate this phrase as "lived in the Holy Spirit" and take it as a reference to Melito's piety.[18] However the use of πάντα as an object with πολιτεύομαι is unusual. Aristophanes uses ἅπαντα as the object of this verb with reference to systems of governance[19] and on this basis we may suggest that Polycrates is speaking of Melito's governance of the church in the Holy Spirit. Of course it is possible that Polycrates was wrong, for instance he makes John the Elder a bishop likewise, which is hardly probable, but the balance of probabilities is that Polycrates is better informed about Melito than about the apostolic period.

Apart from the letter of Polycrates there is little external evidence of any value. Origen attributes to Melito the idea that God is corporeal, but this may mean nothing else than that he was influenced by stoic ideas in the way that Tertullian was. A third century writer attributes to Melito belief in Christ as God and man.[20] This would mean that Melito had been concerned to combat gnosticism and docetism.[21]

So it was that until the nineteenth century Melito was little more than the name of a prolific writer and Quartodeciman luminary from Sardis. In that century Syriac fragments were discovered and identi-

---

[15] Mohrmann "Conflit Pascale" 157-158

[16] The rejection of Nautin's argument does not however mean that Melito should be automatically reinstated, as Giordano "Millenarismo" would appear to suggest.

[17] In accordance with the interpretation offered by Bauckham "Papias and Polycrates" 29

[18] *Eusebius* 186-7

[19] *Lysistrata* 573

[20] Fragment 8a according to the numbering of Hall *Melito of Sardis*

[21] The substantial correctness of this assessment of Melito's christology appears to be upheld by the rediscovered works. So Grillmeier *Christ in Christian Tradition* I 94-98 and refs. See also Cantalamessa "Meliton de Sardes: une Christologie antignostique du IIᵉ Siècle" and Hall "Christology of Melito"

fied as being from his hand. The real breakthrough however came in
1940 when the more or less complete *Peri Pascha* was first published.
It has since then been a constant focus of scholarly attention.

1.1.2 *The Discovery and Identification of Peri Pascha*

The *editio princeps* was based on a single fifth century codex, the leaves
of which had been assembled from two collections.[22] Bonner identified the work as being a homily by Melito on the basis of the heading
ΜΕΛΕΙΤΩΝ (the colophon is missing), on the grounds that its style fulfilled what might have been expected of Melito, and on the basis of
the Syriac fragments already in existence.[23] He entitled it ΕΙΣ ΤΟ ΠΑΘΟΣ
on the basis of a fragment of Anastasius of Sinai.[24] In the following
years further fragments and a Latin epitome were found, but the
most significant discovery was that of a further, almost complete
Greek version in Papyrus Bodmer 13.[25] This was entitled Μελίτωνος
περὶ πάσχα which suggested that the work was related to the Quartodeciman paschal celebrations.

Bonner's identification of the work was questioned on the grounds
that the *Peri Pascha* mentioned by Eusebius is a controversial work,
and on the basis that the attribution to Melito contained in the Chester-Beatty codex is fourth century in origin.[26] The titles and colo-
phons of the papyrus edited by Testuz and of the Coptic codex
Crosby-Schøyen, as well as the earlier date of these codices, and the
fact that the fragments are frequently attributed to Melito all might
be seen as convincing arguments in favour of its authenticity. But
Hyldahl has pointed out that titles in the patristic age served not as
precise indications of the content of the work but as means of identification.[27] From this he deduces (reasonably) that the title of the Bodmer codex is not necessarily the only correct one (Crosby-Schøyen
was as yet unedited), and that therefore the work is not necessarily of
Quartodeciman provenance. He then argues in the same way as
Huber that *Peri Pascha* is not Quartodeciman, and therefore either
that it is not by Melito or that Melito was not a Quartodeciman. He
cannot accept that Melito was not a Quartodeciman and therefore
suggests the second alternative. Similar arguments have recently been

---

[22] Bonner *Homily* 5-8
[23] Bonner *Homily* 7
[24] Fr. 7 in Hall *Melito of Sardis*
[25] Edited by Testuz *Papyrus Bodmer XIII*
[26] Nautin "Homélie"
[27] Hyldahl "Titel"

employed by Cohick[28] who, noting that Melito is not an uncommon name, and suggesting that there is nothing in *Peri Pascha* which is distinctively Quartodeciman, suggests that this work is not that referred to by Eusebius, but a work from the hand of a different Melito altogether.

We have already seen that Huber stands on shaky ground, and so Hyldahl stands with him. Assuming that the complications caused by Eusebius can be cleared up there are good grounds for persisting with the attribution to Melito.[29] These are listed by Hall and include the similarities between the style of the work and that of contemporary Asian orators, the similarities in style and content between the recovered work and other known fragments of Melito, the nature of the use of the Bible, the use of *Evangelium Petri* and the debt to Jewish paschal traditions.[30] These arguments may also be brought to bear against Cohick, who attempts to take issue with some of them. She is for instance unconvinced by the parallels between *Peri Pascha* and the Passover haggadah which Hall notes, suggesting that they are isolated phrases in common Christian currency. However it is not just the appearance of common phrases which allows us to suggest significant parallels between *Peri Pascha* and the haggadah, but a similarity of outline and a weight of parallels.[31] Cohick suggests that there is nothing typically Quartodeciman about *Peri Pascha* such as "an interest in fasting or in dating the passion". But this fails to take account of the nature of the work, which is not a learned defence of Quartodeciman practice but, as we shall see, a celebratory and liturgical realisation of the death, resurrection and return of Jesus.

We have touched here on certain of the scholarly problems related to *Peri Pascha*, namely the establishment of a text and the identification of the author, which are now reasonably assured, and the problems created by the notices in Eusebius and those of reconciling the Quartodeciman practice to any given gospel chronology, which have yet to command any consensus. It is on these aspects, and on questions of style, that the scholarly enquiry thus far has concentrated. There has also been some thinking concerning the form of *Peri Pascha*, although we contend here that this has thus far been inadequate.[32]

---

[28] Cohick "Melito and Israel"

[29] We shall attempt this at 4.1.3 below

[30] Hall *Melito of Sardis* xix. We shall deal further with each of these signs of Melito's authorship

[31] See 3.1.2 below for a detailed investigation of the parallels.

[32] The form of *Peri Pascha* is discussed principally by Hall "Melito in the light of the haggadah". His contribution is discussed in detail in 3.1.2 below.

The aim of this work is to see *Peri Pascha* in the light of the Quartodeciman paschal liturgy. This requires an examination of form, and thus of its *Sitz im Leben*, both in Melito's world and in the setting of Quartodeciman paschal liturgy. The work of form-criticism should bring us to answer the most important questions concerning this major document.

1.1.3 *Sardis*

Since it was from Sardis that Melito came and at Sardis that he worked, it may prove of assistance to have some understanding of the city as he would have known it.[33]

A very ancient city, situated on what had formerly been the great east-west highway through Asia Minor and centred on the Pacteolus River, overlooked by an acropolis and surrounded by a fertile alluvial plain, Sardis had at one time been of great strategic importance. It had ceased to be strategically significant by the time of Melito, but it remained a site of some cultural significance.

Although once the capital of the Lydian Empire, by the time of Melito it had long since been a thoroughly Greek city, since the conquest by Alexander in the fourth century BC, at which time the written Lydian language, apparently a form of Indo-European with affinities to Hittite, dies out altogether. The evidence of the period is of a thoroughgoing Hellenism extending from public buildings and governmental institutions to burial customs.

It is into this Greek context that Babylonian Jews were introduced by Antiochus III;[34] there were however Jews at Sardis even before this, according to *Obadiah* 20. This Jewish population was perhaps supplemented with Palestinian Jews in the years subsequent to the destruction of the temple.

Although the cosmopolitan ambience thus created survived into the time of Melito, and indeed beyond, the physical city was somewhat different as a result of the earthquake in 17 AD, which flattened the city. Mitten notes that those to whom the letter in *Revelation* was addressed would still have memories affected by that event.[35] The city was then rebuilt, largely out of public funds and with imperial assist-

---

[33] On the archaeology of ancient Sardis in general Mitten "New Look" and Hanfmann, Yegül, and Crawford "Roman and Late Antique Period"

[34] Josephus *AJ* 14.235. Zeuxis, Antiochus' general, had his headquarters at Sardis. See Kraabel "ΥΨΙΣΤΟΣ" 86

[35] Mitten "New Look" 61

ance. Construction was slow, proceeding as funds allowed, but by the time of Melito the chief features of this city of 100,000 souls would have been recognizable.

The main Roman street of the city was of marble, 12.5 metres wide and running along the east-west axis. It had an elevated pavement and a colonnade of shops on either side. Behind this main street to the north was the gymnasium complex, which was eventually to consist of a pair of halls 100 metres long with an oiling room. At the time of Melito however only the gymnasium proper stood, having been finished about 166 AD. Between the gymnasium and the main street was a thriving bazaar area, including a Jewish section.

This centre was situated near the Pacteolus, on the east bank, and to the north of the city, while settlement extended to the south and east, up the hillside and away from the valley itself.

It is on the prime, central site that the synagogue was found. It is certainly the largest and perhaps the richest Roman synagogue to have been discovered. Its date, however, is uncertain. Originally it was dated to the fourth century, and was subsequently dated to the time of Melito. It is now thought that its construction began not long after the earthquake, but that it was not originally a synagogue but a civic building, perhaps an adjunct to the gymnasium. It underwent rebuilding and was subsequently given to the Jewish community, perhaps in the third century, when further rebuilding was undergone.[36] There had been Jews in Sardis for a long time, they were free to practise their religion and, apart from simply being prosperous, were citizens. Melito exhibits a great deal of anti-Jewish sentiment and it has been argued that this is the result of the differing social situation of the Christians and the Jews. Moreover, expulsion from the synagogue had been an issue for Christians in Asia Minor late in the first century and by the time of Melito may still have been so.

Apart from Jews, the place of God-fearers in Sardis should be considered briefly. Excavations at the synagogue, whilst affording evidence for a later period, do provide evidence for extensive donations made by persons with Greek names. Thus the large marble *menorah* was given by a Sokrates, a balustrade rail by the sons of Marcus. Other names include Polyhippos, Pegasios, Euphrosynos. These, Mit-

---

[36] Seager "Building History" collects the evidence. His findings are questioned by Botermann "Synagoge". In any event, it may be noted here that the synagogue is not of a date such that it would have been known to Melito. It must therefore be used with extreme caution in assessing Judaism at Sardis in the second century. This subject is treated well by Trebilco *Jewish Communities* 37-55.

ten states, attest the extent of the absorption of Jews into Graeco-
Roman culture.[37] However, that these are Jews is an assumption
only; we should reckon with the possibility that these are gentiles who
are sympathetic to Judaism. Polyhippos for instance is described as
θεοσεβής, as Trebilco notes.[38] John tells of the Greeks who visited
Jerusalem for the Passover and Barrett suggests that they are θεοσε-
βαί and as such may reflect the conduct of Asian gentiles at the time
of John.[39] It is on the basis of such evidence as this that Trebilco
concludes that there was a fair degree of gentile interest in Judaism in
second century Asia.[40]

Of course Judaism and Christianity were not the only religions at
Sardis in the period. Among other religions most notable is the cult of
Artemis, the civic cult. To her was dedicated the large Hellenistic
temple by the Pacteolus. She appears to have taken on some of the
appurtenances of the native Cybele.[41] The worship of Sabazios was
also common in Sardis but he appears to have been identified with
Zeus and also with the god of the Jews;[42] apart from Sabazios the
numismatic evidence indicates that Herakles and Dionysius were also
worshipped. Although Hemer suggests that the identification of Artemis and Cybele may provide some indication of the survival of
native Lydian religion at the time of Melito they are so extensively
Hellenized that there are really no grounds for such an assertion
though native religion would perhaps have been more tenacious in
the countryside than in the city.[43] Melito refers to the Pascha as a
μυστήριον and Hansen suggests that the reference is made in the
context of the mystery religions;[44] but whereas this would accord with
the evidence of a growing interest in native religion at the time of
Melito,[45] particularly among the educated classes, Melito's Judaism
would to an extent exclude him from this interest. Hansen suggests in
similar light that Polycrates' description of Melito as a eunuch is an
indication that he was a converted priest of Cybele. Again the reference is to be seen in the light of his Jewish Christian heritage as an

---

[37] Mitten "New Look" 64-65 assumes that these are Jews. In either instance it
indicates a significant degree of commerce between the synagogue and gentile Sardis
[38] Trebilco *Jewish Communities* 158-159
[39] Barrett *Gospel of John and Judaism* 18-19, with reference to *John* 12:20
[40] Trebilco *Jewish Communities* 164-166
[41] So Hemer *Letters* 138-140
[42] Johnson "Christianity in Sardis" 82 and refs
[43] As indicated by the discovery north of Sardis of an inscription to the mother of
the gods, noted by Mitchell *Anatolia* II 22
[44] Hansen *Sitz* 121
[45] Johnson "Asia Minor" 83

indication of his asceticism. Too much emphasis may perhaps be placed on the mysteries, given the distinctly exoteric nature of pagan religions in the region.[46] Perhaps more significant than the mysteries is the imperial cultus; according to Tacitus, Sardis competed with ten other Asian cities to be the home of a temple to Tiberius, and pleaded its case before the Senate.[47] The evidence of visits from both Marcus Aurelius and Verus is an indication that imperial loyalty continued to run high in the time of Melito.[48]

A prosperous city in Asia Minor, recovered from a devastating earthquake some 150 years before and now expanding. A significant Jewish presence giving a somewhat cosmopolitan atmosphere to a city which was both loyal to Rome and a centre of Hellenistic culture. Such was Sardis at the time of Melito.

1.1.4 *Conclusion*

This has been a preliminary introduction to Melito, his city and his work. In it we have been able to demonstrate that Melito was a Quartodeciman and that *Peri Pascha* is his work. We have also uncovered a suspicion that his work is in some way related to the Jewish tradition. We have also noted that Melito would inevitably have been influenced by the norms of Hellenistic civic and cultural life, which in turn opens up the possibility that Hellenistic rhetorical forms might be present in Melito's work. This much has in turn uncovered the necessity of tracing Melito's Christian tradition, a task to which we now turn.

1.2 The Quartodeciman Christian Tradition

1.2.1 *Christianity at Sardis*

It is not known when Christianity first came to Sardis, however the letter to the Christians at Sardis in *Revelation* would not only indicate that there was a congregation already in existence, but the words that they who had the reputation of being alive are now dead would indicate that the congregation had been in existence for some time.

---

[46] A point noted by Mitchell *Anatolia* II 11-30

[47] *Annales* 4.55

[48] Evidence of these visits is provided by an inscription to Verus found at the synagogue site (for details of which see Trebilco *Jewish Communities* 44) and by the apology of Melito to Marcus Aurelius (on which see in particular Hall *Melito of Sardis* xii)

The question thus arises as to the nature of its origins. We have
already suggested that in order to understand Melito's Christianity
we must trace it back to its Palestinian origins, and so the task is all
the more important. Essentially we intend to suggest that the Christian tradition of Melito was Johannine.

Much has been written on John and the Quartodecimans, but the
greatest amount of nineteenth century scholarship was concerned directly with questions of Johannine history, chronology and authorship
and more recent work with questions of Quartodeciman chronology
directly.[49] The first argument is no longer an issue and it seems to us
that the second cannot be settled without first undertaking a more
general study of John and Melito in isolation from any particular
issue.

Sardis is not far from Ephesus and during the Roman period was
well-connected by road. According to tradition it was at Ephesus that
John wrote his Gospel. Of course the tradition is not unquestioned,
but it is a more probable place of origin than any other suggested.[50]
There are moreover connections between the work of Melito and
that of the fourth evangelist and those in his tradition apart from
geographical proximity, though on the basis of this geographical
proximity we should note the initial similarity between John and
Melito which emerges when one takes account of their attitudes towards Judaism. Barrett paints a picture of John as in a situation akin
to that of Melito, one of uncertainty in definition, where there are
Jewish and anti-Jewish elements together held in tension, neither to
be seen in isolation from the wider Hellenistic world, and where there
is also an element of nascent gnosticism at work.[51] Stewart-Sykes has
shown that the picture regarding relationships to Judaism at least is
analogous. Both are simultaneously Jewish and anti-Jewish, both live
in Asia surrounded by strong Jewish communities, both find a repudi-
ation of Judaism as a necessary concomitant of their acceptance of
Christianity and supersession of the Torah implied in their belief in
Jesus.[52]

Most significant of all, however, is the place which Melito finds in
the letter of Polycrates recorded by Eusebius,[53] where he is listed last

---

[49] Lohse *Passafest* 20-40 provides an interesting review of the early period of scholarship on this issue. The chronological issue is still not settled
[50] The location of Ephesus is most recently and most ably supported by Hengel
Johannine Question and Bauckham "Papias and Polycrates" 29-30
[51] Barrett *Gospel of John* 69-76 in summary
[52] Stewart-Sykes "Melito's Anti-Judaism"
[53] *HE* 5.24

among the apostolic worthies of Asia who await the resurrection. At the head of the list is Philip "one of the twelve" and second is John. Also figuring in the list is Polycarp, according to Irenaeus a disciple of John.[54] Since Eusebius is handling very ancient tradition there would appear to be good historical grounds for linking Melito with the Johannine tradition.[55] Polycrates is attempting to trace Quartodeciman practice to the apostolic period, and in this respect John is a key figure. Although it will be necessary to explore the passion chronology of the Quartodecimans in considerably more depth below, we may suggest that there is a prima facie case that Quartodeciman practice is founded on a Johannine passion chronology, and that the chronology of the fourth Gospel represents the Quartodeciman practice of its author.

Whilst examining the letter of Polycrates one may also note that among the figures mentioned by Polycrates Philip's daughters prophesied,[56] as did Polycarp.[57] It is in this light that we should consider later reports that Melito was considered a prophet.[58] We may moreover perceive this prophetic strand in Melito's Christian tradition as further evidence of its roots in Johannine Christianity. The Jesus of the fourth Gospel is portrayed as an enthusiastic prophet, this in turn perhaps illustrating the prophetic practice of the author of the Gospel[59] and the Johannine community's experience of the paraclete.[60] In particular we may see the "I sayings" of the fourth Gospel as representative of prophecy, and may thus note the parallel with Melito.[61] It is in the light of Melito's repute as a prophet that we should read the climax of *Peri Pascha*:

Come all nations of men compounded with sins,
and receive forgiveness of sins.

---

[54] Recorded at *HE* 3.39, 5.20

[55] A sure sign of the antiquity of Eusebius' sources here is the discrepancy between the sources themselves and the use to which Eusebius puts them. See Zernov "Eusebius"

[56] *HE* 3.37

[57] διδάσκαλος ἀποστολικὸς καὶ προφητικὸς γενόμενος ἐπίσκοπος. (*Martyrium Polycarpi* 16.2)

[58] Jerome *De Viris Illustribus* 24 quoting Tertullian. Eusebius records a λόγος αὐτοῖ (Melito) προφητείας (*HE* 4.26), which may be a discourse, or may be a collection of Melito's own prophecies.

[59] So Boring "Influence"

[60] On the paraclete as the spirit of prophecy and preaching see in particular Johnston *Spirit Paraclete* 135-141

[61] Dunn "Prophetic 'I'-sayings" denies that the "I" sayings of the synoptic gospels are prophetic in origin, but his arguments do not apply to the situation in the fourth Gospel.

> For I am your forgiveness,
> I am the Passover of salvation..[62]

This is directly comparable to the climax of the discourse at John 6:32-58:

> I am the living bread which came down from Heaven.
> If anyone eat of this bread he will live for ever....

Melito and John may be seen as representatives of a type of Asian prophetic Christianity which also emerges in the *Epistula Apostolorum* and in the Montanist controversy.[63]

Given that Melito was seen to stand in the historical tradition established by John and that their Christianity was of the same prophetic type we would expect to find distinct theological similarities. Such similarities are not hard to find. For instance le Guillou notes that for Melito the Resurrection and the Ascension/Glorification are seen as different aspects of the one movement.[64] This emphasis on the exalted Christ is again surely reminiscent of the Johannine tradition, not simply of the visions in *Revelation* but of the exaltation tradition underlying John's Gospel.[65]

Yet more significantly we may note the similar typology of the two authors. Melito has a theory of typology according to which the type, say the first Passover, precedes the reality, the salvation worked by Jesus, which fulfils it. A very similar typological scheme may be seen at work in *John*; for instance the descent of the manna given to the Israelites in the wilderness is a type of Christ's descent as a gift of salvation. Melito's typological theory is given an extensive treatment by Huber, who, apart from expounding this section of *Peri Pascha*, attempts to find the origins of the theory and finds them in the Johannine school.[66] For although he notes similarities between Melito's and Paul's typological treatments of the paschal mystery, he notes the distinct difference between them; for Melito the Old Testament events had their own worth and value in their own time whereas for Paul all attempts to achieve justification through the law are doomed. In *John* on the other hand the law had grace in itself; the grace brought by Christ may be such as to outweigh it, and in outweighing

---

[62] PP103. Hawthorne "Christian Prophets" 117 similarly regards this as an example of prophecy.

[63] See Stewart-Sykes "Asian context"

[64] le Guillou "Résurrection" 540-541

[65] So, throughout the farewell discourses Jesus talks of glorification without once mentioning resurrection.

[66] Huber *Passa und Ostern* 95-104

to invalidate it, but this does not mean that it had not validity on its own. Whilst this argument depends on a somewhat controversial reading of Paul and his attitude towards the law, the truth of its representation of John and the similarity between the Johannine theory and that of Melito stand out clearly. Paul does not speculate on the consequences for the type of its fulfilment, as Huber points out, whereas the validity of the type in itself is as implicit in the work of John as it is explicit in that of Melito.[67]

However, apart from isolated instances of typology there have been various attempts to see a typological scheme based on *Exodus* at work underpinning the entire structure of *John*. These are roundly criticized by Reim.[68] Apart from being over-elaborate they do not reflect the theology of *John*. This derives from the milieu of wisdom, that is concerned with eternal verities. And so it is not a question of the repetition of an event which took place in the *Urzeit* being repeated in the *Endzeit* but rather "das, was in der Urzeit geschah, ist hinweis auf das Geschehen des Eigentlichen in der Christuszeit."[69] As in *John* so in *Peri Pascha*. In this context Reim notes the intrusion of ἀληθινός in *John* 6:32; this is reflected by Melito's ἀλήθεια, the description of the reality as opposed to the type. John has a theory of typology in his armoury, and although he does not use it as consistently as does Melito, it is nonetheless substantially the same theory; whereas the law was given by Moses grace and truth came through Jesus Christ. Both the thought and the language here are as much Melito's as they are John's.[70]

Implicit in Melito's typology is the antithesis between τύπος and ἀλήθεια. Is there an echo of *John* at PP4, ὁ μὲν γὰρ τύπος ἐγένετο, ἡ δὲ ἀλήθεια ηὑρίσκετο?[71] The most striking use of this is made by Melito at PP7, where echoing John's prologue he states ὁ νόμος λόγος ἐγένετο. This is noted by Suggit in an article in which he seeks to argue that John's λόγος would have echoed νόμος for his Jewish readers.[72] He notes that the Septuagint in *Psalm* 118 (119 Hebrew) sometimes translates דבר with νόμος, and suggests that what is predicated of the law in the psalm is in turn predicated of Jesus in the Gospel. He believes that Melito is working in a similar context; we may note that he is working in the same exegetical tradition. ὁ νόμος λόγος ἐγένετο

---

[67] Huber *Passa und Ostern* 102
[68] Reim *Studien* Appendix A "Typologie im Johannesevangelium." Conclusions on 268.
[69] Reim *Studien* 268
[70] So compare PP7 with *John* 1:17
[71] The line is found also in ps-Hippolytus.
[72] Suggit "*John* 17:17"

refers both to Christ and his Gospel. According to Cantalamessa the λόγος-νόμος antithesis which may be found in *Peri Pascha* is an element of catechetical instruction;[73] in this case it is anchored all the more in the Johannine tradition rather than simply being an individual trait of Melito.

Another interesting link is at PP4, in which, in common with John, Melito makes Christ's body an image of the temple, and uses it, in keeping with *John* 2:19-21 as an anti-temple polemic. Finally we should note that just as John's work contains an anti-docetic and anti-gnostic christology, so does that of Melito.[74] We noted this aspect of Melito's work above, and so to establish a link between John and Melito at this point we need only note the similarities. Melito has inherited this part of the theological tradition, and would appear to have inherited its opponents as well.

This emphasis on the unity of Christ and the Father lives on in the Johannine tradition. Hall makes a strong case for *Peri Pascha* and the *Acta Johannis* deriving from the same Asian tradition at the centre of which lies the Gospel of John itself.[75] He notes the way in which *Peri Pascha* 7-9 revolves around certain Johannine key-words, λόγος, νόμος, χάρις, ἀλήθεια, ἀμνός, υἱός, ἄνθρωπος and θεός. Both the *Acta* and Melito are free in their employment of the title θεός of Jesus, deriving from the Gospel tradition. Exceptional and unique however are the employment of χάρις and πατήρ as attributes of Christ; there appear to be direct verbal echoes of the common tradition, since in a list of attributes Melito holds the two together, whereas at the parallel passage in the *Acta*, c95, they occur at each end of the list. In either event these are terms which are emphasized. One may suggest that the reason for this emphasis lies in the anti-docetic polemic of Asian Christianity.[76] More tellingly, the christology of the *Acta* implied in these terms may, like that of Melito, be described as christological monotheism.[77] On this basis, even if the *Acta* are not themselves Asian[78] we may see them as standing within the Johannine tradition

---

[73] Cantalamessa *Omelia* 59

[74] On John's anti-docetism see in particular Schnelle *Antidocetic Christology*; on Melito see in particular Cantalamessa "Christologie anti-gnostique"

[75] Hall "Melito's Paschal Homily and the *Acts of John*"

[76] For further references to this Asian type of christology see Stewart-Sykes "Asian Context"

[77] The term of Hall "Melito's christology". One may compare that employed by Schäferdiek "Herkunft" 266, where he refers to the "Christomonismus" of the *Acta*

[78] For a discussion of this question see Schäferdiek "Herkunft"; widespread scholarly opinion in the past has suggested that they are Alexandrian on the grounds of their gnostic tendencies, but this opinion is now to an extent under review

as a development of the tradition produced within circles stemming from the original Johannine school;[79] in particular, insofar as the *Acta* encourage encratism we may see that they would fit with the attitude of the "eunuch" Melito.

This is not a list of references to the fourth Gospel in Melito's work. These are not in fact particularly numerous, and are allusions attributable to the tradition rather than direct citations of the text. However these links are more significant than simple references because they demonstrate not that Melito had the fourth Gospel at his disposal but that Johannine theology is digested, and provides Melito's theological and mental structure. This would imply that the community originated as a Johannine community and continued in the Johannine tradition, and is therefore Jewish-Christian in its direct antecedent, deriving immediately from the Palestinian tradition.[80]

Yet further evidence of the strong Palestinian links of Melito's Christianity may be provided by his use of the theme of the *aqedah*. One of the most striking things about Melito's list of those who, as types of Christ, suffer in the Old Testament is his mention that Jesus is bound as Isaac.[81] This puts Melito in direct touch with the Jewish traditions of the binding of Isaac; this theme may be present in the New Testament by implication but its statement by Melito is explicit.[82] The binding of Isaac is an event strongly connected with the Passover- it is one of the four nights of salvation, together with creation, Pascha and eschaton, and is given extensive treatment in the targums. The story develops towards one in which Isaac is a mature man, readily giving his consent to the sacrifice and in which the sacrifice is actually offered. This becomes so linked with the Passover lamb that in *Jubilees* 17:15-18:19 the Passover becomes a commemoration of the aqedah. The targum *Neofiti* refers to Isaac as "the lamb of the burnt offering".[83]

---

[79] So Pervo "Johannine Trajectories"

[80] Jewish Christianity is a term which is notoriously difficult to define. However Kraft, a prominent critic of the term's abuse, is himself satisfied that there is a *Zeitgeist* which may lend itself to such a description. So Kraft "In Search of 'Jewish Christianity'"; Kraft "Multiform Jewish Heritage". Whilst there was no self-defining group calling themselves "Jewish Christians" and so no homogeneous theology of that school, Jewish Christianity may be employed as a term to describe a form of Christianity which is in close contact with the Judaism of the first century and continues certain Jewish practices such as the keeping of Pascha.

[81] PP49 and 69

[82] So Wilken "Melito" 62-63. Significant treatments of the *aqedah* in the New Testament may be found in Stegner *Narrative Theology* 13-31, and Daley *Christian Sacrifice* 175-186

[83] Wilken "Melito" 58-62 and references.

This is the tradition of which Melito is in receipt. Not only is it mentioned in *Peri Pascha*, a number of fragments on the subject have survived, which are treated by Wilken.[84] In accordance with his manner of treating the Old Testament he seems to be arguing that in contrast to Isaac, Jesus actually was offered, and that his sacrifice is effective, whereas Isaac was not so offered, and cannot therefore be effective. It provides a type of which Jesus' suffering was the reality. In fragment 9 Isaac himself is the type of Jesus, Abraham is the type of God the Father, who is not ashamed to put his son to death, and Isaac carrying the wood becomes a type of Jesus carrying his cross. There is also a reference to the suffering servant, indicating a certain flexibility of reference between Isaac and the ram. This becomes manifest in fragment 10, Isaac is the type of one redeemed, it is the ram which is offered on his behalf which is the type of Christ. In fragment 11 the same is true, the tree becomes the cross, and interestingly it is situated in Jerusalem, just as for Melito the crucifixion took place in the middle of Jerusalem.[85]

Melito's concern is to demonstrate the truth of the offering of Jesus by use of his typological method of exegesis. He is in receipt of a set of traditions concerning the *aqedah* as a redemptive offering of suffering, and it is also possible that he is aware of the difficulty felt in Judaism to which Wilken adverts, that Isaac's offering was not actually complete. In any case we have a strong link with Jewish tradition here. It is also, again, a link with echoes of *John*, and conceivably mediated through that tradition rather than through the Sardis synagogue, as Wilken suggests.[86] We have noted the description of Isaac in *Neofiti* as "the lamb of the burnt offering"; does the same thought not lie behind John's description of Jesus as "the lamb of God"? This line of argument may be strengthened by noting that for Melito and the Dura Europos synagogue alike there is a link between the temple mount and the *aqedah*/crucifixion, just as for John the crucifixion is so timetabled as to coincide with the slaughter of the lambs in the temple. Although Melito asserts that Jesus died in the evening, this does not mean that he is not in touch with the Johannine tradition, since

---

[84] Wilken "Melito" 64-67 treats the fragments numbered 9-12 in Hall *Melito of Sardis*

[85] Harvey "Melito and Jerusalem" argues that Melito so situates the crucifixion on geographical grounds, on the basis of information gathered on his visit to Palestine. The reasoning is however theological; Melito is thinking of the slaughter of the lambs. The site of the Temple is already identified with Mount Moriah, the place where Isaac was offered, in *II Chronicles* 3:1.

[86] Wilken "Melito" 67-69

the link between the lamb and the Lord is made strongly enough throughout the work.[87] In this light we may perceive Jesus' carrying of his own cross as being a typological representation of Isaac.[88]

Whilst we differ from Wilken in suggesting that Melito has received the *aqedah* tradition through the Christian tradition rather than directly from local Jewish sources, this comes about in part in that we differ from him in our view of the origins of Christianity at Sardis. Wilken suggests that Sardis may have been evangelized by Paul,[89] but it is not Pauline Christianity which took root here, but one deriving from John. Wilken perceives Melito's anti-Judaism deriving from the nearby presence of the synagogue, but as we have already noted, the synagogue is not contemporary with Melito. Moreover no trace of any depiction of the *aqedah* has been found at the Sardis synagogue. Whereas Melito's knowledge of the *aqedah* may have been derived from the Jewish community within Sardis, and the implicit supersessionist theology of his treatment of Isaac may be aimed against that community, this is speculation only given that there is clear evidence of a tradition rooted in Palestine being passed to Melito through the medium of the Quartodeciman Christian tradition.

The Jews of Sardis were mainly Babylonian in origin, and notably little is known of Babylonian Judaism of the period. Attempts to classify *Peri Pascha* as a haggadah or to explain its paschal function are based of necessity on Palestinian evidence. Indeed, if local Jewry were the source of Melito's practice and information this would constitute a fatal objection to any attempt to classify or to understand *Peri Pascha* in this way given Melito's uncompromising views on the guilt of the Jews. The point is that the Quartodecimans were not consciously imitating the Jews but derived their paschal practice from their Johannine Christian roots, and that what holds good of their paschal practice holds good for all aspects of their faith and cult.

However, these links with the Johannine school give rise to further questions given that the first evidence of Christianity at Sardis is provided by the book of Revelation, with its inclusion of a letter to the church at Sardis. Thus the question of the relationship between the Christianity of the seer and that of the fourth Gospel is raised.

---

[87] For Melito's timing of the crucifixion in the evening and the tradition behind this assertion see 4.1.2 below.

[88] cf Schnackenburg *Gospel* 270 who denies a connection on the grounds that he can find no other *aqedah* typology in *John*. However this is to ignore the connection between pascha and *aqedah*.

[89] Wilken "Melito" 55. Wilken admits that there is no direct evidence for this.

This question is of such a nature not to permit a final answer in a work devoted essentially to Melito. Therefore only those indications of a relationship directly pertinent to *Peri Pascha* will be studied here. Thus when Fiorenza argues that there is little common ground between the Fourth Gospel and *Revelation,* she argues this most strongly on the basis of the different theologies of the two works which, she argues, would make a circle improbable, and on the grounds of the different language, which would make a school unlikely.[90] We cannot follow all her arguments here but in this context she discusses the lamb imagery of the two books, and in this discussion we may join since it is of most immediate importance for a discussion concerned to uncover the background of the community which produced *Peri Pascha*. She sees a Passover imagery which is common to the two works but suggests that they have been developed in different ways. She notes that two entirely different words are used, ἀμνός in the Gospel and ἀρνίον in the Apocalypse. (ἀρνίον is used in the 21st chapter of *John* but one cannot pin a redactional argument on one word. Melito uses ἀμνός and, under the influence of *Exodus* 12:3 and *Isaiah* c53, πρόβατον.) She also points out that the function of the lamb in the Gospel is expiatory whereas in *Revelation* the lamb takes on the attributes of the Messiah.

Both these elements are present in *Peri Pascha,* and both transformed, in line with Melito's typological theory. Firstly at PP5 (text uncertain), in a list of types fulfilled, there are the two pairs lamb-son and sheep-man, and the man is revealed to be Christ (Messiah). It is the lamb which suffers (the Gospel) but is nonetheless a type of the Messiah (the Apocalypse.). Substantially the same point is made with the same pairs at PP8. Throughout the treatment of the first Passover the sheep is seen as being slain, but this is understood only because the mystery of the Lord (Κυρίου) is seen in the blood on the doorposts. The sheep has a messianic title. Finally we may note the words of the Messiah in triumph at PP103, "I am the lamb slain for you." The lamb is always the lamb slain or led to slaughter but we are never allowed to forget that he is also Χριστός and Κυρίος, here using the language of divine self-revelation.

Although this is an isolated example, it is an important one. It would indicate in the first case that for both works the Passover is a festival of significance, and that both are still working in a Jewish Christian context. Next it would indicate that by the time of Melito the schools have united. We have already observed that Melito is a

---

[90] Fiorenza "Quest"

disciple of the tradition of the fourth Gospel, but nonetheless he writes about the Apocalypse.[91] His paschal theology shows links with that of the fourth evangelist, links which will have to be further explored, but we shall also note below that the seer likewise has an extensive knowledge of Jewish Passover tradition.[92]

Fiorenza concludes her essay by suggesting that Ephesus was a place where traditions intersected and co-existed. If this is so then it is also likely that they might unite and become co-terminous, and in this case it would seem that this has happened by the time of Melito, in the nearby Sardis at least.[93] Melito is heir to a tradition in which the paschal theology of the fourth Gospel has been fused with that of the seer. Moreover it should be noted that the anti-synagogue polemic combined with strong Jewish elements which is characteristic of *Revelation* is equally characteristic of the fourth Gospel, and of Melito. We intend to suggest therefore that Quartodeciman Christianity is not only Palestinian in origin, but is rooted in Asia. This has come about because of the pervasive influence of the Johannine school and in this sense may be described as Jewish Christian.

An alternative view of Quartodecimanism as Jewish Christian is canvassed by Chilton.[94] He suggests that Quartodeciman practice is founded upon an association of Eucharist and Passover, and that this association was the result of a deliberate policy within Jerusalem circles of restricting the eucharist to Jews. Against this we have to note not only the markedly Johannine flavour of so much Asian Christianity in the second century, a Johannine chronology being part of the Quartodeciman tradition,[95] but also the absence of any actual association between eucharist and Passover in the Quartodeciman literature. Chilton's reconstruction of this attitude within the circle of the Jerusalem disciples is inevitably speculative; this would be permissible did it not contradict the evidence. It is far more likely that the association between Passover and the Last Supper found in the synoptic

---

[91] Eusebius *HE* 4.26. Blank *Meliton* 21 treats Melito's writing on *Revelation* as evidence of his Johannine background without due caution.

[92] 2.1.3

[93] Another example of this happening may be provided by the similarities between *John* 19:37 and *Revelation* 1:7. Both quote *Zechariah* in slightly different ways and yet there is no use of a collection of testimonia here, but rather a piece of text and interpretation which is held in common. See further Freed *Old Testament Quotations* 115-116 and 125

[94] Chilton *Feast of Meanings* 100-103

[95] It is true that some Quartodecimans associated Pascha with a synoptic chronology, but this is for reasons entirely unassociated with the origins of the tradition. We deal with this at 4.1.4 below.

tradition came about for liturgical reasons; the memory of the death of Jesus and Passover were so bound up that the memorial of the death of the Lord became attracted into Passover itself.[96] In support of this we may note indications of a liturgical Sitz im Leben within the Markan text itself.[97]

In supporting the Johannine origin of Quartodeciman practice it becomes necessary to enquire into the possibility of Pauline influence. Might Sardis have been evangelized by Paul? Although Wilken speculates that Paul may have visited Sardis Johnson is followed by Hansen in arguing strongly that even if he did, he did not evangelize there.[98]

If Paul had visited Sardis, he would have done so on either the second or the third of his missionary journeys. Concerning the second, *Acts* 16:7-8 states that when Paul had reached the border of Mysia he attempted to enter Bithynia but was forbidden. So he went to Troas. The question revolves on the route he took; the narrative states that Paul and Silas παρελθόντες δὲ τὴν Μυσίαν κατέβησαν εἰς Τρῳάδα. The most natural understanding of παρέρχομαι is "pass by" and of καταβαίνω "go down". This would seem to indicate a northern route, travelling north first, passing by Mysia, and then west, going down to the sea. If παρέρχομαι is read as "pass through" there is a chance that Paul may have taken a southerly route which would involve travelling west first and going through Sardis, next turning north and going through Pergamum. Hansen seems to think that the latter route is more direct, and so favours a Pauline visit to Sardis on the second missionary journey. An examination of the map that he employs would indicate that this is a moot point, although admittedly there is some unclarity as to where exactly κατὰ Μυσίαν might be.[99] In any case Paul would not have preached on this journey since this would have been in breach of the prohibition to speak the word in Asia.[100]

---

[96] A process suggested by Feneberg *Christliche Passafeier*

[97] So Trocmé *Passion as Liturgy*

[98] So Wilken "Melito" 55, opposed by Johnson "Laodicaea" and Hansen *Sitz* 82-85

[99] The map in question is that of Ramsay *Historical Geography* map facing 24. Metzger *St. Paul's Journeys* is not explicit concerning the route. His map, facing 30, does not seem to take Paul on any road depicted by Ramsay

[100] The reason for the prohibition is unclear. It is possible that this would have been the result of interference in other Christian missions since it is possible that Peter may have been in Bithynia and John in Ephesus. This was suggested by Weiss, who is quoted without reference by Bigg *Epistles* 79

The narrative of *Acts* is even more terse concerning the third missionary journey, stating simply that Paul went through the interior of
the province on the way to Ephesus. The main trade route at this
time was not the royal road through Sardis but one which passed to
the south. It is almost certainly this route which Paul took.

Having said this, Hansen notes the statement of *Acts* 19:10 that
everyone in Asia heard the word.[101] Even allowing for hyperbole this
would indicate that some in Sardis at least may have been touched by
the Pauline gospel. However, whether or not Paul visited Sardis the
evidence points to a form of Christianity in many ways close to Judaism, rather than Pauline gentile Christianity, being prevalent at
Sardis. On the basis of *Galatians* 4:10 a Quartodeciman practice
would hardly be a mark of a Pauline congregation! We have already
observed with approval Johnson's suggestion that the extent of Judaistic practice at Sardis may be a reason why there is no letter to a
Bishop at Sardis from Ignatius of Antioch.[102]

But overmuch speculation is fruitless. We are really in the land of
speculation inhabited by Bauer, who at Ephesus saw an originally
Pauline church refounded by Jewish Christians from Palestine under
the leadership of "John", the main opponent of this "orthodox"
church being gnosticism.[103] Similarly Koester, self-consciously following the steps of Bauer, sees five influences in western Asia Minor.[104]
Insofar as his picture is more complex it is more satisfactory, but he
does not, particularly in view of what has been discussed in this work
concerning the Johannine nature of the church in Sardis, lend sufficient weight to this school. This is particularly surprising since Johnson had long before suggested that Johannine/Palestinian influence
might be dominant in Anatolia during this period.[105] This present
work adds evidence to this claim. Koester sees the school producing
Revelation as an apocalyptic school, but the possibility of it being in any
way linked to the school of the Evangelist is not broached.

With this we may conclude this brief examination of Christianity
in Sardis at the time of Melito and the Christian tradition which he
inherited. However, the most puzzling question that would have to be
answered by any history of Christianity at Sardis is that of what
happened to Christianity in the town after the time of Melito. Did the

---

[101] Hansen *Sitz im Leben* 86
[102] Johnson "Christianity in Sardis" 83 following Bauer *Orthodoxy and Heresy* 79-80
[103] Bauer *Orthodoxy and Heresy* 77-79
[104] Koester "ΓΝΩΜΑΙ ΔΙΑΦΟΡΑΙ" 279-318
[105] Johnson "Early Christianity". However, by the time of "Asia Minor and Early
Christianity" he appears to assent to Koester's reconstruction

synagogue ever become a church? Kraabel suggests that it continued
to flourish well into the Constantinian era, receiving a renewal under
Julian. He further notes that both Chrysanthios, the teacher of Julian,
and Eunapios, his biographer, were natives of Sardis, and suggests
that Julian's policy was to support the Jewish population in the town
at the expense of the Christians. The point is that the Jews were still
strong enough to be supported in this manner, and Kraabel suggests
that their economic power was such that they gained the sympathy of
the native population;[106] that Sardis, in fact, was never Christianized.

Botermann, however, reads the archaeological evidence from the
synagogue differently, and suggests that this odd building could quite
well have been taken over for Christian worship.[107] There were certainly a number of churches built in the post-Constantinian era and
there was a Christian quarter in the south-west of the city. However,
the archaeological evidence points to a highly syncretistic version of
Christianity and to slow progress being made by the new faith.[108]
Whether there are reasons for this other than the economic power of
the Jews is hard to say. It is possible that the Church was weakened
after the intervention of Victor in the paschal controversy, or that in
view of the similarity between the two cults a number of Sardis Christians formally Judaized. One of these is impossible to say; the other is
quite possible in view of the Syrian evidence. Syrian Christians found
Judaism amenable in view of the similarity between the religious
practices of the two faiths; the same may have been the case at Sardis.
It is certainly true that in the later imperial era Christians and Jews in
Sardis traded alongside one another.[109] This shows us that Melito's
attitudes are not necessarily typical. It may be the case that his polemic, like that of the Syriac fathers, is partly called forth by the Judaizing
tendency of his congregation. In similar vein MacLennan shows the
difficulties undergone by Christianity in those parts of Syria in which
Judaism was strongest.[110]

For whatever reason, Christianity seems not to have taken root in
Sardis. It cannot be said whether this was the result of the economic
and social position of the Jews, the manner in which they were adapt-
ed to the prevailing culture by contrast to the sectarian Christians
(which would be less true of the period after that of Melito), or the

---

[106] Kraabel *Judaism* 240
[107] Botermann "Synagoge" 120-121
[108] Hanfmann, Yegül and Crawford "Roman and Late Antique Period" 166
[109] Hanfmann and Buchwald "Christianity: Churches and Cemeteries" 191-210
[110] MacLennan *Early Christian Texts* 108. See also Stewart-Sykes "Melito's Anti-
Judaism" 281-283

simple fact that Judaism succeeded in answering the religious questions which were at issue in Sardis in a way which Christianity did not.

1.2.2 *Other Manifestations of Quartodeciman Tradition*

We have explored something of Christianity at Sardis and have indicated that this tradition is not restricted to Sardis but was common throughout Asia and derived from the tradition on which the fourth Gospel is founded. We may note the *Epistula Apostolorum* as a Quartodeciman representative of this Johannine tradition.[111] The *Epistula Apostolorum* was first claimed as Quartodeciman by Schmidt who argued this on the grounds that this was the prima facie probability on the basis of its Asian origin, which Asian origin was indicated by its Johannine bias and by the prominence of Cerinthus as the arch-heretic.[112] Some opposition to this Asian setting came from Bardy and Lietzmann who suggested that Alexandria was a more probable place of origin;[113] were this the case then *Epistula Apostolorum* could not be claimed, in speaking of the Pascha, to be speaking of a specifically Quartodeciman Pascha since no date was given for this festival. Support was given to Schmidt by van der Veken and to Lietzmann and Bardy by Hornschuh.[114] However Stewart-Sykes has recently observed significant theological, literary and verbal parallels between *Epistula Apostolorum* and the new prophecy, which is of undisputed Asian origin.[115] The demonstrated Asian origin of *Epistula Apostolorum* means that it is hardly conceivable that the Pascha which it describes is anything other than a Quartodeciman Pascha.

Additional to the *Epistula Apostolorum* there is a work preserved among the spuria of Chrysostom, earlier believed to be a fourth century work, but shown by Cantalamessa to be roughly contemporary with *Peri Pascha* and from the same Asian milieu.[116] The author of this work we shall refer to as ps-Hippolytus in keeping with common usage. Rouwhorst suggests that this work is slightly later than that of

---

[111] On *Epistula Apostolorum* as a Johannine document see Hills *Tradition and Composition* who, at 161, speaks of the "marked, if not pervasive, Johannine character of much of the author's language and theology", as well as Stewart-Sykes "Asian Context"

[112] Schmidt *Gespräche Jesu* 364-370

[113] Bardy (review of Schmidt); Lietzmann "*Epistula Apostolorum*"

[114] van der Veken "De Sensu Paschatis"; Hornschuh *Studien* 99-115

[115] Stewart-Sykes "Asian Context"

[116] Cantalamessa *Omelia*

Melito,[117] and we shall produce evidence below to support this assessment.

Further evidence for the faith and practice of Asian Quartodecimans may be provided by the *Evangelium Petri*. The common points between Melito's work and the *Evangelium Petri*, which cover the whole extent of Melito's treatment of the passion, are noted by Perler and highlighted in the notes to Hall's text.[118] Perler does not find it necessary to postulate a common source and suggests that the relationship is one of Melito's direct literary dependence on the *Evangelium Petri*; the parallels are certainly striking and extensive. In essence, *Evangelium Petri* shifts the blame for the crucifixion away from Pilate and firmly onto the Jews under Herod, a tendency we have already seen in the fourth Gospel; in each instance it is under Jewish judgement that Jesus is condemned. All of this corresponds to Melito's belief in the responsibility of the Jews for the death of the Lord; Pilate washes his hands of the matter, in *Evangelium Petri* as in *Peri Pascha*, and in both Herod plays a key role in the condemnation of Christ.[119]

Peter's liturgical response to the death of the Lord is to fast until the Sabbath of the resurrection,[120] which was, we shall note a Quartodeciman practice to which the Syriac *Didascalia* also bear witness. We may therefore note that Peter has a Johannine chronology of the passion, the death of the Lord is explicitly stated to have taken place πρὸ μιᾶς τῶν ἀζύμων.[121] These are all indications of Quartodecimanism which taken together with the extensive parallels with Melito's work lead Mara to attribute an Asian origin to *Evangelium Petri*.[122]

Most significant however is the evidence of a Quartodeciman past in Syriac Christianity, which may cast light backward upon the Asian Quartodecimans of an earlier period, like Melito. need only note the definite Quartodeciman sections in the Syriac *Didascalia* c21. Although the whole has been "de-Quartodecimanized"[123] more recent

---

[117] Rouwhorst "Quartodeciman Passover" 156-157

[118] Perler "L'Évangile de Pierre"; Hall *Melito of Sardis* 39, 43, 53

[119] PP93; EvP 2

[120] EvP 27: seen as a reflection of liturgy by Vaganay *Évangile de Pierre* 273-5

[121] EvP 5

[122] Mara *Évangile de Pierre* 217; Vaganay *Évangile de Pierre* 216-217 and 273-275 finds these as reasons to deny that *Evangelium Petri* is Quartodeciman. He is thinking of the Quartodecimans keeping a synoptic chronology, and concludes from the manner in which Peter fasts during the Passover that this is deliberately anti-Quartodeciman. We shall note below that the practice described is anti-Jewish, and distinctively Quartodeciman.

[123] So Connolly *Didascalia Apostolorum* 192 disputes that there is Quartodeciman practice here, but he is looking at the whole chapter as currently extant.

studies confirm that a Quartodeciman source is contained within the *Didascalia*;[124] in particular the *Didascalia* drew upon a document known as the diataxis, now preserved in Epiphanius, which is definitely Quartodeciman. The Jews in this passage are called "the people", recalling Melito's constant ὁ λαός, the timing of the fast is co-ordinated with reference to the paschal celebrations of the Jews as is the time at which the fast is to be broken, that is when the Jews conclude their celebration. What is being described is a vigil which, as Rouwhorst notes, presupposes a Quartodeciman pascha.

Although later sources such as the 12th Demonstration of Aphraahat and the paschal hymns of Ephrem no longer betray Quartodeciman practice, according to Rouwhorst they continue to betray traces of a Quartodeciman past and may therefore be employed as evidence in reconstructing the Quartodeciman past of Syrian Christianity.[125] The 12th Demonstration in particular gives indications that this Quartodeciman past is quite recent, in particular in its concern at 12.12 for those who may be "troubled by this time of the Passover". These are Christians who would be familiar with keeping Pascha.[126] This Quartodeciman past explains how it is that Theodoret in the fifth century might still have first-hand knowledge of Quartodecimans.[127]

The extensive Jewish influence on Syrian Christianity[128] may either be traced to origins in a Palestinian mission, or one retaining strong Palestinian links which feed into the tradition, or alternatively to the influence of Jewish populations in Syria on the ways in which Christians understood their faith.[129] Rouwhorst suggests that this question may best be answered by observing liturgical practice since liturgy is a corporate activity rather than one expressing simply the understanding of an individual. He concludes that whereas some Syrian liturgical peculiarities, such as the use of the bema for the liturgy of the word, may best be attributed to localized Jewish influence, the widespread nature of Quartodeciman Christianity indicates that this manner of keeping Pascha had derived from a Palestinian tradition, and that this is the best means by which we may explain its long life in Syrian Christianity.[130] In this he reaches similar conclusions to those of Kazan who notes the Jewish nature of the method of argu-

---

[124] Notably that of Rouwhorst *Hymnes* 157-190, conclusions at 186-190
[125] Rouwhorst "Quartodeciman Passover" 156; Rouwhorst *Hymnes* 128
[126] So Rouwhorst "Date of Easter" 1379
[127] *Haer. Fab. Comp* 3.4.
[128] See for instance Murray *Symbols* 7-18 with references.
[129] So Rouwhorst "Jewish Liturgical Traditions" 72-3
[130] Rouwhorst "Jewish Liturgical Traditions" 81-83

mentation employed by Aphraahat, and concludes that Ephrem and Aphraahat are in receipt of a common Christian tradition.[131] He does not attempt to locate it, but suggests it is Aramaic speaking, not Greek, because of the highly Semitic colouring of the whole of Aphraahat's style. It is this common Palestinian tradition which undergirds the similarities between the paschal traditions of the Asian Quartodecimans and Syrian Christianity, the liturgical expressions of which we shall note further below.[132] It is no co-incidence that both Aphraahat and Ephrem are significant witnesses to us of a paschal theology and practice which displays its Quartodeciman origin.

It is interesting in this light to observe the existence of significant fragments of Melito's work, in particularly rendering the anti-Jewish passages of *Peri Pascha*. These are translations of a high quality, of rhythmic quality and with generous use of suffix rhyme, almost literary productions in their own right. This is so much the case that the suggestion was made by Kahle in the years after the first publication of the Greek text of *Peri Pascha* that the original was written in Syriac![133] Although this is untenable, the literary quality of the translation implies that use was still made of *Peri Pascha* in the Syrian churches and that the anti-Jewish tradition which is so much bound up to the self-definition of Quartodeciman Christianity was maintained for perhaps the same reasons.[134]

It was precisely the possibility of links of this nature between the Syrian and the Asian traditions which first brought Kahle to make his suggestion. Wellesz had sought to demonstrate the links between *Peri Pascha* and the metrical homilies of Ephrem the Syrian, which in time gave rise to the kontakia of Romanos.[135] In his view, Melito was a representative of a purely Semitic school, both in verse structure and thought. Whatever questions may now be raised about whether there is such a thing as purely Semitic versification in the Hellenistic world, or indeed whether there is such a thing as a Semitic cast of mind, the fact that there may indeed be some connection between *Peri Pascha*

---

[131] Kazan "Isaac of Antioch" (1962) 92-3, (1965) 73-74

[132] At 4.2.6

[133] By Kahle "Was Melito's Homily on the Passion Originally Written in Syriac?" Zuntz "Melito—Syriac?" marshals the arguments against this: at PP46 Melito states that the Pascha (πάσχα) gets its name from its characteristic, suffering (πάσχειν), a construction impossible in any language but Greek, that to create Syriac with rhyming suffixes is not difficult, and that it is unlikely that Syriac would have been known as far west as Sardis. Nonetheless Werner "Melito of Sardes" 204-205 seems still to think that Melito knew the language.

[134] A suggestion of Rouwhorst "Quartodeciman Passover" 168

[135] Wellesz "Melito's Homily on the Passion"

and the style and versification of Ephrem may certainly be explored.[136] Kahle's belief that Melito was a representative of a Semitic
school was in turn founded upon Bonner's suggestion that Melito's
style was essentially Semitic.[137] We shall see below that this is by no
means the case. But on the basis of the Quartodeciman origins of
Syriac Christianity we may now state that the search for Melito's
Semitic "feel" is not, however to begin in his language, as Kahle
would have it, nor in his subject matter as Zuntz suggests against
Kahle,[138] but in his tradition, reaching back into Palestinian Aramaic
Christianity. Thus, if Wellesz were right, he would not be right in the
way in which he thought he was. Rather than Melito simply being
cast in the same mould as Ephrem with a direct link between them,
we can see that there is rather a common background.

1.3 CONCLUSION

In this chapter we set out to give a general introduction to *Peri Pascha*
and its author; this led us to examine the origins of Christianity in
Sardis, concerned that the Palestinian roots of the Christianity of
Melito should be laid bare. This we have done by noting the strong
association between the Johannine Christianity of Ephesus and that
of Sardis. The book of Revelation had left some influence upon the
church at the time of Melito, in that it had been absorbed into the
wider Johannine Christianity, but the Pauline mission made little
headway here. Christianity at Sardis was Johannine Christianity.
This is important for us because this provides the means by which the
paschal tradition of Judaism might be transmitted to Melito, and so
provides a basis on which it is possible to claim, as we intend, that *Peri
Pascha* is in part a Passover haggadah.

Having demonstrated that Melito was a Johannine Christian we
must therefore turn now to the examination of Jewish Pascha, and
seek to show how Jewish paschal traditions and forms might be transmitted to Melito through the Johannine tradition. This in turn will set
out the necessary groundwork for our examination of the Quartodeciman Pascha.

---

[136] We shall attempt this at 3.1.8 below. This case can be overstated; for instance
Wellesz notes the significance of the counting of syllables in Syriac versification,
whereas this is also a mark of the Asianist Greek style. (So Smit Sibinga "Melito of
Sardis")

[137] Bonner *Homily* 23, 27

[138] Zuntz "Melito—Syriac?" 198-200

CHAPTER TWO

JEWISH AND CHRISTIAN PASCHA

Having established that Christians at Sardis were heirs to a Jewish form of Christianity, and that this was the probable source of their paschal practice we must explore the paschal practice of Jews and Christians in more detail. It has been axiomatic from the first that *Peri Pascha* is in some way related to the Quartodeciman paschal liturgy; it is moreover axiomatic that the Quartodeciman Pascha was in some way a continuation of the Jewish practice of Passover. Clearly there were, as a result of the parting of the ways, differences between Jews and Christians in their Passover ritual, quite apart from matters of theology, and developments in paschal ritual and theology would take place in both communities. However it is reasonable to proceed on the assumption that there will be continuity if only on the basis that the date of the celebration is preserved among the Quartodeciman Christians. Whilst *Peri Pascha* may contain internal clues to the Quartodeciman liturgy, it is necessary to examine both Jewish and Christian paschal ritual in order to be in a position to evaluate these clues.

In this chapter we intend to demonstrate that the paschal haggadah existed in some form before the parting of the ways, and that a domestic seder was practised at this time. This enables us to locate *Peri Pascha* in such a context, and is a necessary preliminary to our formal examination of *Peri Pascha* in which it is intended to demonstrate that it is in part a Passover haggadah. Further to this we intend to demonstrate that the haggadah was intended as a means of commemoration within a commemorative rite, and that this understanding of commemoration was passed on to Christians, and so to Melito. This may provide a rationale for Melito's paschal practice and for his adoption of the form of the haggadah for his work. These are limited aims; in particular there will be no attempt to chart in detail the development of the Jewish seder between the fall of the Temple and the codification of the Mishnah and so a limited selection of studies is cited.

2.1 THE FORM OF THE PASCHAL CELEBRATION

2.1.1 *The Origins of the Passover Haggadah*

The writings preserved only in late collections like the *Talmud* and the *Mishnah* are notoriously difficult to date. This applies equally to the Passover haggadah, presupposing as it does a liturgy such as that described by the *Mishnah*. However, if any external evidence concerning Melito's Pascha is to be gathered, then it must come from our knowledge of Jewish Passover liturgy and ritual. Since our certain knowledge of this derives from the time after the destruction of the Temple, and in particular from the *Mishnah*, we must further be able to show that the seeds of this later ritual at least had been planted before the ways of Christianity and Judaism began to part, in order that it may have been passed to Melito through his tradition.

A number of factors militate against this possibility. Most notable is the silence from Jewish Hellenistic writers such as Philo and Josephus. These mention the Passover and the slaughter of the lambs but have no reference to a domestic seder. It is also to be noted that non-rabbinic Jewish groups such as the Samaritans have no elaborate seder ritual, and that none survives from the Elephantine papyri.[1] On the other hand there have been attempts to date several of the texts making up the Passover liturgy to pre-Maccabean times.[2]

There are therefore two related questions. The first is that of whether the literary texts comprising the haggadah could have been in existence before the time of the parting of the ways of Judaism and Christianity, and the second is that of whether there existed a liturgical context for such a practice, a seder in other words. We shall attempt to answer these questions in turn.

The first, and most thorough, attempt to date the texts making up the haggadah is that of Finkelstein. The basis of his attempts consist firstly in finding an appropriate political *Sitz im Leben* for the texts and secondly in producing internal theological evidence by way of support for his historical contentions.

We may begin with his dating of the midrash of *Deuteronomy* 26:5-8 which is contained in all extant rituals and is the basis for the haggadah.[3] He sees a possible *Sitz im Leben* for this work as a Jerusa-

---

[1] This silence is found a compelling objection by Stein "Influence" 15 followed by Segal *Hebrew Passover* 241
[2] Notably those of Finkelstein "Oldest Midrash" and "Pre-Maccabean Documents"
[3] Finkelstein "Oldest Midrash"

lem under Ptolemaic rule. Its anti-Egyptian tone is, he argues, somewhat soft, and the opening phrase, reading "a wandering Aramaean
was my father", is pointed to read "An Aramaean sought to destroy
my father." This rather odd reading may be explained, Finkelstein
contends, as an attempt to distinguish the Israelites from the Seleucid
Syrians in Ptolemaic eyes. Having established, he believes, a *Sitz* on
this basis, he produces supporting evidence which, he claims, would
make it most unlikely to derive from a later rabbinic milieu. The
assertion contained in the midrash that it was no angel but God
himself who passed over the Israelites and destroyed the Egyptians
not only contradicts scripture but seems to imply a polemic against
belief in angels as the intermediaries of God. This belief came in time
to be characteristic of rabbinic Judaism, but during the third century
BC, the time to which Finkelstein would date the midrash, was being
hotly contested by the priestly classes. Finkelstein goes on to claim
that the assertion in the midrash that the Divine Presence is visibly
manifested is a typically priestly assertion, in direct contradiction to
the pharisaic belief in the invisibility of God; were they not hallowed
by long tradition, later rabbis would not have repeated these asser-
tions. On the basis of the political and theological arguments
Finkelstein concludes that the midrash is the work of a High Priest,
anxious to influence pilgrims coming to Jerusalem for the Passover,
especially the Egyptians, and to minimise the anti-Egyptian sentiment
inherent in the festival.

In subsequent works Finkelstein gave a similar treatment to other
texts making up the seder.[4] The introduction to the Passover
Haggadah, based on *Deuteronomy* 6:21ff he also sees as deriving from
the temple at the time of Ptolemaic suzerainty over Palestine, again
introducing changes aimed at lessening the offence to Egyptian sensi-
bilities, hence the vivid description of the suffering of the Israelites at
Deuteronomy 6:22ff is omitted. Again, he seeks to give internal justification to his historical argument.

To all this Zeitlin makes the interesting objection that since the
Ptolemies were Greeks and not Egyptians, there was no need to mod-
erate anti-Egyptian sentiment.[5] This much may be true, but we must
distinguish sentiment against Egyptian people and against Egyptian
rule. Whereas the first would not affect the feelings of the Ptolemaic
government the second would. Zeitlin also suggests that the term "the
Holy One, Blessed be he", which is contained in this section of the

---

[4] Finkelstein "Pre-Maccabean Documents" and "Origin of the Hallel"
[5] Zeitlin "Liturgy" 451

haggadah cannot derive from the period of the second commonwealth, since it was not in use at the time. However, he does admit
that there is a much older prototype to the haggadah.[6]

The problem with Finkelstein's arguments is that they are so
speculative. The theological evidence that he cites by way of support
for his historical arguments is debatable, and the attempt to secure a
historical context is really undemonstrable. Finkelstein, however, is
not the only scholar to have investigated the date of the haggadah; we
have already noted the opposition of Zeitlin. However he too, whilst
concluding that the shape and order of the present seder are late,
concurs with Finkelstein that the basis of the haggadah is of the
period of the second temple.[7] Likewise Manns reviews all the existing
evidence. He notes how difficult it is to give a date to the haggadah,
but concludes that many of the traditions, particularly those pointing
to a messianic understanding of the Passover, date from the time of
the Temple and thus precede Christianity.[8] One dissenting voice is
that of Bokser, who believes that the existing midrash which forms
the haggadah is typical of rabbinic Judaism.[9] But although this kind
of encounter with the biblical text might be said to typify rabbinic
Judaism, it is not therefore exclusively the preserve of the rabbis;
moreover even Bokser admits that the Passover would from early
times admit a retelling of the biblical account.

Although Finkelstein cannot be said to have proved his case, it is at
least possible that the haggadah as a literary form could have been
transmitted to Melito. We should note the widespread circulation of
the midrash through the extant rituals, and its anonymity as being
signs of its possible antiquity. If we were able to demonstrate the
existence of a liturgical *Sitz* for the haggadah at a stage at which
Melito might have inherited a corpus of liturgical Passover material
then the possibility of a literary relationship between *Peri Pascha* and
the haggadah would be all the greater.

2.1.2 *The Date and Origin of the Passover Seder*

We have referred to the lack of external reference to a liturgical
practice among Jewish writers and to the fact that this is thought by
Stein sufficient in itself to dispense with Finkelstein's argument con-

---

[6] Zeitlin "Liturgy" 451
[7] Zeitlin "Liturgy" 460
[8] Manns "Traces" 269-278
[9] Bokser *Origins* 72, followed by Rouwhorst "Quartodeciman Passover" 170

cerning the haggadah.[10] Stein further shows strong Hellenistic parallels between symposiastic literature and the seder liturgy and believes that this too makes it impossible that there should be an early date for the haggadah. However, given that Hellenistic influence was widespread in Palestine from the time of the Seleucid occupation these Hellenistic parallels do not make the development of the liturgy any less likely to be early. The argument from silence is no better than those of Finkelstein. This silence surely indicates only that the domestic ritual is of less significance than the Temple ritual. It does not indicate that it did not exist. Had there been ño possibility of celebrating the Passover outside of the Temple, then it is more than likely that the celebration would have disappeared altogether.

The silence, moreover, is not total. At *Antiquitates Judaicae* 14.214 Josephus informs us that the Jews of Delos were given permission to conduct their συνδεῖπνα καὶ τὰ ἱερά. If the Jews had permission to keep the festivals prescribed by the law this would surely include Passover. Philo, moreover, in describing the Passover at *De Specialibus Legibus* 145ff, indicates a domestic celebration. This is the evidence on which Segal argues for a domestication of the Passover rite in the latter days of the temple.[11]

And so, if the keeping of Passover outside of Jerusalem was possible, it is quite likely that some form of liturgy developed in the diaspora and in the outlying regions of Palestine. Of course, we cannot be certain that the form was that of the later seder liturgies, but it would most probably have contained elements which had been imported from the Jerusalem festival. Although it derives from a different place altogether, we must also note what is said of the common meals of the *therapeutae* by Philo, containing an explanation of Holy Scripture by the πρόεδρος and community singing after the meal.[12] This would seem to show that a basic model was in existence, whether among the *therapeutae* themselves, or in Philo's Alexandria.

Finally we may take the evidence of the synoptic Gospels which would indicate a domestic rite which was practised separately from, although connected to, the Temple sacrifice. It is a rite like this which Zeitlin would see as the typical Passover meal in the period of the second temple.[13]

Thus we may claim a reasonable certainty, and indeed unanimity among authorities, about there being a domestic Passover rite of

---

[10] Stein "Influence" 15
[11] Segal *Hebrew Passover* 26-30, 240
[12] Philo *De Vita Contemplativa* 64
[13] Zeitlin "Liturgy" 445

some description before the parting of the Jewish and Christian ways. Far less certain is the form which it might have taken. However, in view of the work of Stein we may suggest that it the rite would fit the general conditions of a formal Hellenistic meal,[14] and that the domestic liturgy would include the treatment of Scripture and some hymnic element, even if the full liturgy of the *Mishnah* is a later development.

At a later stage of our investigation we may enquire in more detail into the seder of Melito's tradition. For the moment however we may proceed to see whether the haggadah as a form might have been transmitted to him through the medium of his Johannine tradition, and that the seder as a liturgical event might likewise have been known to him.

2.1.3 *The Passover in the Johannine Tradition*

If there was indeed the possibility of some elements of the later seder being used as part of a Passover liturgy independent of the temple, which might in time be passed to Melito as part of a traditional ritual, these are to be sought in the Johannine tradition. We have shown that Melito is heir to this tradition and so should seek traces in the fourth gospel, and indeed in *Revelation*[15], of what we have claimed as the traditional paschal practice of the Christians of Sardis

It may be objected that this is an unnecessary hypothesis. Is it not possible, indeed simpler to suppose, that the Passover practice of the Christians at Sardis had been imported directly from Judaism within Sardis? In determining the origin of Jewish elements in Melito's pascha we are in the same situation with regard to determining Jewish elements in Syriac speaking Christianity. Just as there it was noted that liturgical elements would reflect not the insights of an individual but also the expectations of the community so here we may suggest that the origins of Quartodeciman practice at least derive from within the Christian tradition. A rite would not be imported and planted where it did not belong. Lieu similarly notes that although there may have been a number of elements in common between the Pascha of Melito and his congregation and the Passover kept by the Jews of Sardis there must have been some significant development of the Christian understanding of the paschal celebration quite separate from Judaism in the hundred or so years of development which pre-

---

[14] In agreement with Stein "Influence", whilst differing on the subject of date

[15] For connections between the Gospel and the Apocalypse in the Johannine tradition see 1.2.2 above.

cedes the time of Melito,[16] and Cohick argues along similar lines that the paschal tradition of Melito is purely Christian.[17]

We have already suggested that Melito came from a Jewish family and it is possible that he imported elements of the Passover with which he was already familiar. Of course, these are then given an anti-Jewish bent. But the broader Quartodeciman tradition is not restricted to Sardis; Polycrates argues for the propriety of Quartodeciman practice on the grounds of its antiquity deriving from its Jewish origin and on the grounds of its conformity with the fourth Gospel and these are the bases on which we should seek the origin of Melito's practice. It is conceivable that the Judaism of Sardis might exercise some influence on the paschal rite celebrated by Melito, but this would be grafted onto an existing rite.

Moreover, our knowledge of the Judaism of Asia Minor in this period is so limited, being chiefly archaeological and epigraphic, that it is impossible to show for certain the precise nature of the observance of Passover at Sardis. Perversely, Melito himself is the best witness we have to the Jewish observance of the Passover at Sardis. However, we may suggest that the Jews of Sardis had a Passover ritual of some sort, and that this is reflected in Melito's description of Jewish rejoicing at the time of Jesus' suffering. We may also suggest that, in view of the extensive Hellenization of the Jews of Sardis, their Passover rite, like that of Melito, was a tradition of Palestinian origin clothed in Hellenistic dress.

Had the Passover tradition of the church at Sardis come directly from local Judaism, it would have been an innovation, and this kind of originality accords ill with the fact that liturgy is essentially conservative and traditional, and not therefore prone to huge changes. Although a certain degree of cross-fertilization is possible, wholesale adoption by the Christian community is rather less likely. If the Jewish community influenced the celebration of the Christians then this would have lain in the manner of the celebration rather than in the texts employed, although even this is an unnecessary hypothesis, since the origins of the rite are more likely to be found in the Christian theological and liturgical tradition.

And so we are led to seek the origins of Melito's paschal observation in the evidence provided by the Johannine literature. There is an inbuilt difficulty here, however, in that John does not treat of the Last Supper. In the synoptic Gospels a Passover seder takes place, indeed

---

[16] Lieu *Image and Reality* 228
[17] Cohick "Israel"

a domestic occasion of sorts, which clearly contains elements of the later seder. John's Last Supper does not contain these elements. It is quite clear, however, that the Passover was a season of significance for John,[18] not least since the Gospel is structured around three Passovers.

We shall note below that there are theological reasons why the fourth Gospel does not treat of the Passover. We may, however, note that the discourse concerning the bread of life in c6 is given the setting of the synagogue at Passover. The reasoning behind this is explained by Gärtner with reference to a number of rabbinic texts which link the giving of the manna to the Passover;[19] a discourse on the manna might well fit in with synagogal practice in the month of Nisan. So, just as the manna ceased to fall on the day of Passover, celebrated according to *Joshua* 5 overlooking the promised land, so according to the *Exodus Mekilta* the manna began to fall at Passover time. Other rabbinic texts speak of the unleavened bread taken by the Israelites at the Passover tasting like manna, and of the bread baked by Abraham for the three strangers, who called at Passover time, being a prefiguration of the manna.[20] Evidence that this linkage of manna and Red Sea crossing is not a peculiarity of the later midrashim to which Gärtner is perforce indebted may be provided by Melito, who makes the same connection, and by the *dayyenu*, where once again the miracles are linked together.[21] On the basis of this tradition Gärtner proceeds to seek formal parallels between this discourse and the Passover haggadah.

Part of this may be seen in the bread of the three ages which is spoken of in the haggadah, that of the Mosaic age, that of the present, and the bread of the messianic age. Gärtner interprets the discourse in this way, that the bread of the feedings is interpreted as being messianic bread by those who seek to crown Jesus as king, whereas it is still in fact the bread of the present age; in seeing the bread of the feeding as messianic the people show their misinterpretation of Jesus' messiahship.[22] The bread of the age to come is fulfilled in the eucharist, which cannot come about until Jesus has inaugurated the new age by his death. However, although this conception, found in the haggadah, may cast light on the interpretation of the discourse, it

---

[18] See e.g. Howard "Passover and Eucharist"
[19] Gärtner *John 6* 25-29
[20] Gärtner *John 6* 20-25
[21] So Gärtner *John 6* 15
[22] Gärtner *John 6* 20-24

does not establish it as a haggadah, but simply as a discourse which shares ideas in common with the haggadah.

The same is true of Gärtner's statement that the shape of the section may be explained by its parallel with that of the haggadah as prescribed in the Mishnah, that is event, followed by question, followed by interpretation.[23] Daube points out that much traditional material in the Gospels is built up in this way; a gesture or action of Jesus brings forth a question, as an answer to which Jesus gives his teaching on a particular matter.[24] The fact that the haggadah and *John* 6 share a teaching method does not join them to the same genre, since this is a method which is widespread. *John* 6 and the Passover haggadah may share a background and a set of assumptions and ideas, and this is interesting in itself, but *John* 6 is not a Passover haggadah.[25]

A further echo of the haggadah, but again one which does not establish a positive link, is the ἐγώ εἰμι formula, met at the great festivals in the narrative of the fourth Gospel and evinced in this chapter. This is given liturgical expression in the haggadah in the passage where God describes the wonders he will work:

> *I* will pass through the land of Egypt, *I* and no angel;
> and *I* will smite all the first-born, *I* and no seraph.....

We may cite a closer parallel in *Peri Pascha*, at PP103:

> ἐγὼ γάρ εἰμι ὑμῶν ἡ ἄφεσις
> ἐγὼ τὸ πάσχα τῆς σωτηρίας

The clearest link between *John* 6 and the haggadah is the invitation of Jesus to come and eat, corresponding to the lifting up of the seder dish at the beginning of the meal, and the invitation there for all the hungry to come and eat the Passover meal. But this link is one in no way evinced by *Peri Pascha*. There is an invitation to receive forgiveness of sins at PP103, but that is at the end of *Peri Pascha*, not at the beginning. There is in fact only one possible reference to *John* 6, a somewhat oblique one at PP79, and one reference to the manna although notably it is linked, as in the *dayyenu* to the miracle of the exodus. However, we have not claimed that Melito worked with a copy of the Gospel in front of him, but that he is heir to a common theological, and possibly liturgical, tradition. Verbal similarity is not to be expected.

---

[23] Gärtner *John 6* 28
[24] David Daube *New Testament and Rabbinic Judaism* 166-169
[25] cf. Kilmartin "Liturgical Influence"

From our criticism of the work of Gärtner we may conclude that John probably knew some of the Passover haggadah, and employed Passover traditions in his construction of c6, but that the haggadah as later known did not supply the shape of the discourse. In view of the uncertainty we have expressed concerning the precise form which the haggadah known to John may have taken, we must conclude that the form of haggadah which continued to be part of the Johannine liturgical tradition and which Melito may thus have inherited cannot be shown with certainty from the Johannine sources. A further problem is created by the fact that whereas *John* 6 is concerned to interpret the miracle of the manna, *Peri Pascha* is concerned with *Exodus* 12. If a link is to be demonstrated then the change in the reading of the Old Testament would have to be explained. Gärtner in fact employs *Peri Pascha* as supporting evidence for his hypothesis, but this cannot be admitted.[26]

An attempt is made by Ziener, followed by Kilmartin, to see the haggadic section of *Wisdom* lying behind the structure of the entire Johannine Gospel.[27] He sees a Jewish Christian, Quartodeciman, congregation as the source of the fourth Gospel and sees the Passover celebration as being the particular basis by which the Gospel was built up. Thus he draws elaborate parallels between *Wisdom* and the miracles in *John*. The parallels are not only too elaborate to be credible, but this leads him into missing parallels which are also there but do not fit into this scheme.[28] What is positive about Ziener's work, however, is that it shows up again the importance for John of the Passover events and the way in which this importance is mirrored among the Quartodecimans. There is indeed a typology operating here, one which we have shown to be the same as that of Melito.[29] And typology is the key to the Johannine understanding of the fulfilment of the Passover in Christ.

We can conclude on this basis that whilst the themes treated in the haggadah were part of the Johannine theological tradition, it cannot be demonstrated from *John* that the seder as later known was part of the Johannine liturgical tradition. This is hardly surprising since it is unlikely that the seder had as yet been canonized into its later shape. What is more serious is the absence of any element of liturgical Passover keeping, let alone the particular elements which may be discerned in Melito's work. This, however, can be explained.

---

[26] Gärtner *John 6* 29-31
[27] Ziener "Johannesevangelium" followed by Kilmartin "Liturgical Influence"
[28] So Reim *Studien* 193-204
[29] See 1.2.2 above and 3.1.6 below

The one place where one would expect elements of the seder to appear, where indeed they do in the synoptic Gospels, is the Last Supper. The Johannine Last Supper is not however a Passover celebration; such is precluded both by chronology and theology. The same is equally true of the Last Supper reported in the *Acta Johannis,* although it contains paschal elements.[30] John's Last Supper takes place before the slaughter of the lambs, and a true Johannine Passover celebration can only take place after the exaltation of Jesus. Such is Melito's context, Christ has been exalted and as exalted saviour calls the gentiles to their salvation. Such is the basis for Melito's Johannine Pascha; although there is no evidence within the fourth Gospel that John kept the Passover not only must we note that this is a priori probable, we may also note that this claim is made by Polycrates, and my finally note that Melito shares a theological system with John by which the Pascha could not come to fulfillment until after the true lamb is slain. This takes outside the time-frame of the Gospel, but into the time-frame of Melito when the promise that the Father might be worshipped in spirit and in truth is brought to fulfillment.

In *Revelation* we may likewise find Passover themes. According to Manns the crystal sea of *Revelation* 4 is a reference to the Red Sea and in the following chapter the handing over of the βιβλίον to the lamb a reference to the establishment of the covenant on the basis of the giving of the law.[31] In view of the many other potential references these cannot be held as certain, although Manns presents a wealth of rabbinic material to support his case. On the other hand the reference to creation in *Revelation* 4:11 is clear enough, and the immolated lamb is surely a reference to the Passover lamb. The verb σφάζω is used of the Passover lamb as of the intended slaughter of Isaac in the Septuagint. In the haggadah of the Cairo Genizah the sacrifice of the Passover is to be greeted with a "new song", a new song reflected in the words of *Revelation* 5:9. In the Jewish tradition this term generally refers to the song of *Exodus* 15, but according to *Exodus Rabbah* 23:5 characterises the messianic age.[32]

The significant difference between the treatment of Passover themes in the Apocalypse and the Gospel is that there is liturgical material present here. As in *Peri Pascha* there is christological reference to the lamb, and it is the lamb who is hymned. The Apocalypse works on a different time-frame from the Gospel, the lamb is exalted,

---

[30] See below 3.2.3
[31] Manns "Traces" 285-290
[32] Manns "Traces" 293

and so the faithful may celebrate. We may therefore see the hymns of *Revelation* 4-5 as reflections of the Passover liturgy of the school which produced this document. As in PP68 it is through the death of the lamb that the people become a Kingdom. Manns notes throughout his work the possible links between *Revelation* and *Peri Pascha*.[33]

And so despite the absence of any specific parallels in the Gospel there is a strong possibility that John was acquainted with a form of Passover liturgy containing elements found in the haggadah. The uncovering of the synagogue homily form in his work and the central importance of the exodus events for him are clues to his intimate acquaintance with Jewish Passover tradition. Ideas have been found which are held in common, even if the haggadah form has not.

As Melito received the tradition, the school of the evangelist had become bound up to the circle of the seer,[34] and here there is evidence not only of an acquaintance with Passover themes but of liturgical celebration. Whereas *Peri Pascha* is most certainly not a synagogue homily, as we shall see, it is quite possible for elements of the haggadah to have been transmitted to Melito. Such would be consistent with the picture of a Jewish Christian congregation in the Johannine tradition which we have been building throughout this work.

2.1.4 *The Haggadah within the Seder*

Having established that both the literary form of the Passover haggadah itself and the liturgical event of the seder might both have been in existence before the fall of the Temple and the consequent reformation of Judaism, and thus that these items of the Passover tradition might have been passed to Melito, we may examine the manner in which they belonged together within Judaism. If *Peri Pascha* is linked to the Quartodeciman seder, we must ask whether this seder is a table rite.

The basic document for the Jewish seder is the Tractate *Pesahim* of the *Mishnah*, which contains instructions for the seder as at the end of the second century, a rabbinic rite assuming the end of the temple, a Passover without the lamb. We must seek to go behind this, in order to find out what kind of domestic rite might have passed into Melito's tradition. For having shown at 2.1.2 above that there was a domestic rite already in existence before the fall of the temple, we must see

---

[33] Manns "Traces" passim, but especially 284-294
[34] See 1.2.2 above

whether it may be reconstructed in any detail. Although our basic source is a product of the second century, the *Mishnah* reports the transformation of a rite already in existence rather than creating a new one entirely, this rite being that hinted at in the synoptic Gospels, and by Josephus. The rite, moreover, is presented in a way which stresses its continuity with what has gone before and so we may have reasonable confidence in using the *Mishnah* to reconstruct the seder at a time before the parting of the ways for Judaism and Christianity, in that a more primitive rite lies behind the newer. We must seek the extent to which the rite has undergone transformation as a result of the destruction of the temple.

Presumably Melito's seder would also be transformed, for whilst originating with the same domestic rite Melito's community would alter it in the same way as did the rabbis, albeit in a different direction, since in this case it is not a change due to the unavailability of a lamb, rather that the necessity for the lamb would be superseded. In other words, in Judaism, as in Christianity, traditional actions were taken and given new interpretations; thus whereas the interpretations contained in the *Mishnah* are of the second century, lying behind them are actions which date to a time when the temple was standing.

We may see an example of this with regard to the three questions of the Palestinian *Mishnah*, which concern dipping, the eating of unleavened bread and the eating of only roast meat. According to Zeitlin these derive from domestic ritual which results from the following of the pentateuchal instructions.[35] The fourth question, concerning bitter herbs, which is found in the Babylonian *Mishnah*, he sees as later, since it is asked from a perspective of slavery and not freedom.

The answers to the questions, in effect the haggadah, are again the same as the biblical answers; Bokser however sees a difference in what elicits the questions, a difference which, he believes, affects the form of the questions themselves.[36] For whereas in *Exodus* the questions are elicited by the sacrificial ritual, in the *Mishnah* it is the nature of the meal which causes questions to be asked. However, two questions at least, those concerning the roasted meat and the dipping, must derive from a time when the pentateuchal ritual is being followed. The development and expansion of the questions must then have had some basis in the domestic ritual previous to the destruction of the temple. What happens is that it develops further; the

---

[35] Zeitlin "Liturgy" 433-437
[36] Bokser *Origins* 40-41

pentateuchal questions are dropped, and the domestic questions expand. This tendency is in line with Bokser's thesis of continuity in alteration and explains the addition of a fourth question by the Babylonian *Mishnah*.

Zeitlin also deals with the interpretation of Rabbi Gamaliel contained in the *Mishnah* of the things of which mention must be made at the Passover.[37] He argues that the interpretations are not traditional as they are now found, but that they take their form because they cover up the omission of any reference to dipping. The question concerning dipping is a traditional one but is nowhere answered. The saying of Gamaliel passes over this question in silence, and is in effect an argument that the question should no longer be asked. Zeitlin explains that this is because the dipping had been into the blood of the paschal lamb in order to mark the houses, a following of the action of the first Passover. This ancient rite had long since been discontinued, but the question remained as a relic, and an embarrassing one after the destruction of the temple. Gamaliel had sought its effective deletion; the editors of the *Mishnah* on the other hand sought to give it a new application.

This saying of Gamaliel is also considered by Bokser who sees the verbalisation of them as being equivalent to their presence.[38] The lamb is of course no longer present, so mention of it suffices, and an explanation of it is given which covers up its absence; Pesah can be focused on those items which are available in the domestic ritual. It is this tendency which Bokser sees beneath the whole of the rite described by the *Mishnah*. Even the section in which the ritual is described, *Mishnah Pesahim* 10, is written in a somewhat less fragmented manner than the rest of the *Mishnah*, lending to the rite a timeless quality, intended to stress the continuity of the domestic rite with the ancient ritual.[39] Philo and Josephus are witnesses to the centrality of the sacrifice in the former rite, but it is this element which needs to be replaced, and in the *Mishnah* it is replaced by the meal which was always there.

For Melito however, the sacrifice has been superseded, and the question at PP46 has reference to nothing, it comes out of nowhere. It is the traditional question found, like those of the *Mishnah*, in a revised rite. Again this is an example of the retention of the traditional, all the more clear in this case because it is so uncomfortable.

---

[37] Zeitlin "Liturgy" 440-443
[38] Bokser *Origins* 42, 44
[39] Bokser *Origins* 85-89

Thus we may see that just as the rabbinic transformation of the rite seeks to retain the traditional, so does the transformation undergone in Christian circles. The question is answered by the haggadah, in the *Mishnah* as in *Peri Pascha*.

Being thus assured of the basic trustworthiness of the *Mishnah* as a means of gaining an outline of the Passover rite of the first century, and reasonably confident of having a methodology which may enable to us to tell the difference between what is primitive and what has accrued between the destruction of the temple and the compilation of the *Mishnah*, we may attempt to see this haggadah within a seder setting.

As we suggested above in 2.1.2 the shape of the meal appears to have been the same as the basic shape of any formal meal. This is something which would be unaffected by the changes in Judaism after 70 AD. Bahr very neatly collects together the evidence concerning the Passover seder and moreover collects the classical evidence to show how similar this is to a Graeco-Roman symposium, a conclusion we would expect having studied the work of Stein.[40]

This basic shape was then as follows:

   I Hors d'oevres
     First Cup

   II *Main Course* (bread served at this point)
     Second cup
     Meal
     Third Cup

(III Dessert)
     (Fourth Cup)

This is the shape of any formal meal, here however the third section is bracketed because the Passover seder ended with the *aphikomen*.[41] The accompanying cup of wine is also bracketed. Bokser argues that this fourth cup is added to the rite as the accompaniment to the singing of the hallel, which in temple times would have accompanied the slaughter of the lambs.[42] Zeitlin however seems to indicate that this singing of the hallel has been transferred to the synagogue service for the first day of unleavened bread, and that the hallel was part of

---

[40] Bahr "Seder" NB especially 188. Again we may have reference to Stein "Influence of Symposia." Note however that Bokser *Origins* 50-66 shows the slight but significant differences between the seder and the classical symposium

[41] On the *aphikomen* see especially Daube *He That Cometh* and 4.2.5 below.

[42] Bokser *Origins* 43-44

the domestic rite from early on.[43] It would seem that the hallel was only sung in part originally; as it is the hallel is divided after *Psalm* 114. Perhaps the best speculation is that at first the first two psalms only were sung, the rest of the psalms being added at a later date.[44] *Jubilees* 49 hints at an element of psalmody in the rite.[45] The disciples moreover are said by the synoptic Gospels to leave the Last Supper singing a hymn. A hymnic response to the seder would seem probable, and so it must be considered a possibility that a fourth cup was added to the seder, though this need not be universally true. It is even possible that the Mishnaic prohibition on the seder extending beyond midnight is an indication that the seder was frequently prolonged in that way, and that like Graeco-Roman symposia it may have involved the consumption of several cups of wine extending into the night.

Returning to the meal, we may state that the first two courses would have been the outline of the seder known to Jews before the fall of the temple, and that which was thus transmitted to Christians. Its similarity with Hellenistic custom would, of course, make it congenial and comprehensible to Melito. It is at the mixing of the second cup that the *Mishnah* indicates that the questions should be asked and the haggadah recited.

The impression might be given that the haggadah is to be declared before the meal, already served, is eaten; this however would reflect practice after the fall of the temple. Just as the Greek symposium follows the meal proper, so it would seem more likely that in the days of the temple the haggadah would be delivered after the main course, in Jerusalem the paschal lamb, had been served.

It is significant that the unleavened bread is served here for the first time. That bread should be served at this point was usual both in Jewish and in Hellenistic formal meals, that it should of necessity be unleavened was peculiar to Passover. In the context of the seder its proximity to the serving of the lamb makes it possible for the later fluidity of reference between the lamb and the bread to become established.[46]

Thus we may see the haggadah of the Passover in its context as a repetition of the acts of God in the exodus, taking place over the festal

---

[43] Zeitlin "Hallel"; also "Liturgy" 445

[44] Finkelstein "Origin of the Hallel" 320, 323-324 points out this division of the hallel. However, his explanation, again bound up to the historical circumstances surrounding the second commonwealth, is once again speculative in the extreme

[45] So Segal *Hebrew Passover* 22

[46] On which see Daube *He That Cometh* 10

meal. There is no reason to believe that this would be any different for Melito than for his Jewish predecessors. In seeking a function for *Peri Pascha* within the Quartodeciman Pascha, we must be aware that it is a table rite.

2.1.5 *Conclusion*

We have shown that Judaism was in possession of a paschal haggadah before the parting of the ways, and that John was probably acquainted with these paschal traditions, which might therefore be passed on to Melito. We have also shown that there was such a thing as a table rite distinct from the celebrations which took place in the Temple, and that this too might have been passed on to the Christian tradition. Having shown a reasonable possibility that the form at least in outline of the Passover rite would remain the same in Christianity as it had been in Judaism before the parting of the ways, we may now examine the function of the Passover ritual within Judaism, in order to see whether the continuity of liturgical form encompasses a continuity of liturgical function.

2.2 THE FUNCTION OF PASCHAL OBSERVANCE

The haggadah was recited in obedience to the biblical precept to tell of the acts of God in the Passover. It tells of the event which is being celebrated. Likewise the entire festival was celebrated in obedience to biblical command, that the festival was to be a memorial to Israel for ever of the Passover of Egypt. *Jubilees* 49 in the second century likewise sees the festival as a memorial, ordering Israel to keep the festival, to remember it, and stating that the keeping of the festival is a memorial pleasing to God.[47] Thus as the function of the haggadah, to tell of the deeds of God, is subsumed into the context of the festival its function becomes identical with that of the festival, to remember. As remembering is the function of the seder, a function stated in the opening benediction, so the haggadah focuses the act of remembrance. So it is that among Sephardic Jews the entire seder is referred to as a haggadah. However, in order more fully to understand this act of commemoration we must understand the significance of remembering in the Judaism which Melito inherited.

All these words which are translated with "remember" are derived from the root זכר. Its basic meaning, as de Boer points out, is "to

---

[47] See Segal *Hebrew Passover* 20-23

name" or "to mention".[48] Thus to translate the word simply as "remember" is far too cold-blooded a rendition, since what is taking
place when the Hebrew Bible uses a form of זכר is not simply an
intellectual remembering but an expression of what is remembered.
So it is that זכר roots are frequent in the Hebrew Bible, and have
particular significance in the cult.[49] We might primarily cite as an
example the commandment in *Exodus* 12 to keep the feast of the
Passover as a זכרון, a word translated in the Septuagint with
μνημόσυνον. The portion of the meal offering which is burnt (*Leviticus*
2:2) is called אזכרה (a word translated here with ἀνάμνησις but also
as μνημόσυνον, the words are near synonymous)[50] likewise the incense
which is put on the shewbread is to serve as an אזכרה (*Leviticus* 24:7).
The blowing of the trumpets by the priests over the burnt offerings
and the peace offerings is to be a זכרון (*Numbers* 10:10), as are the
stones bearing the names of the tribes of Israel which were worn by
Aaron on his shoulders (*Exodus* 28:12). These are all examples by
which memory goes far beyond simply remembering in the mind but
is to take place concretely and cultically, the thing to be remembered
being expressed before God. Thus when the verb is used with God as
subject (and in this instance with the covenant frequently as object) it
is implicit in the meaning not simply that God should remember but
that God should act. Thus at *Numbers* 10:9 God's remembering of his
people is the first stage in his rescue of them. And when in the liturgical setting people remember past actions of God it is implicit that
the past act of mercy is to continue to be expressed in the present. It
is in this sense that the ancient prayers for Rosh haShanah known as
the *zikronoth* ask that God remember the sacrifice of Isaac. These
prayers have such antiquity that they may be assumed to have derived from the temple cult, so again this shows the cultic primacy of
ideas of God's remembrance.[51]

This receives expression at the centre of the haggadah in the
midrash which, according to Finkelstein derived from the temple liturgy, when it states that God remembered his covenant with the
patriarchs when he heard the groaning of Israel under Egyptian oppression.[52] Remembering here is the basis of his action in sending the

---

[48] de Boer *Gedenken und Gedächtnis* especially 12-16
[49] For all these uses of זכר in the Old Testament and for its significance see de
Boer *Gedenken und Gedächtnis* and Gross "Wurzel". See moreover Chenderlin *Do This*
who, studying the Septuagint rather than the Masoretic text, comes to similar conclusions; finally note Macina "Fonction"
[50] Chenderlin *Do This* 228; Macina "Fonction" 5
[51] Chenderlin *Do This* 160
[52] Finkelstein "Oldest Midrash". Note however our comments at 2.1.1 above.

plagues upon Egypt. Thus, when the Passover of Egypt is remembered in the context of the seder, implicit in this is that the mercies of the Passover should be shown again, just as in the seder the Israelites relive the Passover.[53] The past deliverance is typical, and the present re-enactment of that deliverance ensures a deliverance in the present as well.[54] As the Israelites remember God, so they ensure that God remembers them.[55] Whereas there are many indications of the centrality of remembrance at Passover, we may note as an example the paschal embolism in the *birkath hamazon* calling upon God to remember the remembrances of his people, the act of remembrance is focused in the haggadah. The remembrance is a saving remembrance as continuing saving mercies are appropriated through this festal commemoration, and so the haggadah is much more than simply a midrash.

The past mercies which are remembered, through the act of commemoration come to have a strong eschatological element, pointing not simply to the present but to the assurance of God's future rescue of his people by the sending of the Messiah.[56] The function of the haggadah was then to be a memorial of the Passover, memorial here being a memorial both for the participants and for God, that the participants should be as those who first kept the Passover both in their own minds (and indeed bodies, since the meal, the very dishes of which are concrete reminders of the Egyptian Passover, is eaten in haste) and hence in their standing before God. The haggadah, together with the haroseth and bitter herbs, is part of the re-enactment, a making present of the Egyptian Passover. This is what the *Mishnah* means when it says that in every generation a man is to regard himself as though he had himself come out of Egypt; such is the nature of the remembering that not only does it enable the individual to feel as though he were a participant, but it ensures that the blessings appropriated in the events of history are made authentic for the present. So it is that in the haggadah, in obedience to the *Mishnah*, the father tells the son who is unable to ask that "this (the seder) is because of what the Lord did when he brought me out of Egypt". Likewise this theory of remembrance explains the statement of *Jubilees* that the memorial

---

[53] Which is why, according to *Tosefta Pesahim* 10.9, they do not give thanks for the exodus at the seder, namely because it has not happened yet

[54] זכר in the context of the Passover celebration is examined by Thurian *Eucharistic Memorial* 27-39

[55] This double sense is given expression in the targums. See le Déaut *Nuit Pascale* 70, n152

[56] le Déaut *Nuit Pascale* 281

will protect Israel. The remembering ensures Israel the same protection that it received at the Egyptian Passover.

The Passover which is remembered by the Christians of Sardis is
of course ultimately not the Egyptian Passover but the mysteries
which that Passover prefigured. However it is quite possible that the
same idea of remembering may lie behind Melito's work, as of
Melito's rite. Hall states that it is never made clear how the benefits of
Christ are appropriated to the individual.[57] Could it not be that just
as the benefits of the Egyptian Passover are extended to the Jews who
commemorate it that the events of the Christian Pascha are extended
by those who likewise remember in this concrete sense? We may
reasonably suppose that the context of the delivery of *Peri Pascha*
conforms to that in which Jewish tradition would deliver the
haggadah, that is to say it is delivered in the context of a table rite.
On this basis we may equally suggest that *Peri Pascha* and the
haggadah are functionally comparable. Clearly they are not identical
in view of the different mysteries which are being commemorated,
but they may be compared on the basis that both intend to commemorate what, in different ways, are paschal mysteries. Testuz
speaks of *Peri Pascha* as bound up to commemoration but does not
construct any argument on this basis.[58] Nonetheless it is a real possibility that *Peri Pascha*, like the Passover haggadah, is intended to frame
an act of ritual commemoration. But before such a conclusion is
reached, we should see how Christianity received the Jewish idea of
remembrance.

The Hebrew conception of remembrance is found unreconstruct-
ed in the canticles at the beginning of *Luke* (*Luke* 1:48, 54, 72). Given
the Old Testament background and Jewish origin of this part of *Luke*
this is to be expected. Interestingly in *Acts* 10:4 and 10:31 there are
similar, cultic, uses of the concept and vocabulary of remembrance.
However, although these direct parallels are noticeable by virtue of
their being unusual, any intellectual or mental idea of remembering is
equally not present in the New Testament. There is always something
concrete and active about it.[59]

Remembering in the New Testament is generally either of the
apostles, their preaching and their actions, or of the tradition. In such

---

[57] Hall *Melito of Sardis* xlv
[58] Testuz *Papyrus Bodmer XIII* 19-20
[59] For the New Testament understanding of remembrance in general and its Old
Testament background see Dahl "Anamnesis" to which these paragraphs are indebted for many of the points made.

a way it is the basis for present action, in imitation; in remembering, the early Christians acted. This is the sense of *II Peter* 3:1-2. See also *I Corinthians* 4:17 where Paul is to be remembered by imitation. The early Christians recalled the tradition (*Acts* 11:16, *I Corinthians* 11:2) and the kerygma (*II Timothy* 2:14). This is analogous to the Jewish remembrance of the acts of God in their own history since it becomes the basis for action, the reminding of the apostles re-presents the actions and words of Christ to the communities which they address. This conception unites the whole New Testament. It may be linked to the tradition of Sardis by noting that this message is explicitly relayed to Christians at Sardis in *Revelation* 3:3, where the Christians of Sardis are instructed to remember what they had received, to obey it and to repent. It is also present in John's Gospel, although here it is something more yet.

For John, remembering is essentially a means of understanding the events which are remembered, both those of the Old Testament and the events of Jesus. So it is that at the cleansing of the temple the disciples remember an Old Testament text. In the same chapter, when John relates Jesus' saying about the temple to the body of Christ, he adds an explanatory note that after the resurrection the disciples recalled this saying, and then understood it. At 16:4 Jesus warns his disciples of what will happen to them, and informs them that they will remember what he had told them; and at 12:16 they remember the triumphal entry into Jerusalem after the glorification of Jesus, only then understanding it.

Remembering is then a term for recognising the messianic fulfilment of Scripture in the person of Jesus. As such it may be linked to John's typological scheme. Jesus provides the true meaning of the Old Testament, and so remembering Jesus is the way in which Old Testament texts may in turn be remembered and understood. The types which lie behind Jesus and the depth of Old Testament allusion in *John* with regard to Jesus may be understood with reference to this idea of remembrance. Likewise, in the context of his exaltation Jesus himself becomes a subject of remembrance, the events of his earthly ministry being so understood. Insofar as Melito is the heir to John's typological scheme so we may also suggest that he is heir to this means of remembrance mediated through the Scriptures of the Old covenant.

However, in the Pauline tradition Jesus is remembered primarily at the Lord's Supper. Thus there is the command to enact the supper in remembrance of Jesus recorded at *I Corinthians* 11:24-25. This is not the place to engage in the argument concerning whether or not the Last Supper was a Passover; on the other hand it is clear that the

synoptic accounts at least are full of Passover colouring.[60] This may
lend a clue to the interpretation of the command to enact the supper
in remembrance of Jesus as found in Paul, with no comment as to
whether these are the words of Jesus or Pauline interpretation.

This interpretative effort is confused by the suggestion of Jeremias
that the words mean "Do this that God may remember me", stated in
such a way as to exclude any human act of remembrance.[61] This has
received notable rejoinders from Jones and from Kosmala.[62] These
have argued that whilst the meaning is possible, it is unlikely. Although the forms of זכר in the Old Testament are polyvalent, referring to God or to people, if the meaning is not clear from the context
then the verb is qualified. Here there is no qualification and so the
obvious meaning must be imputed. "Do this to remember me".
Chenderlin has moved the debate along by pointing out the Old
Testament background, in view of which there is no such thing as an
"obvious" meaning behind the sentence. Rather the verb is polyvalent by its very nature.[63] Thus there is no question that the disciples
will actually forget Jesus, rather the remembering taking place here is
cultic, occurring at what was from the beginning a festival of commemoration. Likewise it is not possible to exclude God's action from
the equation. So it is that Davies suggests that the haggadah is here
being recalled, mention of Jesus being substituted for the departure
from Egypt.[64] It is interesting that Paul should use the word
καταγγέλλειν when he speaks of declaring the death of the Lord in
eating and drinking the eucharistic gifts, since this is the word used by
the Septuagint to render הגיד, the hiphil of נגד and the basis of the
noun "haggadah".

A final point on this may be made with reference to the work of
Petuchowski who notes that a sandwich of unleavened bread and
bitter herbs is made in remembrance of Hillel at the seder.[65] He
suggests that this way of remembering with symbolic foods may provide a parallel for the action of Jesus. This remembrance however
seems to have more in common with the remembrance of the actions
of the apostles encouraged in the epistles. This point is made to
demonstrate that the Jewish idea of remembrance, especially around

[60] Note in particular Feneberg *Paschafeier und Abendmahl* for the extent of this colouring and for an explanation
[61] Jeremias *Eucharistic Words* 273
[62] Jones "ANAMNHΣIΣ"; Kosmala "Das tut"
[63] Chenderlin *Do This* 120-122
[64] Davies *Paul and Rabbinic Judaism* 257
[65] Petuchowski "Do This" 296

the Passover, was distinctly alive in early Christianity. Moreover that remembering Jesus was an essential part of the eucharistic rite of the early church. However, this evidence is restricted to the Pauline witness, and may not readily be imputed to other Christian communities. Unfortunately *I Corinthians* 11 is the nearest thing to a Passover haggadah contained in the New Testament.[66] If this is typical then it would seem that the function of the haggadah was identical, albeit with a different subject of commemoration.

On the other hand it is noteworthy that the eucharistic teaching contained in *John* 6 is expressed typologically. Thus it is bound up to the process of understanding the Old Testament through remembering Jesus which was discussed above. Although we were previously unable to show any definitive link between *John* 6 and the haggadah, it is possible that they held a commemorative element in common. We did in fact find that John was indebted to Jewish Passover traditions.[67] As the glorified Jesus is present in the eucharistic assembly so the cultic act of commemoration of him may take place, and he, together with the Old Testament type lying behind him, may be understood.

Despite the lack of explicit New Testament evidence, the very fact that the Quartodeciman Passover derives directly from the Jewish celebration would indicate that the motivating factor of remembrance would in some way be transmitted to Christianity. The great opponent of this view of the Quartodeciman Pascha is Lohse, who on the assumption of the continuation of the Jewish festival believes the emphasis to be purely eschatological.[68] However, we have seen that past commemoration and future eschatology were not mutually exclusive in the Jewish setting, and so there is no reason to suppose that they were considered so by the Christians.

There is then a common liturgical context and a common purpose. This is not to minimize the differences between the Jewish Passover and the Christian Pascha. Apart from the theological differences in the subject of celebration/commemoration to which we have alluded throughout, there are liturgical differences too.[69] Most significant for our contention that the table rite was common to both is that

---

[66] Gärtner *John 6* and Manns "Traces" stop short of claiming that these works are actual haggadoth

[67] 2.1.3 above

[68] Lohse *Passafest* 78-84. cf the approach of Blank *Meliton* 38-40. We deal with this question in detail at 4.2.3 below.

[69] These distinctions, both theological and liturgical, are enumerated by Huber *Passa und Ostern* 8-11

the Jews celebrated in families, in which context the place of the table
is clear, whereas the Christians celebrated as an *ekklesia*.

However, the earliest Christian churches originated in domestic
households, a table rite being central to their worship; such is the
locus of the pastoral epistles. There was thus little distinction between
family and church. The eucharist, a domestic rite, was celebrated as
such by the entire Christian community, and there is no reason why
the same should not be true of the Passover seder. Although the seder
was inherited from mainstream Judaism, whereas the eucharist was
native to the Christian movement there is still no reason why a family
rite should not be extended to the οἶκος θεοῦ. The invitation at the
end of *Peri Pascha* is made to πατριαί; we may read into this the
implication that πατριαί are being invited to join into one πατριά
around one table.[70] It is thus that forgiveness and resurrection are to
be given and received. Such is the offer which is made, the means by
which it is gained having been remembered.

2.3 Conclusion

We have established that it is possible for there to have been conformity between the Passover ritual of Judaism and the paschal ritual
of the Quartodecimans. We have moreover been able to suggest that
the function of the ritual, and of its accompanying texts, that is to say
remembrance, each continued to be upheld within the church. An
analysis of the genre of *Peri Pascha* is necessary to see whether the
form of the document supports this identification of its function. If
this is the case, then we shall be able to go on to locate *Peri Pascha* in
the table rite of the Christians of Sardis.

---

[70] See on this transference Kretschmar "Christliches Passa"

CHAPTER THREE

THE FORM AND FUNCTION OF PERI PASCHA

Having established the form and function of paschal observance in Judaism, and established a reasonable possibility that such practice was passed to the Quartodeciman Christians, the next part of the argument must concern the form and function of *Peri Pascha*. The first part of this chapter will establish a genre for the document, the second then attempts to see how this genre fits into the Quartodeciman rite.

This chapter is the central plank in our overall case. An identification of the genre of *Peri Pascha* as haggadah is what will enable us to see it as a primarily liturgical document. We have already argued that *Peri Pascha*, being delivered in the context of a table rite, is functionally equivalent to the haggadah,[1] but for this to be sustained a formal equivalence needs to be shown likewise.

3.1 THE GENRE OF PERI PASCHA

3.1.1 *Peri Pascha as Homily*

When Bonner first published the work he classified it as "a Good Friday Sermon".[2] This is a description which has continued to be maintained. Salzmann, for instance, continues to claim *Peri Pascha* as a homily and attempts to account for the absence of paraenesis on the basis that it is inappropriate in a festal homily, that the praises of God take precedence.[3] To this one must ask whether a piece given over so entirely to the praises of God is a homily at all. A subtle variation on this theme is suggested by Hall, who proposes that *Peri Pascha* be divided at 46,[4] and that the first half, that is to say *Peri Pascha* before this point, may be seen as a homily for one of the Sabbaths preceding Passover. We will examine the division of *Peri Pascha* in due course; for the moment we must seek to see whether the form of any part of the work is susceptible of such a description. We begin here since this

---

[1] 2.2 above
[2] Bonner *Homily* 19
[3] Salzmann *Lehren und Ermahnen* 270
[4] Hall "Melito in the Light of the Passover Haggadah" 36-37

is still the most common answer offered to the question of the genre
of *Peri Pascha*, and is one which has dictated the place assigned to *Peri
Pascha* in the paschal liturgy of the Quartodecimans.

A problem with this is that the term "homily" is largely undefined.
However, if Melito's tradition is Johannine, then a homily according
to his understanding may be seen as being the same as that understood by John. Although there has been little research into the discourses as such since the abandonment of Bultmann's theory of a
Redenquelle,[5] there is a tendency to see them as in some way reflecting
the homilies delivered in the Johannine assembly. So for instance
Borgen argues that John shows awareness of the rabbinic synagogue
homily, and that such is the rationale for the discourse of *John* 6.[6]
This would be indicated by *John* 6:59, which states that the discourse
had been given in the synagogue. This would presumably be an
example of the pre-Passover preaching to which Hall has reference,
and which he claims explains the shape of the first part of *Peri Pascha*.
Working along similar lines to Borgen, Lindars has sought to show
that the Gospel is in part built up out of homilies delivered at the
eucharistic assemblies of the Johannine community, these homilies
having been redacted into the Gospel.[7]

Borgen's conclusion concerning John 6 is not far different from
that reached by Gärtner, who saw the discourse as originating in a
Sabbath homily preceding Passover,[8] but Borgen goes further in that
he discusses not only the Jewish background of the chapter but gives
us a form-critical analysis of the synagogue homily as well. In creating
this he is fundamentally indebted to the work of Maybaum and
Bacher in describing homiletic forms in the Palestinian midrash.[9] He
also finds similar forms in the work of Philo.[10] Indeed we may point
out that something like this is evinced in the midrashic part of the
haggadah isolated by Finkelstein.[11]

Other synagogue homilies have been reconstructed, but many of
the reconstructions are the work of Mann,[12] and are themselves based
on his own reconstruction of the triennial Palestinian lectionary. His
work, however, is far from universally accepted. Heinemann for instance suggests that the inductive method which he employed in or-

---

[5] This point is made by Meeks "Am I a Jew?" 161
[6] Borgen *Bread from Heaven*
[7] Lindars *Behind the Fourth Gospel* 43-60 and *Gospel of John* 46-54
[8] Gärtner *John 6*
[9] Maybaum *ältesten Phasen* and Bacher *Proömien*
[10] Borgen *Bread from Heaven* 46-51
[11] Finkelstein "Oldest Midrash"
[12] Mann *Bible*

der to isolate the *haftaroth* is flawed in that it is not based on any principle, that the number of *sedarim* in the Masoretic text makes it impossible to create a three-year lectionary cycle, and that the evidence for a regular lectionary is too late to be of validity for the first century.[13] Mann's reconstructions are, however, accepted by Bowker, who finds these forms displayed in certain of the speeches in *Acts*.[14]

In view of the controversy surrounding this area we are not entitled to ground any conclusions too firmly on this evidence. The consensus would seem to be that attempts to find synagogue homilies in the New Testament are anachronistic; however there is some Tannaitic evidence for the use of this form.[15] To gloss over an extensive discussion, we may suggest that a variety of forms may have been employed in synagogue preaching in the first century. Simply because something does not conform to the exegetical shape described by Borgen is not sufficient reason baldly to state that it is not a homily. Moreover, although it may be possible to reconstruct some homilies, we should not be fooled by their literary shape into making their shape prescriptive of a homily, since they have of necessity undergone a degree of literary editing.[16] We may, nonetheless, seek to discover whether any of these alleged forms are exhibited by *Peri Pascha*. If they are not prescriptive, they may be descriptive, and if one of them is exhibited here then it may be claimed.

The basic content of one of these homilies is a paraphrase of Old Testament material into which material from the haggadic tradition is interleaved. So, *John* 6:31ff is mainly made up of paraphrase of the Old Testament, with the exception of the word καταβαίνων. This is not found in the Old Testament but in both *Mekilta Exodus* and *Exodus Rabbah* the fact that the bread came down is treated as significant.[17] Perhaps John drew on a similar tradition. This basic content is shared by the Palestinian midrashim, although these tend to be more stylised, not wedding in paraphrase and haggadah, but simply quoting haggadic material by way of interpretation of the passage. According to Borgen the paraphrase begins with the citation of the initial text which is then interpreted in its constituent parts, by which process the wider setting of the text is drawn in, and subordinate Old Testament texts are supplied in order further to illustrate the interpretation being

---

[13] Heinemann "Triennial Lectionary Cycle"

[14] Bowker "Speeches in Acts"

[15] Aune, for instance in *New Testament* 202 expresses the consensus that these attempts are anachronistic, but himself admits the existence of Tannaitic proems.

[16] This is a bald summary of some of the conclusions reached by Heinemann "Proem" and Shivan "Sermons"

given. The closing statement of the homily picks up the opening citation.

Borgen's conclusion has been disputed in part by Richter who suggests that 51b-58 form a separate and distinct section added by a later hand.[18] He suggests that the form is complete within 31-51a. This argument is more important for the exegesis of *John* than for the provision of comparative material relating to the study of *Peri Pascha*; however one may note with Lindars that one cannot expect to find the synagogue lecture form followed too closely here, in that the redactional needs of the Gospel have also had to be met.[19] It is also true that the division sought by Richter is the result of the distinction between the sapiential and eucharistic interpretations of the manna, the sapiential predominating in 31-51a, the eucharistic in 51bff. However, the two cannot really be seen as mutually exclusive, the distinction being one obvious to the modern mind, but perhaps less obvious in the second century. It is adequate for our purposes to say that the homiletic pattern is discernible in this passage, and that the association between eucharist and Passover is clearly established this early in the history of the Johannine tradition.

The problem to which Richter draws our attention is essentially the extent to which the overarching genre of the Gospel has affected the individual forms which are redacted into that overarching form. Thus we may compare Lindars' discussion of *John* 8:31-58,[20] where he argues that the homily form is present as an exegetical treatment of the parable of the son and the slave, to his examination of the literary construction of c5,[21] in which he shows that in the construction of the Gospel part of the homily has been held over. In the same way the discourses at the Last Supper are constructed out of the elements of a number of homilies.[22] The point is sufficiently made that the discourses are based on homilies and that these homilies are exegetical homilies of the kind preached in the synagogue, based however not on Scripture but on elements of the Jesus tradition; but there cannot be absolute security on the extent to which the Johannine discourse follows the exegetical shape of the synagogue homily because the needs of the Gospel form in the redactional employment of the homilies should be taken into account.

---

[17] Borgen *Bread from Heaven* 20-21
[18] Richter "Formgeschichte"
[19] Lindars *John* 250
[20] Lindars *Behind the Fourth Gospel* 43-47
[21] Lindars *John* 51-54
[22] Lindars *John* 468

Although Borgen's work has not found universal acceptance we may nonetheless for the moment accept his analysis of *John* 6 as consisting of citation and paraphrase in order to enquire whether this Johannine method has found a practitioner in Melito, whether it has been transmitted to him in the tradition and may so provide a basis for the form-critical classification of *Peri Pascha*. Something like this may, perhaps, be seen in fragment 9, discussed at 1.2.1 above, where Melito begins with a text from *Isaiah*, and goes on to discuss it in haggadic detail, using traditions concerning the *aqedah*. Parts of *Genesis* 22 are mixed in to the fragment and the text is not only paraphrased but typologically treated in order to make a theological point. The text is fragmentary, however, to such an extent that beginning and end cannot be said to have been established. We cannot even be clear which of *Isaiah* and *Genesis* is the text actually under discussion.

The section of *Peri Pascha* where a text might be found as a preliminary citation is that following PP12. We may begin to see a citation from *Exodus* 12 in PP12-15. There he explicitly refers to the text, saying several times φησίν, and sets forth the content of *Exodus* 12. However, a closer examination reveals that this is not a citation of the text at all. For although there is little in this section which does not occur in the original text, the word ἄσπιλον being the only word which is entirely unparalleled in either the Masoretic text or the Septuagint, large amounts are omitted as he jumps from verse 3 (the instruction to take a lamb) to verse 6 (the instruction to slaughter it) to verse 11 (the instruction to eat it at night.) This is a paraphrase rather than a citation.[23] Subsequently he returns to verse 7, the command to smear the blood on the doorposts.

Although this paraphrase in itself might be claimed as being itself the homily, consisting of paraphrase without preliminary citation, one should note that the text is not worked through in any detail, and indeed is left behind altogether in what follows. Along similar lines it may be suggested that this section is the remainder of a synagogue homily, because it has developed out of one. However, even if this is so, it does not answer the form-critical question as to what it is now.

---

[23] It is interesting to observe in this respect that the text is not being paraphrased according to the Septuagint, since the phrase שׂה תמים is rendered ἀμνὸν ἄμωμον as opposed to the Septuagint's πρόβατον τέλειον, and yet the command not to break any bone of the animal is brought to prominence in a way which reflects the Septuagintal position of the command at verse 11 rather than the later position of the Masoretic text. The citation of this command is different again from the version recorded at *John* 19:36, which Freed *Old Testament Quotations* 108, with good reason, believes to be a citation from memory of the Septuagint.

Of course, given the possibility that a variety of homilies existed, the fact that *Peri Pascha* does not conform to this kind of synagogue homily does not mean to say that it is absolutely not a homily, but nonetheless, whatever *Peri Pascha* is, it is not an exegetical synagogue homily along rabbinic lines.

Further enquiries need to be made. In particular we may enquire into the other suggested genre, that which we intend to lend support, namely the possibility that *Peri Pascha* is a paschal haggadah.

3.1.2 *Peri Pascha as Haggadah*

Although *Peri Pascha* has been generally assumed to be a homily, there have been dissenting voices. Most particularly Cross took issue with this and pointed out certain links between *Peri Pascha* and the Jewish Passover haggadah.[24] On internal grounds he concluded that *Peri Pascha* was in fact precisely this, a Christian Passover haggadah. The most thorough treatment of the question of whether *Peri Pascha* is a haggadah is, however, that of Hall.[25] Hall's work follows on from that of Cross, and of Werner, who whilst not pursuing that specific idea had suggested certain links between the haggadah and Melito's work.[26] It must be added that Hansen had also attempted to classify *Peri Pascha* as a haggadah, but failed to produce any firm evidence for his assertion.[27] After Hall's criticism of certain of the arguments of Cross and Werner has been taken into account, the following positive internal links emerge.

First there is a close verbal correspondence between *Mishnah Pesahim* 10.5, which appears in the haggadah, and PP68. This correspondence had first been noticed by Cross, and was independently noted by le Déaut.[28]

The relevant texts are as follow:

---

[24] Cross (Review) 162-163; idem *Early Christian Fathers*; at 107 he states "what we have here is nothing else than a Christian Paschal Haggadah."

[25] Hall "Melito in the Light of the Passover Haggadah"

[26] Werner "Melito of Sardes". Werner's main argument is that the improperia of the Latin Good Friday rite had their origin with Melito. This is not so, they originate in a Byzantine treatment of a Jewish catalogue of benefits. See Yahalom "Piyyut as Poetry"; also Flusser "Hebrew Improperia" and Brocke "Jewish Origin"

[27] Hansen *Sitz* passim, but inconsistently!

[28] Cross *Early Christian Writers* 108; le Déaut *Nuit Pascale* 233-234

Mishnah Pesahim 10.5	*Peri Pascha* 68
He brought us out	It is he who rescued us
from bondage to freedom	from bondage to freedom
from sorrow to gladness	
and from mourning to a festival day	from death to life
and from darkness	from darkness
to a great light	to light
and from tyranny	and from servitude
to redemption...	to an eternal Kingdom

Hall shows that the correspondence can be brought even closer since the extra couplet in the haggadah text, omitted in *Peri Pascha*, derives from the book of *Esther* and may be inferred to have been directly incorporated into the original haggadah text.[29] He goes on to quote further comparable Jewish and early Christian texts, most notably *Exodus Rabbah* 12.2, which includes the reference to life found in *Peri Pascha* but not in the haggadah.[30] All this would indicate that both Melito and the haggadah, as well as the passage from *Exodus Rabbah*, are dependent on the same pre-Christian Passover text.[31] Le Déaut likewise demonstrates extensive parallels from the Jewish paschal tradition.[32]

Secondly it must be noted that the set themes which, according to Rabbi Gamaliel in the Mishnah are to be covered in the haggadah are all covered by *Peri Pascha*, namely the lamb, the deliverance from Egypt, the bitter herbs and the unleavened bread. Again this had been observed by Cross.[33] Significantly, whereas according to Gamaliel the justification for the mention of the lamb is the passing of God over the Israelites, the significance in Melito is the saving effect of the blood of the lamb which is put on the doorposts of the Israelites. In Christian terms, the blood of the paschal lamb is seen as the basis for the sparing of Israel, as it is of the salvation of Christians.[34] This is significant because it is the ancient reason for mentioning the Passover as part of the Jewish observance. Gamaliel had changed it, as Zeitlin pointed out.[35] Thus Melito preserves a piece of Jewish

---

[29] Hall "Melito in the Light of the Passover Haggadah" 31-32

[30] Pines "From Darkness into Great Light" 49 points out that it is also to be found in a similar series of transition statements in Joseph and Asenath

[31] Apart from the texts cited by Hall we should note the connection with *Revelation* 5:10

[32] Le Déaut *Nuit Pascale* 232-236

[33] Cross *Early Christian Writers* 108-109

[34] PP30

[35] Zeitlin "Liturgy" 440-443. For the change see 2.1.4 above.

tradition more ancient yet than the *Mishnah*. This may have been readily comprehensible to him since it could be seen as a Hellenistic apotropaic rite.[36]

Thirdly there is the use of the term ἀφικόμενος of Christ at *Peri Pascha* 66 and 86. In these places it is used of Christ in respect of his coming to earth to heal the suffering. This is significant because it reflects the *aphikomen* of the Jewish Passover rite. Daube sought to show that *aphikomen* is derived from the Greek ἀφικόμενος and is originally a messianic title.[37] It is precisely this messianic significance which the term carries in *Peri Pascha* and this may be seen as lending fuel to Daube's argument. It is moreover again indicative of primitive Passover traditions being known to the Church at Sardis. Werner had noticed the allusion but reckoned it a parodic imitation of Jewish practice.[38] We may note that this is an indication that a degree of eschatological expectation is bound up to the Quartodeciman rite, again a link with Judaism, and one which goes some way to answer the arguments of Huber and Hyldahl referred to at 1.1.1[39]

Fourthly we must notice the links between *Peri Pascha* and the *dayyenu*. These were noted by Werner, who argued that PP87-89 were a parody of the *dayyenu*.[40] His case is overstated, as there is no direct parallel in terms of verses or numbers of benefits recounted, but there is indeed something in common with the repeated refrain and the list of wonders worked for Israel. In particular we may note the close linking of the exodus and the giving of the manna, and the prose conclusion to the catalogue of benefits.

In addition to these major points of agreement we may note smaller ones, such as the repeated refrain of ἐγώ noted in 2.1.3 above, and the question placed at PP46 corresponding, as Hall notes, to that asked in the course of the seder.[41] This much goes to support our hypothesis, that *Peri Pascha* is a haggadah derived from the Jewish tradition and treated in a way which would accord with Hellenistic oratory. The problem, however, is that the shape of *Peri Pascha* as it stands does not correspond with the shape of the haggadah, however loosely that term is treated. This is seen by Hall who proposes a very ingenious solution.[42]

---

[36] See Young *Sacrificial Ideas* 154

[37] On the *aphikomen* see Daube *He that Cometh* and 4.2.4 below

[38] Werner "Melito" 205-206

[39] Huber *Passa und Ostern*; Hyldahl "Titel"; see further on the messianic expectation of the Quartodecimans at 4.2.3 below

[40] Werner "Melito of Sardes"

[41] Hall *Melito of Sardis* 23

[42] Hall "Melito in the Light of the Passover Haggadah" 36-37

The prescribed shape of the haggadah is that it should "begin with the disgrace and end with the glory". That, according to the *Mishnah*, is the overall manner of the treatment of *Deuteronomy* 26:5ff. Stein believes this to demonstrate a form of encomiastic rhetoric, and quotes classical parallels, to the effect that a panegyric may be more effective if one begins with deprecatory material concerning the object of praise and goes on to overshadow this with the praise that is due.[43] It is interesting that this section of the midrash is that which according to Finkelstein derived from the time of the Ptolemaic government of Palestine.[44] Moreover it is on this basis a pattern all the more liable to commend itself to the Hellenist Melito. And yet *Peri Pascha* does not appear to exhibit this shape. A further problem lies in the fact that the work is partly concerned to elucidate *Exodus* 12, a passage which is nowhere recorded to be the substance of the reading of Scripture for the eve of Passover, but is nonetheless material for synagogal lections on the Sabbaths preceding Passover. On this basis Hall proposes to divide the work as we possess it into two, with the break at PP46. A major division at this point is upheld by virtually all who have studied *Peri Pascha*. It is to be maintained not only on the grounds of sense, but, as we shall see below, on the basis of the role of the doxologies in dividing the work. Hall suggests that if the work be divided at that point, then the second half may be seen to have the shape for the haggadah as prescribed by the Mishnah, whereas the first half may then be seen as a homily for one of the Sabbaths preceding Passover, when *Exodus* 12 would have been one of the readings. We may note that the same setting was allotted to *John* 6.

That the second "half" may be seen as a haggadah in itself, and not simply a division in the text, may be supported by the fact that this is the point at which the introductory question is asked; this is the part of the work in which occur all the Passover themes and allusions mentioned above. We may also note that the first half is described as a *diegema*, a distinct part of an epideictic whole, whereas the second half is given its own rhetorical identity.[45] But most important of all, this division of the work has the shape prescribed for the haggadah which was found wanting over the work as a whole, it begins with the disgrace and ends with the glory. So it begins with the fall of Adam and ends with the exaltation of Christ. Hall shows how the details of

---

[43] Stein "Influence" 36-37; Zeitlin "Liturgy" 450 had argued that this prescription was late, on the grounds of a rabbinic disputation concerning its meaning. However this does not mean that the original prescription is contemporary with the argument

[44] Finkelstein "Pre-Maccabean Documents"

[45] On which see further 3.1.4 below.

Melito's account of the fall and exaltation mirror those details given concerning the decline of Israel into Egypt and their rescue which are found in the set passage of *Deuteronomy* 26:5ff.[46] Thus the fall may be compared to the descent into Egypt, (as well as being understandable in Platonic terms!), the Israel which became great in number to the prolific Adam, the rescue of the Israelites to the redemption wrought by Christ.

In this context he notes that the passage in the haggadah which expresses most clearly that it was God himself and no angel who rescued Israel is paralleled at a point where Melito gives us his fullest expression of incarnational theology. There are, of course, difficulties with this. The incarnational statement is difficult to reconcile to PP32, where in agreement with *Exodus* and in distinction from the haggadah it is clear that it was an angel who had undertaken the slaying. It is impossible that the angel is Jesus since Jesus has already been typified in the lamb, whose blood protects the doorposts of the Israelites. This can only be reconciled if the division into two discrete halves is upheld; indeed this may be seen as further support for the division.

Hall also sees the difficulty of reconciling the passage concerning the indictment of Israel to the haggadic pattern. However, he sees numerous good reasons for seeing it as part of the pattern, the manner in which it treats the mishnaic subjects of the unleavened bread and the bitter herbs, the fact that in part it mirrors the *dayyenu*, the fact that it treats the signs and wonders surrounding the crucifixion, mirroring in turn the terror and the signs and wonders surrounding the exodus which are treated in *Deuteronomy*. Finally he notes that the exaltation (the glory is that of humanity in Christ just as the disgrace is that of Adam) is only complete after this passage is complete.

Overall he sees the passage as a substructure within the disgrace-glory pattern which itself follows the pattern. We may add to this that it makes the work complete as a piece of epideictic oratory in that it apportions blame as well as praise. If the subject is God then there can be no possibility of enumerating the less endearing points about the subject before going on to praise him, and so the focus of blame is shifted elsewhere, onto those who are already traditional objects of blame for the passion.

Thus we may see that Hall makes out a very strong case indeed for the classification of *Peri Pascha* as a Christian paschal haggadah, on the basis of its ultimate dependence on a Jewish model. It is a case

---

[46] Hall "Melito in the Light of the Passover Haggadah" 38-39

which depends entirely, however, on the division into two discrete parts. Nonetheless further arguments may be adduced.

As Hall notes, the overall structure of PP46-103 was of disgrace-glory; we may perceive that within *Peri Pascha* this structure occurs in two substructures, PP46-71 and 72-103, and note that these two parts each have hymnic conclusions. In the Jewish haggadah likewise there is a (much interpolated) pattern of treatment of scripture and hymnic response.[47] In both haggadoth, the Jewish and the Christian, we may see the question being answered by the haggadah and the rite con-cluded hymnically, the chief difference being that in *Peri Pascha* the material is divided into two, being re-arranged to create a more com-plex structure. In this light we may note the suggestion that the hymnic conclusion to Melito's work, including the recounting of the mercies of God towards Israel, owes something to the *dayyenu*.[48] Of course the benefits extend beyond the building of the Temple and for this reason Melito's hymn is extended beyond the blessings of God upon Israel to climax in Christ's resurrected presence.

Differences in detail between the two rites should neither surprise nor alarm us; our studies have shown that whereas the context and basic content of the seder are stable there is a fluidity in order.[49] Melito's version of the haggadah is sufficiently close to that of the Jews to make it a reasonable assumption that the table context re-mained, as did the motivation for the haggadah, in Melito's tradition. This would gain support from the evidence of the *Epistula Apostolorum*, which concludes its celebration with the agape. In the paschal con-text, this agape could well have grown from the seder.

---

[47] This pattern is not only that of *Peri Pascha*, but is that which Philo's report on the *therapeutae* (on which see 2.1.2 above) would lead us to expect. In the currently extant haggadah the midrash on *Deuteronomy* concludes with the *dayyenu*. We may note in this context the claim of Finkelstein "Pre-Maccabean Documents" that the *dayyenu* de-rives from the pre-Maccabean period. He reasons that the lack of any mention in this hymn of early military victories by Israel indicate a time at which Israel is under a foreign military occupation, and more convincingly that since the temple is consid-ered to be the climax of God's mercies it must therefore still be standing (though this would not make it pre-Maccabean, simply pre-70). This alone however may be sufficient for our purposes. Cavaletti "Fonti" states that Finkelstein's arguments at this point are unconvincing, but without lending anything to the discussion. Flusser "Hebrew Improperia" assents to dating the dayyenu before AD 70. As was noted in 2.1.4 a hymn was sung at the conclusion of the Passover rite, and whilst this could have been the hallel, a reference to the *dayyenu* is also possible

[48] So Flusser "Notes"

[49] Daube "Earliest Structures" likewise warns us to expect variety in the shape of the primitive seder. Because the primary emphasis was on the temple rites, the seder was not canonized into a particular shape before the second century

For the moment we may accept Hall's division, and seek further possible genres for the work, either in parts of as a whole, and on the basis of the conclusions reached on the matter of form, turn to the question of whether the work should be divided. In particular one further suggestion has been made as to the genre of *Peri Pascha* which requires examination.

3.1.3 *Peri Pascha as Diatribe*

Hall's work in uncovering the haggadah in the second part of *Peri Pascha* has received criticism from McDonald.[50] He too attempted to answer the form-critical question, arguing that the work may properly be called a homily, and suggesting that haggadah and homily are really fruits of the same tree. He also suggests that the stoic-cynic diatribe lies somewhere in the ancestry of *Peri Pascha*. The *diatribe* was a brief moral essay, examples of which are preserved in the discourses of Epictetus, which Arrian, his editor, called *diatribai*. McDonald makes his suggestion on the grounds that elements of the diatribe found their way into Christian preaching and because elements of rhetorical technique appear in Epictetus' *diatribai*. However, in order to suggest that *Peri Pascha* is a diatribe, a Greek rhetorical form, probably with a schoolroom origin,[51] it is necessary to show that Melito has been rhetorically educated to such an extent that he may employ such a form in his work.

This has been achieved already. The investigation of the style of *Peri Pascha* originated when Bonner suggested *Peri Pascha* was strongly Semitic in cast, pointing in particular to the Septuagint as the source of its style.[52] Wifstrand responded not long afterwards and pointed out numerous parallels with the second sophistic in order to argue for its essentially Hellenistic background.[53] Wifstrand quotes extensive stylistic parallels to Melito from Asians of the second sophistic, using chiefly Maximus of Tyre, but also Favorinus, Lucian and Polemo. His chief object is to demonstrate that the parallelisms in Melito's isocola show a formal balance which is lacking in Hebrew poetry, but is demonstrated frequently by the Greeks of the Asianist style. He also demonstrates that Melito's anaphorae are more elaborate than those found in the Septuagint, whilst being matched by those of Maximus. He goes on to show extensive homoioteleuton (e.g. at PP73),

---

[50] McDonald "Comments"
[51] On the scholastic origin of the diatribe see Stowers *Diatribe* 48-78
[52] Bonner *Homily* 23
[53] Wifstrand "Homily"

homoiarcton (e.g. PP69), antithesis with paronomasia in the middle (the example he quotes at PP11 no longer demonstrates this, due to the revision of Bonner's text, but PP34 demonstrates the same features, albeit not so clearly) and long series of two membered isocola with anaphora (e.g. at PP44.) All these are typical of the Asianist style. Other typical Asianist features are address to persons and objects not present (e.g. PP32, to the angel) and exclamations with " Ω followed by the genitive (e.g. PP97). Bonner assented to the correctness of Wifstrand's case.[54] If Melito is an imitator of the second sophistic he must therefore have received an education in the rhetorical schools. This education was centred on the gymnasium;[55] we have already observed that Sardis possessed a gymnasium.[56]

Since Wifstrand there have been further treatments of Melito's style. One of the marks of the Asianist style, as opposed to the Atticist, which used only vocabulary known from the classical Attic orators, was the coining of neologisms. This aspect of Melito's style has been studied by Ruiz who finds not only neologisms in the text but also some hapax legomena.[57] He cites extensive contemporary parallels to this process of neologism. A broader study of Melito's style is that of Halton.[58] Halton begins with the prologue and noting that the antithetic adjectives build up to the preliminary announcement of the resurrection. The introduction of the types of the old and the new are dealt with so skilfully, PP7 being antistrophic to the first part of PP4 just as they are theologically antithetical, the whole summed up in PP9, that Halton is forced to exclaim that "This is less a display of architectonic virtuosity than an impressive fusion of rhetoric and theology".[59] He goes on to show debts to Homer in the treatment of the suffering of Egypt, the very kind of treatment of Homer that was customarily learnt under the sophist. This graphic description is contrasted with the protection of Israel. The rhetorical question to the angel at PP32 is answered immediately, this pair of antithetic isocola recalling the prologue. The didactic section is thus introduced, again employing much parallelism and enabling him to give free play to paronomasia (PP38 contains a delightful example: ποιεῖς τὸν τύπον. τοῦτον ποθεῖς). So Halton continues through the entire work, showing at all stages the high art employed not only in the figures of sound but

---

[54] Bonner "Text"
[55] Marrou *History* 181
[56] At 1.1.3 above
[57] Ruiz "Hapax Legomena"
[58] Halton "Stylistic Device"
[59] Halton "Stylistic Device" 251

in the construction of the work. This is not the place to repeat all of
Halton's findings, but simply to point out that as a result of his work
we are able to see that *Peri Pascha* is a piece of rhetorical brilliance.
From this we can deduce that Melito must have had a rhetorical
education. That this is the case is not only demonstrable from *Peri
Pascha*, Grant has demonstrated that, in his *Apology* to Marcus
Aurelius, Melito follows the advice laid down by Menander for an
address of this kind, in dwelling on the history of the imperial family
and in pledging loyalty to the Emperor and to his succession.[60]

It is in view of all this work that we must note that not only does
Peri Pascha display the Asianist Greek style, but that far from being a
clumsy composition it displays rhetorical skill to a very high degree.
The implication of the work of those who have studied the style of
Peri Pascha must be spelt out; Melito was not an amateur imitator of
the sophists but was himself a sophist in the very first rank, indeed an
"elegans et declamatorium ingenium."[61]

There is thus no reason why Melito might not have been an expo-
nent of the diatribe, a form with a schoolroom origin tinged with
rhetorical elements. But although *diatribai* are tinged with a rhetorical
style the presence of a rhetorical style is not a sufficient condition to
enable us to label any piece of writing as a diatribe. Informality is
nearer the mark; Wendland speaks of "Wärme und Lebhaftigkeit des
Gefühls, Reichtum der Erfahrung, Originalität der Formen".[62] This
is not *Peri Pascha*.

The diatribe has frequently been claimed as the nearest thing to a
Christian homily produced by the Hellenistic world, to the extent
that for Thyen the terms are virtually interchangeable.[63] One should
indeed note that the diatribe did exercise some influence over rabbinic preaching.[64] Thus it is natural that these moral sermons would
be imitated by Christians, and equally natural that, coming from
Hierapolis, Epictetus would employ rhetorical techniques in his
works. Often they take the form of a chreia, betraying in these cases
the influence of Arrian. Epictetus and Melito are each Asians, and
would each inevitably be touched by the influence of the second
sophistic, but that may be the entire extent of their affinity.

Peri Pascha neither as a whole nor in its constituent parts, bears any
resemblance to the lectures of Epictetus. Epictetus may use oratorical

---

[60] Grant "Five Apologists" 6-7
[61] The words are Tertullian's, quoted by Jerome, *De Viris Illustribus* 24
[62] So Wendland *Hellenistisch-Romanische Kultur* 80
[63] Thyen *Stil* passim but notably at 1-16
[64] Marmorstein "Background"

techniques and in doing so holds something in common with Melito, but even though the diatribe grew in part from the meeting of philosophy with the sophistic movement[65] the use of oratorical technique is not in itself a mark of form. Not even the more technical parts of *Peri Pascha*, such as the discussion of what constitutes a type, owe anything to this form, even though it may be considered a philosophical discussion.

The form of the diatribe is difficult precisely to ascertain. A foothold may be found however in one distinct difference which Thyen notes between the classical and Christian models. That is the different extent to which the addressee of the diatribe appears. In the classical diatribe the addressee is very present as an entity, and is often an individual, whereas in the Christian models that he examines the addressee is either a group, or completely absent, and in any case makes little appearance. The fact that the classical and Christian models should exhibit such important differences and yet their basic similarity be recognisable indicates a certain flexibility of form. Thus form alone need not exclude *Peri Pascha* from classification as a diatribe.

The similarity between the Christian and classical models of the diatribe is actually to be sustained on the basis of content; it is this which enables us categorically to state that *Peri Pascha* cannot be described as a diatribe. Late stoicism, the philosophical movement which gave rise to this form was essentially a moral creed. Although it held metaphysical suppositions which were the basis for its ethic, it expressed itself primarily in ethical terms; it "was less a system of thought than a way of life".[66] This is the form in which stoicism became popularized, and thus how the essentially populist diatribe became its typical medium.[67] So it is that Thyen can see the function of the Hellenistic sermon as *parainesis*; that is to say it was hortatory, encouraging the conduct of a good life.[68] This is true also of the Christian models, *parainesis* is again the key, even if the assumptions behind the *parainesis* are different. Thus, although there is indeed an abstract discussion of the (often theological) principles by which these ethical conclusions are reached, both in the classical and the Christian models, they are always brought home, more directly so by the classical writers, but without exception in either school.

---

[65] So Wendland *Hellenistische-Romanische Kultur* 75-80
[66] So Clarke *Roman Mind* 124
[67] Wendland *Hellenistische-Romanische Kultur* 75-80 outlines this history
[68] Thyen *Stil* passim. This is an underlying assumption behind Thyen's work, to the extent that he can conflate moral exhortation and preaching.

However, Melito in no part of his work, least of all in that which is under particular scrutiny, draws out any moral lesson for his hearers. There is nothing here of *parainesis*, although some have claimed to see it. Epictetus intends "to persuade, to move, to actuate (not simply to inform)"[69] whereas Melito has no persuasory intent. His rhetoric is not sumbouleutic. He is concerned to elucidate a text, a canonical text moreover, and to state what God has done, not what his hearers should do, to interpret a historical event, and not a moral creed. It is not difficult to find any parallel to any of this in the classical world; the statement of the works of God may be paralleled by the prose hymns of Aelius Aristides, the discussion of a text seen in terms of the technical exegesis of Homer practised in the schools, the interpretation of history seen in terms of classical and sophistic historiography.[70] But these are separate and distinct enterprises; more to the point, none is homiletic.

Parainesis is the key to a diatribe, and it is this which is most notably lacking in Melito's work, either ethical encouragement, or indeed, as Hansen purports to see, encouragement for a church under persecution.[71] On this basis it cannot be seen as a diatribe. Of course this does not itself mean that it is not a homily of a recognisable shape in the pagan Hellenistic world, it simply means that it does not correspond to the form which is most frequently proposed as being the Hellenistic precursor of the homily.

McDonald's suggestion is partly motivated by his assumption that a work employing Hellenistic media excludes the possibility that Jewish media may be likewise employed. If the *diatribe*, a Hellenistic form, lies in the ancestry of *Peri Pascha*, then that excludes the notion of haggadah, because that is a Jewish form. However, Jewish and Hellenistic forms may interrelate in a complex way. It may at one point have been accepted that Judaism and the Hellenistic world were two separate spheres of influence that at no point interacted, but such was never actually the case. So Hengel notes that by the time of Jesus Palestine had been subjected to Hellenistic influences for more than three centuries.[72] His study is chiefly centred on Palestine in the early years of Hellenistic influence, but this is relevant because it is from Palestine that the mission which we believe to have founded the church at Sardis derived. Apart from the generally complex nature of

---

[69] So White *Melito of Sardis Sermon* 2 (wrongly) describes Melito's purpose

[70] For a detailed discussion of the similarity between Melito's enterprise and each of these classical endeavours see 3.1.4 and 3.1.8 below

[71] Hansen *Sitz im Leben* 93

[72] Hengel *Judaism and Hellenism*

the relationship between the two cultures we should note for the purposes of our study certain facts which may cast light on the particular problem which we are facing.

Firstly, in view of the shadow of the stoa in the background of Melito's work there is the influence which Hellenistic philosophy exerted on Jewish thought. Hengel notes that in the pre-Christian period all the philosophical schools were represented in Syria and Palestine but that in common with the whole of the Hellenistic world a form of eclectic stoicism was predominant.[73] This found an easy home in the Jewish world since it had a large degree of common interest. Of course Alexandria was the natural home of the philosophically interested Jew but philosophical influence on Judaism was by no means confined there.

Secondly there is the example of the wide degree of Jewish-Palestinian history writing in the Hellenistic period. As Hengel notes, this is no co-incidence, since it reflects the interest in history which is shown in Judaism throughout the post-exilic period.[74] It is significant for our study because it shows the manner in which it became natural for Jewish history to be expressed in a Hellenistic medium, just as Melito describes the Passover of Egypt using a full armoury of rhetorical devices. We should also note the use of haggadah made by the anonymous Samaritan mistakenly assimilated to the name of Eupolemos.[75] Haggadah is assimilated to Hellenistic myth to create a Jewish euhemeristic theogony. This indicates that haggadah, although an essentially Jewish process, could thrive in Hellenistic soil.

Finally, in view of the influence of philosophy in Alexandria and the extent to which Hellenistic literature, both poetic and historical, was practised in Syria and Palestine, we should note the absence of any mention of rhetoric in Hengel's book, even though membership of the gymnasium among Jews was widespread.[76] Hengel does not really cover Asia Minor, so we may reasonably guess that the same pattern was followed here that appears to have been followed elsewhere, that Jews adopted into their own system whatever literary form was widespread among the Greek population. It could be done and, within a Christian form of Judaism, Melito appears to have done it.[77]

---

[73] Hengel *Judaism and Hellenism* 87, 311

[74] Hengel *Judaism and Hellenism* 99

[75] Hengel *Judaism and Hellenism* 88

[76] Hengel *Judaism and Hellenism* 67. He notes here the evidence from Sardis.

[77] Although Daube "Rabbinic Methods" notes links between Talmudic legal thinking and Hellenistic rhetoric, it is forensic oratory and not epideictic with which he concerns himself

Thus Judaism had a complex relationship with the rest of the Hellenistic world. Whereas Wellesz may write of the sermons of Basil of Seleucia that "only the language is Greek; the thoughts expressed and the formal structure is of eastern origin",[78] (the point being made by way of implicitly comparing this to *Peri Pascha*) and Bonner may characterize Melito's style as "Semitic",[79] we must see that such easy characterizations do not fit the evidence. It is quite possible for Melito's work to be at once a haggadah and an item of Hellenistic rhetoric. A haggadah may have been rooted in Melito's tradition, but he would be equipped to give that tradition renewed expression according to the canons of classical rhetoric.

Thus far we have concluded that *Peri Pascha* is not an expository homily, nor is it an ethical homily. Rather it would appear to be a sacred retelling of the works of God at Passover, a haggadah in other words. As such we may describe it as a liturgical homily, as long as we are clear that here we are describing an ancient form, and are not confusing it with any kind of homily that is experienced in the church today.

The genre of the paschal haggadah is a satisfactory description of the second half of *Peri Pascha*. But the other part of Hall's classification, that the first half is a synagogue homily must stand rejected. We must discover what this is. Moreover, although a paschal haggadah may be a valid expression of Melito's religious heritage, we must seek the manner in which he would understand his heritage, standing in the second century as a trained sophist.

To an extent we have already begun that task, by noting that *Peri Pascha* is not sumbouleutic oratory, but epideictic. It is thus to the practice of epideictic oratory in second century Asia that we now turn.

3.1.4 *Peri Pascha as Epideixis*

When Cantalamessa sought a classical work to which he might fruitfully compare ps-Hippolytus *In Sanctum Pascha* he suggested that the *hieroi logoi* of Aelius Aristides could be the basis of a comparison.[80] However, even a superficial examination of the *hieroi logoi* would reveal that this is not the case. They are cast in the first person and are essentially autobiographical accounts, almost in diary form, concerning not only Asclepius but Aristides' diet. Far more helpful is Canta-

---

[78] Wellesz "Melito's Homily" 44
[79] Bonner *Homily* 23
[80] Cantalamessa *Omelia* 337

Iamessa's other suggestion of the encomiastic form. Although the *encomium* is a *progymnasmaton* it is one which continues to be practised by advanced sophists. Epideictic oratory was divided by Aristotle into the giving of praise or blame,[81] and although this classification was widely accepted, it represents only the epideictic oratory known to him; as the functions of orators grew, so did what may be subsumed under these headings.

If the prose hymns of Aristides may be described as encomiastic then perhaps this is a useful point. We may take as an example his *Hymn to Zeus*, No. 43, an oration made in fulfilment of a vow. On a first reading we may note a similar etymological process to that which we noticed in Melito in his derivation of the word *Pascha*. Here there are plays on Δία, the accusative of Zeus, and the preposition διά, and on Zeus and ζάω, both made in all apparent seriousness in section 23. In terms of form, after the proem, Aristides tells of the creation of the universe, preceded by the existence of Zeus himself, and then of the creation and ordering of the world of gods and of people. So he hymns Zeus, always in the third person, as the one who sustains the world, and then in his peroration turns to high rhetorical style with a string of attributes anaphorically linked by οὗτος at the beginning of each asyndetic list. So, the etymological word-play, the story of creation leading to a hymning of the one who is first of all things, the repetition of οὗτος and the asyndeton are all reminiscent of *Peri Pascha*.

The study of prose hymns is made more complex by the instructions in the first treatise attributed to Menander Rhetor. A list of the types of hymns possible is given, together with how to construct them, but nothing therein relates either to this hymn of Aristides or to anything in *Peri Pascha* which we might be tempted to note as a hymn. However, Anderson points out that by the time of Menander the prose hymn, a form which Aelius had transformed into much more than a literary genre had by the time of Menander reverted to being simply that, rather than a living expression of religious commitment.[82]

Whereas there may in fact be no direct parallel extant, Wifstrand noted that if more of what he calls *declamationes* were extant then it might be possible to find further parallels to *Peri Pascha*,[83] we may certainly conclude that we have a piece of epideictic oratory in the most general sense of the word, and having reached this preliminary

---

[81] Aristotle *Rhetorica* I 9
[82] Anderson *Second Sophistic* 201
[83] Wifstrand "Homily" 214

conclusion we may examine *Peri Pascha* further, attempting to see
what features of rhetorical forms may be found within the work.

After the obvious proemium, ending in a doxology at PP10, Melito
says that he will now give a *diegema* of the words of Scripture
(διηγήσομαι, PP11). This internal clue is repeated at PP46 where he
states:

> You have heard the *diegema* of the type and of its correspondence.
> Now hear also the *kataskeue* of the mystery.

The word *diegema* may simply mean "story" as it does in normal post-
classical Greek and in the Septuagint.[84] However another strong possibility presents itself. We have already observed that Melito is a
practitioner of rhetorical technique; is it not possible that the term is
employed here as a rhetorical term? *Diegema* is one of the exercises
that make up the *progymnasmata*. The fact that it is found in a work
showing clear signs of the influence of the rhetorical schools, and that
it is linked here to the word *kataskeue*, likewise a *progymnasmaton*, makes
it a near certainty that the word here is used with its full rhetorical
force. The *diegema* was an exercise designed to train the aspiring sophist in the basic techniques of storytelling, but the use of narrative was
not restricted to the school-exercises. *Diegesis*, a related term, referred
to the statement of the facts of a case in forensic oratory or to the
statement of the grounds of encomium in epideictic.[85] Quintilian tells
us that the exercise of narratio is usefully followed by ἀνασκευή and
κατασκευή,[86] and so in proceeding from the *diegema* to the confirmation of his narrative Melito is once again following the practice of the
rhetorical schools.

The section which precedes PP46 may be subdivided into two
parts, the first of which is the *diegema* proper and the second the
explanation of the theory of typology. This, being reasoned and not
narrative, may perhaps owe something to philosophical writing. The
fact that it too is written in high rhetorical style is not surprising since
Melito's fragment on baptism contains much philosophical material
but is written in a similarly rhetorical manner.

As we have noted, the *diegema* is followed by *kataskeue*. *Kataskeue* was
half of a pair, comprising *kataskeue* and *anaskeue* (refutation). The basis
for this procedure is to train the aspiring sophist to argue either side

---

[84] e.g. LXX *Deuteronomy* 28:37, *Ezekiel* 17:2
[85] Aristotle *Rhetorica* III 16. The terms are distinguished in the *progymnasmata* (so
Hermogenes c2, Aphthonius c2) in that *diegema* concerns a single subject whereas
diegesis is less focused
[86] *Institutio Oratoria* 2.4.18

of a case; in the *progymnasmata* it treats of mythical or historical themes, fundamentally in the defence of a given narrative in terms of its clarity, credibility, feasibility, significance, propriety. Thus Hermogenes and Aphthonius both define the term as βεβαίωσις.[87] However, there is something defensive about this procedure, a tendency which is entirely lacking in *Peri Pascha*, as indeed is any hint of these categories of βεβαίωσις.

Perler renders the term as "construction" and suggests that the history of salvation is intended, quoting patristic examples.[88] He is not apparently aware of the rhetorical use of the term, but since it is indeed the history of salvation which follows from this point, the use of that rhetorical term in this sense needs to be explained. The association of *kataskeue* with narrative is made explicit by Theon when he states that it is useful ἐν δὲ τοῖς διηγήμασι; moreover he goes on to state that it is useful under these circumstances if there is something about a *diegema* that is obscure, impossible or incredible.[89] Melito, presumably, felt that none of these things applied to the history of salvation. However, *kataskeue* was part of the armoury of the Hellenistic mythographer and should nonetheless be understood in this light. The scrutiny and explanation of myths was part of the discipline of literary criticism,[90] and it is this that Melito has practised in his passage on the principles of typology, to show not that there is anything incredible about the pascha, but that Christ is its true fulfillment. Thus we may see the term employed as an extension of the narrative content of *Peri Pascha*. It is used to indicate that it is the foundation of the mystery of salvation that Melito is now describing, that there is *bebaiosis* of this in the prophetic testimonies (PP61-64), and finally to indicate an affirmative continuation of narrative without repetition of the word *diegema*, so adding parallelism to the clause. If this section is to be described as *kataskeue*, an attempt should be made to see how far this section extends. The task is made easier in that, like the first, the second part of *Peri Pascha* is subdivided with a doxology, after which there is a definite change of tone, as the narrative falls away into a string of attributes linked by οὗτος.

---

[87] Hermogenes c5, Aphthonius c6
[88] Perler *Méliton* 158-159. He is followed by Halton "Stylistic Device" 250
[89] Theon c6
[90] See 3.1.6 below. Melito presumably avoids the word μῦθος in that this was applied in the progymnasmata to the purely legendary. So Theon (c3) describes μῦθος as a λόγος ψευδής, and Hermogenes (c5) counts myth as so clearly false that it is not to be subjected to *kataskeue* or *anaskeue*. This perhaps is what Josephus means when he charges sophistic historians with using mythology (*Contra Apionem* 1.2.5)

At this point we may note the similarities with the prose hymn to
Zeus by Aelius Aristides mentioned above. This passage too begins
with creation and ends in a string of attributes linked by οὗτος; even
if the preceding sub-section is to be seen as narrative rather than
hymnic, this section in itself is surely a hymn; the presence of narrative does not exclude the section as a whole from being considered as
a hymn, since those of Aristides contain narrative as well. In view of
the similarities with Aristides, we would do well to class this section as
a prose hymn.[91] The fact that it is described as a *kataskeue* should not
prevent us from making this classification. The sophist was not restricted by the categories of the progymnasmata, but rather used
them and played on them in forming his own work. The progymnasmata were not forms as much as techniques. It is important to remember this in using them to classify the parts of *Peri Pascha*.

It is in this section that Melito moves towards an indictment of the
Jews. However, there is more here than indictment, the story is in fact
brought to its climax as the subject turns directly to the crucifixion
and the resurrection, the indictment of Jews being a kind of counter-
point to this. Although this indictment is expressed in forensic language, this does not make it forensic oratory; it is simply an image.
Apart from encomium the Aristotelian function of epideictic oratory
was the apportionment of blame,[92] and *psogos* was indeed a
progymnasmaton. The forensic metaphor is continued in a piece of
ethopoiia (yet again, a progymnasmatic exercise) as the risen Lord appears and asks, who it is who judges (κρινόμενος) and who speaks
against him (ἀντιλέγων) and making a courtroom speech offering forgiveness. More important however than the indictment of the Jews is
the climaxing story of redemption. The section concludes with a
hymn, a string of attributes linked by οὗτος, and a final doxology.

The whole of *Peri Pascha* is marked by the influence of rhetoric.
The first part contains a *diegema*, whereas the second part, the *kataskeue*
of the narrative, hinging on 46, may be described on the basis of the
comparison with the work of Aelius Aristides as a prose hymn. One
piece of evidence makes this conclusion likely. Theodoret of Cyrus[93]
states of the Quartodecimans πανηγυρίζονται τὴν μνήμην τοῦ πάθους. It
would seem that to the eyes of Theodoret, as to those of Melito, a
festival oration is the centre of the Quartodeciman liturgy.

---

[91] We note at 3.2.3 below the action of Polemo delivering an oration at the
dedication of a Temple. This likewise is considered a hymn (ἐφυμνῆσαι)

[92] Aristotle *Rhetorica* I 9. cf Josephus *Bellum Judaicum* 1 1

[93] *Haer. Fab. Comp.* 3.4. For the trustworthiness of Theodoret's witness see 1.1.3
above

Having recognised the whole of *Peri Pascha* as a piece of epideictic oratory, and recognised the parallels between the second part and prose hymns from his pagan contemporaries as well as with the Passover haggadah of his religious heritage, we may seek to explore Melito's *diegema* of the Egyptian Passover in order to understand its role in Melito's construction of *Peri Pascha* and so of his understanding of the liturgy.

3.1.5 *Peri Pascha as Rhetorical History*

In examining Melito's diegema of the Pascha the obvious place to seek comparative material is among the Graeco-Roman historians, and among Graeco-Roman historians who might be compared with Melito Josephus is a particularly interesting case, for he is a Jew who has been so thoroughgoingly Hellenized that it is virtually impossible to say what in his work comes from the Palestinian tradition and what he has gained from his sojourn in the wider Graeco-Roman world. Although Melito is a Christian (albeit Jewish) and not a direct contemporary, the comparison is nonetheless a fruitful one since in the same way there is a fusion of Jewish religious tradition and Hellenistic culture in his work.

If we examine the chapters of the *Antiquitates Judaicae* in which Josephus deals with the same scriptural material as does Melito, we see that the biblical source is recognisable as it is in *Peri Pascha*, but that it is likewise much changed in the retelling.[94] In the same way the narrative is abbreviated, in order to bring out what were the significant points for the author; like Melito he is uninterested in *halakhah* and in the same way there is material interpolated.

However, if changes are made to the same wholescale extent the manner of the deviations from the text are of a different order; there is a clear difference between the works deriving from their differing inspiration. Josephus is not interested in the dramatic detail of the slaughter, simply in getting the point across that it was as a result of this slaughter that the Israelites were able to go free. The interpolations are of the nature of geographical and historical notes. The two works are not directly comparable for the same reason that Josephus' *Antiquitates Judaicae* is not comparable with ps-Philo's *Liber Antiquitatum Biblicarum*; their interests are essentially different.[95] The difference

---

[94] *AJ* 2. 311-319. One should note that the targums are considerably closer to the text; cf the comments of Bilde *Flavius Josephus* 96-97 who seeks to see *AJ* as some kind of targum

[95] See our comments at 3.1.9 below

between their accounts may best be explained by noting that Melito is a sophist rather than a historian. In this light we may note Melito's designation of this section as a *diegema*.[96] Josephus is clearly conscious of the significance of the term. In the preface to his own work he condemns those historians who διηγήματα σοφιστικῶς ἀναγράφουσιν.[97]

These first impressions gleaned from one chapter seem to be borne out by more extensive studies of Josephus' form and technique. Josephus intends to be an objective historian primarily of the oriental school. So he makes extensive use of Nicolaos of Damascus for instance in the latter part of the *Antiquitates*.[98] In the *Contra Apionem* he shows his admiration for the oriental historians Manetho, the Egyptian, and Berossus the Babylonian, who made use of ancient archives and writings in their histories. It is in the same spirit that he uses the Hebrew Bible in the *Antiquitates*.[99] Among Greek models we may compare Thucydides and Polybius as objective historians.[100] We may moreover add that this is clearly not the task that Melito set himself. The graphic nature of his description of the slaughter of the first-born precludes this.

Josephus is not directly comparable to Melito as a historian then, but we must ask who therefore is. By way of answering this question we may ask not simply on whom Josephus models himself but against whom he ranges himself. His polemic against rhetorical historians is clearly a matter of some significance to him, it is found not only in the preface to the *Bellum Judaicum* but is repeated in *Contra Apionem* I 5; *Antiquitates* 14 1-3 also considers the subject, where Josephus claims that he wishes to give entertainment, but in no wise at the expense of truth.

In looking for Josephus' counter-model, we may note that it has long been suggested that Josephus' *Antiquitates Judaicae* is some kind of response to the *Antiquitates Romanae* of Dionysius of Halicarnassus. Thackeray for instance points out that the title is the same,[101] but we may respond by noting that ἀρχαιολογία was a recognised category of the period, a history beginning with prehistory and coming down to most recent times. Both are in twenty books, but this may be co-incidental. They share the tendency to invite the reader to reach an individual conclusion on disputed facts (κρινέτω τις ὡς βουλέται, or

---

[96] PP46

[97] *Bellum Judaicum* 1.1. That he has sophists in mind is clear from his comment that their histories are concerned to attribute praise and blame

[98] Bilde *Flavius Josephus* 85-88

[99] Pointed out especially by Rajak *Flavius Josephus* 200-208

[100] Josephus in fact compares himself favourably to Thucydides at *Contra Apionem* 1. 3

[101] Thackeray *Josephus* ix

words to this effect) but this is a trait of other writers besides. In other words, there was a case but it was not proven.

In an attempt to prove it Shutt undertook an analysis of common stylistic traits between the two, and concluded that Josephus was consciously imitating Dionysius, since the parallels were, he concluded, "considerable".[102] However, Ladouceur has shown that these stylistic parallels are non-existent- the alleged common vocabulary between the two is also held in common by a host of other writers, and peculiarities of vocabulary such as the use of ἴδιος for the reflexive and doubly compounded verbs are common in the *koine* of the period.[103] Dionysius, moreover, is never mentioned in Josephus' work. Thus the idea that Josephus is deliberately imitating Dionysius is without stylistic foundation. Other parallels noted derive from the fact that a common rhetorical and philosophical inheritance is held between the two; it is the common inheritance which explains the fact that *Contra Apionem* II 145-295 and *Antiquitates Romanae* I.9-II.29 both fall into the shape prescribed by Menander for an encomium of a city;[104] the same explains the parallels of form and theology which have been noted between *Antiquitates Judaicae* II 20-31 and *Antiquitates Romanae* VI 1-95.[105] Josephus is not imitating Dionysius.

And yet the parallels continue to strike us. Apart from those already noted, Daube points out the fact that both men came from eastern parts of the Empire and were made welcome in Rome, and that both saw their task as reconciling their own nations to Roman authority.[106] There are differences, Dionysius suggests that the *parvenus* Romans are in fact Greeks, whereas Josephus is concerned to rub the Roman nose in their comparatively short history; but herein lies the key. Dionysius is not the model for Josephus but his countermodel. Not only is the *Antiquities Judaicae* a response to the work of Dionysius, but Josephus' very historical method is a response to that of Dionysius. Dionysius is precisely an example of the rhetorical historian against whom Josephus ranges himself. Small wonder there is little held stylistically in common, when the construction of rhetorical *diegemata* is as much part of Dionysius' avowed aim as it is part of what Josephus eschews.[107]

---

[102] Shutt *Studies* 101
[103] Ladouceur "Language"
[104] Balch "Two Apologetic Encomia"
[105] Noted by Downing "Ethical Pagan Theism" 544-563
[106] Daube "Typology"
[107] So cf *Antiquitates Romanae* 1.8 and *Antiquitates Judaicae* 1.1

The relevance of all this for the work of Melito is this. We have seen the profound differences between Josephus and Melito in their treatment of the slaughter of the first-born and attributed this to their different functions, Josephus as historian and Melito as sophist. But this is likewise the ultimate difference between Josephus and Dionysius; Dionysius is at bottom a sophist. Melito does what he sees being done by Dionysius and his type, presenting a historical narrative in a rhetorical manner. Although Dionysius himself does not refer to his works as διηγήματα, however he does employ the term διήγησεις in reference to his narratives, a term of similar significance.[108]

It is not possible to support this argument with stylistic analysis since Dionysius was a strict Atticist as much as Melito was a thoroughgoing Asianist, and so the suggestion that Melito in PP16-33 considers himself to be incorporating into his work a historical narrative in the style of a rhetorical historian must remain no more than a reasonable supposition. Like Dionysius he was a loyal Roman citizen (witnessed by his Apology) and likewise he is from Asia Minor, similarly educated under the sophist. And so in giving us a historical narrative the medium of the sophistic historian would seem an appropriate one for him to choose. Of course there are were other sophistic historians; Dionysius is here taken as a model because of his Asian origin, sophistic interests and fundamentally because of his relationship with Josephus. The extent to which these histories were "infected" by rhetoric is in fact debatable.[109]

An alternative model to the sophistic historians might be to see the way in which historical subjects are treated in the *meletai*. We have extant that of Plutarch on Alexander.[110] This makes no claim to be history as such, but is purely a work of rhetoric. Beginning with two pieces of ethopoiia, in the opening chapters we can discern homoioteleuton,[111] paronomasia,[112] asyndetic catalogues[113] and an address to an abstract object (in the genitive).[114] The only difference between this and the work of Melito is that Melito is more extreme.

---

[108] *Antiquitates Romanae* 4.84
[109] Anderson *Second Sophistic* 109-114 defends sophistic historians against being "unhistorical"
[110] *De Alexandri Magni Fortuna*
[111] So eg βέλεσιν ἔπεσεν (327C), ἀτρώτοις καὶ ἀναμάκτοις (327A) (here also with homoiarcton.)
[112] Eg ποταμοὺς ἀπεράτους καὶ πέτρας (326E)
[113] Eg χειμῶνες, αὐξμοί, βάθη ποταμῶν, ἄορνα ὕψη, θηρίων ὑπερφυεῖς ὕψεις, ἄγριοι δίαιται, μεταβολαὶ δυναστῶν, παλιμπροδοσίαι (327C)
[114] Ω θαυμαστῆς φιλοσοφίας (328C)

The entire piece is intended not as a history but as a piece of sophistry in praise of Alexander, demonstrating his skill and bravery (as opposed to good luck) and depicting him as a sophistic philosopher, teaching the nations. This, however, is not a narrative, and in that it is distinct from the work of Melito. Perhaps we could suggest that, under the obligation to tell of the Passover, Melito has turned the historical form into a *melete*, or rather has taken the historical *melete* and given it a narrative form, calling it a *diegema*. In this he has joined the two disciplines in a way entirely consonant with sophistic practice.

Most significant however for understanding Melito's use of the sophistic historical medium is his attitude to history itself and to his Scriptural source. Josephus criticises his Graeco-Roman contemporaries on the grounds of their tendency to employ mythology in the construction of the early part of their histories, because nothing else was available.[115] The Jews on the other hand had reliable historical records, and he treats his biblical material as such. His geographical notes in the account of the exodus result from the treatment of the scriptural record as a contemporary archive. Thus his attitude to Scripture is defensive. Melito, on the other hand, had no such axe to grind. Whilst he expresses no doubt concerning the historicity of the first Passover, it is not its historicity which is of primary importance but its abiding significance. He is free to tell the tale without apologetic motive and is free therefore in the way that a Hellenistic rhetorician could be free.

Having established a connection between Melito and Dionysius, and rhetorical historians in general, it may be worth spending some time considering further the reasons behind Melito's adoption of this style. Is it simply a matter of an obvious style coming to hand or is there slightly more to it than that? We have briefly examined the stylistic analyses of others already, what we seek here is to see the theoretical basis behind certain elements of Melito's style; Halton has already shown that there is more than mere ostentation in Melito's choice of stylistic traits.[116] We have moreover already noted with him the similarities between the description of the blind cyclops in Homer and death's grasping for victims;[117] here we may additionally note that the Homeric passage is one which attracts praise from Dionysius.[118]

---

[115] Josephus *Contra Apionem* I 2-5. This may be seen again as a polemic against rhetorical history in that he goes on to suggest that some used mythology whereas others sought to win favour through encomia.

[116] Halton "Stylistic Device"

[117] Halton "Stylistic Device" 251-252

[118] *De Compositione* 15

One of the basic theories of the Pergamene school of literary criticism, adopted from Aristotle through the stoics, was that ποίησις was the imitation (μίμησις) of reality. If the thing described was not present, then it was a μίμησις of the φαντασία of the author, the author bringing events to his own mind and then presenting a μίμησις of that mental picture to his audience. This φαντασία might be historical, of ἀλήθεια, in which the events are real, or alternatively entirely imaginative or the product of the operation of imagination in surpassing reality. Delivery was all important, for the πάθη were communicated in this manner and the audience brought as though face to face with the action. The μίμησις is such that the emotions it creates in the author are to be communicated to the audience.[119] Is there a clue to the manner of the delivery of this part of *Peri Pascha* such that we can see this theory in operation?

Melito is certainly conscious of his audience. He addresses them at PP22 and 23, referring to what they are hearing and the emotions of wonder and dread that they are experiencing. This would indicate that what he is attempting is indeed a *mimesis* of what he is describing. This idea is supported by the conscious theatricality, the use of the word θέαμα, the apparent reference to a chorus and to the pharaoh at centre stage.[120] He seeks to achieve this *mimesis* through sound and in doing this has much in common with his contemporaries.[121]

According to Longinus asyndeton and hyperbaton reproduce excited and disordered speech.[122] We see elements of this in PP24 in the speech of the Egyptian first-born, asyndetic and at the end disordered. Dionysius recommended the avoidance of sigma,[123] and yet this sound is found alliterated at PP19 as part of the description of pharaoh. The same is true at PP20 and at PP22, with the phrase σκότος ψηλαφητόν, repeated several times in different forms. This is not a solecism on the part of Melito but a communication in sound of the terror of the situation.[124] Melito uses the same sounds as Homer, to produce the same effect. Thus just as according to Plato psi and

---

[119] For μίμησις in general and its relationship with φαντασία see Russell *Criticism* 108-113

[120] Pointed out by Halton "Stylistic Device" 251. The use of theatrical imagery originated with Plato; in the time of Melito the simile of the tragic actor was a very common one. See thus Anderson *Second Sophistic* 80 and refs

[121] See Wilkinson *Golden Latin Artistry* for an overview of the use of sound in expression in the ancient world

[122] Longinus *De Sublimate* 19.22

[123] Dionysius *De Compositione* 14

[124] It is on these grounds that Dionysius praises the passage.

phi produce agitation,[125] so this is clearly Melito's intention here. Alliteration with assonance is employed in the second part of PP26, presumably to draw the attention of the audience to the tragedy he is describing. Crates sought euphony, but it is cacophony which is here more appropriate to the expression of the events described.[126] The underlying intention is however the same, the construction of an imitative relationship between words and what they are describing. The figures of sound are therefore chosen with some care, Melito's intention being to present a graphic scene to his audience.

The literary theory behind his presentation is basically stoic, as practised by the Pergamene school, and as taught by Dionysius of Halicarnassus. Melito brings to his mind a rhetorical *phantasia*, one which is of a basic (though not present) reality, and makes it effectively present to his audience. In doing this he follows Hellenistic literary theory and does what a rhetorical historian might seek to do. More than this however, in following Hellenistic precepts and methods he does what the Jewish tradition which he has inherited would have him do! In his telling (διήγημα) he tells of the acts of God in order that God may be praised and in making the events of the exodus most graphically real and present for his listeners he is enabling them to participate in a process of remembrance. He brings these events immediately to their minds, so ensuring that their remembering of them is more than a mental process.

However, having completed the *diegema* proper, and before proceeding to *kataskeue*, at PP35 Melito inserts a discussion of the hermeneutical principles by which he has interpreted the Passover of Egypt. In order to explain the presence of this section we should turn to the work of literary criticism as carried on in Asia at the time of Melito. We have noted that Dionysius and Melito live in the same intellectual world and that Dionysius, apart from his historical work, was a literary critic. The question of whether the considerations of the literary critics have left their mark on this part of *Peri Pascha* is entirely reasonable.

---

[125] *Cratylus* 427a. There is an extensive discussion in this passage of the imitative significance of various sounds and letters

[126] So Theon, in describing *ekphrasis* as putting an object before one's eyes, stresses that if a subject is sordid or horrific the description should not shrink from conveying such aspects. Likewise Dionysius *Demosthenes* 55 defends Demosthenes for using harsh words when such words were appropriate.

3.1.6 *Peri Pascha as Allegory*

We have seen that Melito underwent a rhetorical education and that part of the curriculum was the study of Homer.[127] We may also note that Melito employs Hellenistic etymological technique in his derivation of *Pascha*[128], and may note that this technique, although stoic in inspiration, was one he shared with Aelius Aristides, who, we have noted, derived Zeus from ζάω.[129] There was, it seems, a common stock of Hellenistic etymologies, this latter derivation appearing in Cornutus' *Compendium*[130], etymology being no longer the preserve of the philosophers but part of the *koine* of Hellenistic culture. Etymology was not however an end in itself but a key tool in the allegorical interpretation of Homer. Thus if Melito was adept at this part of the interpretative technique it would seem more than likely that he was aware of the allegoristic technique as a whole.

It is a commonplace to see rhetoric and philosophy in the ancient world as diametrically opposed disciplines. On the other hand Philostratus is happy to accept certain philosophers as sophists on the grounds of their fluency of expression, and several of his sophists are also philosophers.[131] Epictetus used rhetorical techniques in the presentation of his philosophy and the stoics took a keen interest in matters of literary criticism. Bowersock demonstrates that these are not isolated instances by citing evidence from inscriptions that sophistry and philosophy are not mutually exclusive disciplines.[132] Apart from the examples cited by Philostratus we may also note the case of Maximus of Tyre who was really a sophist, but whose *dialexeis* are on philosophical themes.[133] The function of this section is not to argue that Melito in *Peri Pascha* is doing anything of this kind, indeed everything we have discovered so far would militate against that conclusion. Nonetheless we may suggest that Melito was aware of the philosophical background to the literary criticism of the schools and suggest that this lies behind his epideictic oratory.

We may begin with an article by Grant in which he notes remarkable parallels between Melito's fragment on baptism and stoic ex-

---

[127] 3.1.2 above
[128] See 4.1.1 below
[129] 3.1.4
[130] Cornutus *Theologiae Graeciae Compendium* c2
[131] e.g. Aristocles (*VS* II 3 567), Alexander "Clay Plato" (*VS* II 5 570)
[132] Bowersock *Greek Sophists* 11-12. See also Anderson *Second Sophistic* 133-143 for a slightly different view of sophistic philosophy
[133] One should note here that the word *Dialexis* is similar in meaning to *epideixis*. We note below at 3.2.3 that Polemo graced the dedication of a Temple with an oration, and that this action is described as διελέχθη.

egesis of Homer.[134] Thus the first section, concerning the uses of water, contains images generally found in stoic treatments of the doctrine of providence. There follows, interestingly enough, an example from Greek mythology, concerning the action of Iris. And then he talks of the bathing of the sun and the heavenly bodies in the warmth of the ocean. On this passage Grant concludes that "every item in it is derived from stoic exegesis of Homer." He argues then that the particular stoic school that Melito is following is that of Cleanthes and Poseidonius. This is interesting since it is these stoics who had a particular interest in the interpretation of poetry. The technical background to Melito's study is therefore almost certainly Homeric exegesis, learnt at the feet of the sophist. His philosophy is then part of the common fund of stoic wisdom similar to that taught by Maximus of Tyre and employed by literary critics in the ancient world.

We have noted the link with stoicism in the etymology of πάσχα. Another piece of etymology, also found in Philo, is that of *Israel* found in PP82. Hall suggests that it is first found in *De Mutatione Nominum*, and also notes the link with *John* 9:35-41.[135] It is in fact commonplace in Philo. We would suggest that rather than deriving from a confusion with the etymology of Penuel as Hall states, it is another piece of stoic etymology deriving from אִישׁ רֹאֶה אֵל, or "man seeing God". Since Melito shows no knowledge of Hebrew[136] and, more significantly, since the etymology is so widespread in its occurrence, this is an indication that, like that of πάσχα, this is a traditional etymology, not an indication that Melito is an original stoic thinker. Nonetheless it again shows that he was comfortable with stoic modes of thought.

Melito's theory of typology may also owe something to this common fund of philosophical wisdom. The process by which events in history occur beforehand as types which are ultimately fulfilled, so making it possible for the event to be interpreted in the light of the prefiguration, leads Melito to state that there are specific and proper times for each stage of this process. The extended image of the pre-

---

[134] Grant "Melito of Sardis on Baptism". The fragment is 8b in Hall *Melito of Sardis*. Hall (*Melito of Sardis* xxxii) counts this fragment as "doubtfully authentic" but recognises that there are ample grounds for seeing it as possibly authentic. His main reason for suggesting inauthenticity is stylistic. However the difference in style between this fragment (which is reminiscent in many ways of a school exercise) may be accounted for by recognising the difference in genre. *Peri Pascha* is liturgical, this fragment is controversial.

[135] Hall *Melito of Sardis* 45

[136] Although there is no knowledge of Hebrew demonstrated, the possibility that he had some Hebrew can not be ruled out as Hebrew graffiti have been found in Sardis. See Trebilco *Jewish Communities* 44-5

liminary sketch is taken from sculpture but this may in fact be a pedagogic explanation of an interpretative theory which has already come to him in a developed form. The idea of prefiguring in time may owe something to the cyclical view of history which was espoused by certain Hellenistic philosophers. This view is not, however, explicit in Melito. Melito's philosophical knowledge is that of the stoic interpreter of Homer. This in turn leads us to ask whether this treatment of Homer may have influenced Melito's treatment of *Exodus*. Both were in their ways canonical texts and so a hermeneutic developed on Homer might naturally have been extended to Moses.

It was as a canonical text that Homer began first to be treated in this way, as early as 600 BC, according to Tate by Pherecydes of Syros, who sought to recover philosophical opinions from the Homeric text.[137] Subsequently the method was employed by grammarians anxious to defend Homer from his critics. The entire practice was frowned upon by Plato, but was taken up enthusiastically by the stoics, again concerned to find philosophical opinions (this time stoic) in the authoritative text.[138] Whilst the masters of this method were the older stoics, it would seem that this method underwent something of a revival among their successors in the first century. For while the entire enterprise was rejected by Seneca, his contemporary Cornutus treated the whole Greek mythological system allegorically, in particular reviving the etymological method of Cleanthes, seeking to see a hidden primal wisdom behind the language of myth, believing that the old poets communicated their wisdom in riddles.[139] This belief in the encoded nature of the poets' wisdom was a common one, held not only by philosophers but by grammarians like Heraclitus and sophists like Maximus of Tyre, who saw poetry and philosophy as essentially common tasks, and mythology and poetic form as the sugar on the philosophical pill.[140]

A work of immense value in understanding the practice of literary criticism in the first and second centuries is that of Heraclitus, a somewhat shadowy figure whose work on the Homeric text has been preserved and usually dated to the first century.[141] His work is of immense value because it preserves so much of the allegorical interpretation of the period. A defender of Homer against his critics, he has a variety of exegetical methods, described by Buffière as the

---

[137] Tate "Beginnings"
[138] So Tate "Plato"
[139] So Tate "Plato"
[140] See *Dialexis* 5 and the discussion of this discourse by de la Faye *Origéne* 154-164
[141] Buffière *Heraclitus* ix-x

physical, the moral and the historical.[142] These are the means by which Homer's true meaning may be uncovered.

The physical method is that by which myths become descriptions of physical phenomena, and the gods natural phenomena. So Apollo becomes the sun and the plague with which he struck the camp of the Greeks an allegorical description of sunstroke![143] In the moral method the Gods become moral attributes, virtues and vices; Athena becomes an embodiment of wisdom, Aphrodite of passion.[144] The historical is a method by which the myths become representations of everyday life, for instance the adultery of Ares and Aphrodite is understood to represent the working of a forge.[145] These methods may at times be amalgamated into one, certain of the Gods may be polyvalent, but the whole adds up to a complete treatment of the Homeric corpus, the epics being seen as one extensive allegory.

What is interesting is the absence of what Buffière calls "mystical allegory", which sought in the Homeric texts teaching concerning the mysteries above.[146] Like Melito he may use the language of the mystery religions,[147] but the text is not considered oracular. He may also attract comparison with Melito in that he treats whole passages of the text, rather than general principles of interpretation. However, his approach is different, it is a discourse, with occasional quotations of the text, whereas Melito has melded the text into a *diegema*.

In the following century, that of Melito, Plutarch also turned himself to the interpretation of the poets and of myth in general. He rejected the physical interpretation of myth, considering this unimportant, but rather sought moral and philosophical meanings, being prone also to use etymology in the establishment of his interpretations.[148] He turns his attention to this particularly in his discourse on the legends concerning Isis and Osiris. We see here a growing philosophical interest in the mystery religions, which is reflected not only in Melito's language but in the pagan revival of second century Sardis.

So we may see that in the time of Melito the subject of allegorization both of ancient religious myth and of poetry was a live one. May we not see Melito's typological system in this context, as a re-

---

[142] Buffière *Heraclitus* xxi-xxiii
[143] *Quaestiones Homericae* 6
[144] *Quaestiones Homericae* 28
[145] *Quaestiones Homericae* 69
[146] Buffière *Heraclitus* xxvi
[147] e.g. at *Quaestiones Homericae* 6
[148] Hanson *Allegory and Event* 60-62

sponse to the debate about the value and function of allegorical interpretation in the rhetorical schools? Not, of course, that his theory is
identical to any of those produced by the pagan thinkers, but that he
sees himself in a similar context, both in interpreting an authoritative
text and in interpreting its religious content. It is highly unlikely that
Melito in Sardis could have been unaware of the debate, Plutarch
spoke in Sardis and had other connections with the town.[149] More
particularly, Heraclitus reflects the scholarship of Pergamum in Asia
Minor, in his citations of Crates and his disciples, in his use of etymology, and in his overall view of poetry as an imitation of reality.[150] In
view of the stoic origins of this school and its Asian location it is
probably the Pergamenes with whom Melito has most in common.

Melito's exegetical method may be characterised as "historical typology", the events of the Old Testament are seen to be typified in
the New Testament, and there is a correlation seen between the Old
Testament events of liberation and the New Testament events of
salvation. The events of *Exodus* are described as τύποι, a word employed by Justin and Barnabas, although employed by Melito with a
rather different significance from that of Barnabas.[151] The word appears in the Pauline correspondence, but the theory itself as presented
by Melito has more in common with John than with Paul. These
τύποι are temporary in effect. Thus the blood of the paschal lamb is
a type, or prefiguration, of the blood of Christ, as is the law of the
Gospel. The sufferings of the just, like Abel and Joseph, are types of
the sufferings of Christ.[152] Melito compares these types to sculptors'
working models, and to metaphors (παραβολαί), they are of use only
until the finished work has been made. The people of Israel are as the
artist's model, a preliminary sketch for the Church. The Law is the
comparison by which the Gospel is elucidated.[153] Apart from his
treatment of *Exodus* we may note his use of *Psalm* 69 and of the
suffering servant in his treatment of the passion; these may be understood in the same manner.

Although this exegetical method and typological scheme is ultimately that which was communicated to Melito through the
Johannine tradition[154] his reception of the tradition would surely be
shaped by the ongoing argument in the Hellenistic world at the time.

---

[149] Russell *Plutarch* 7
[150] Buffière *Heraclitus* xxxvi and xxxviii-xlvi
[151] For these differences see Huber *Passa und Ostern* 97-98
[152] PP59
[153] PP40
[154] As observed in 1.2.2 above

He would naturally read the scripture in the way in which Cornutus read the poets, as a riddle which hides a wisdom. The wisdom, for Melito, would be the eternal wisdom of God. The typological method would be the means by which the riddle is understood. Form-critically, too, his methodological explanation at PP34-45 may be accounted for by reference to Cornutus, who after his treatment of the Greek myths appends his rationale in a post-script. Heraclitus likewise will leave behind his treatment of the Homeric text in order to deal with a point of interpretative principle.

Apart, however, from the Melito's use of the image of the sculptors' working models,[155] there is a significant difference between Melito and his pagan contemporaries in their differing attitudes to history. Whereas the pagans differed in the extent to which they would consider the events described to be historical, this consideration was not of central relevance to their treatments of the texts. On the whole the literal meaning is to be altogether rejected. This is certainly true of Heraclitus, to an extent of Plutarch, and apparently the meaning of Cornutus and of Maximus of Tyre (although this is not explicitly stated). Whereas for Melito the significance of the events he describes inheres in their historical character. Had they not taken place then his theory of typology would not be possible. The literal meaning is no longer significant, but it is not simply a construction to hide a greater intended significance. The παραβολή is understood in the light of the gospel, but must retain its literal and historical significance in order to be a παραβολή at all.[156]

This is not the claim made by scholars of an earlier generation who would contrast what they saw as the ahistorical allegory of Philo and Hellenistic writers with typology, which they saw as concerned with the saving significance of history and Palestinian in character.[157] That claim reflected not only the false dichotomy between Palestinian and Hellenistic but also the theological concerns of the decade in which it was made rather than those of the fathers themselves, among whom allegory and typologies of various kinds are mixed together. It is dubious whether the fathers would have recognised this distinction. Rather it simply the point made by Quintilian that historical narratives are to be preferred to those which are fictitious or merely realis-

---

[155] Quintilian frequently employs the image of the sculptor and the statue for the construction of a speech by an orator, but does not make use of the idea of working models.

[156] A point made by Daniélou "Figure et Événement"

[157] So Hanson *Allegory and Event* passim; Lampe and Woollcombe *Essays*

tic, since the force of such a narrative is in proportion to its truth.[158] However, the only scholar to whom it has occurred to see Melito's exegetical scheme in the light of the works of Cornutus and Heraclitus rejects such an association precisely on these grounds, that Melito reflects Palestinian practice with his historical typology whereas Cornutus and Heraclitus reflect ahistorical Hellenistic allegory.[159] Whilst Melito would have recognised differences between himself and Heraclitus, these are certainly not the terms in which he would have expressed his difference. As we have seen, the situation is far more complex than any of these constructions would recognise.

Among Jewish exegetes too the situation was rather more complex than this. There appear to have been two schools of interpreters whose method could, broadly speaking, be called allegorical, known as the *dorse resumot* and the *dorse hamurot*. Their methods did not survive into the rabbinic era, and so much about them is hypothetical and uncertain, to be deduced from their remaining writings, embedded as they are in rabbinic sources. They are but infrequently cited in these rabbinic writings, spread over a wide geographical and chronological area, which implies that their methods predated the rabbis and were at one time widespread. Lauterbach sees the difference between these two classes of interpreters as lying in their differing attitudes towards the law, in that the *hamurot* sat rather more lightly on the literal meaning of the commandments.[160] This he sees as un-Palestinian, reckoning this class of interpreters to originate in a Hellenistic/Alexandrian milieu. The *resumot* he reckons as being a native Palestinian group, because of their more literal attitude in this respect. The methods of both are employed by Philo, and so both in fact could reasonably be described as being Hellenistic in inspiration; however, the processes of both have clearly undergone a degree of assimilation into the Jewish context in which they are being employed. There is really no evidence by which one could be seen as Palestinian, the other Hellenistic/Alexandrian. It is unlikely that Philo, since he employs methods used by both classes, would have perceived this difference. Although by virtue of method these two classes are distinct, to ground this distinction as Lauterbach does in the distinction between Hellenistic and Palestinian Judaism is again to be guided by a construct and not by the evidence.

Nonetheless Melito is a clear example of a practitioner of a typology in which the place of history is significant, and in this lies a

---

[158] Quintilian *Institutio Oratoria* 2.4.2
[159] Manis "Melito of Sardis"
[160] Lauterbach "Ancient Jewish Allegorists"

significant difference between Melito's treatment of his authoritative text and that of his pagan contemporaries.

Although we have so far used the word "allegory" we must note here that this word was a comparatively new one at the time of Melito, although coming into general use.[161] The poets had previously referred to ὑπονόαι, or undersenses, meanings lying under the text. It would seem that this is not quite Melito's (or John's) theory; for them, the meaning of the type is not implicit in the text but in the historical events described. This difference emerges clearly if we compare Melito's treatment of the striking down of the Egyptian first-born to Heraclitus' treatment of the plague in the *Iliad*. Melito does not reason the event away, but sees it as indeed the action of God; he does not have the same compulsion to create a theodicy since the justice of God is clear. God's choice of the Israelites is qualitatively different from Apollo's choice of the Trojans.

Whilst these differences in literary theory must be recognised, not too much should be made of them. As we have seen, there were differences among the pagans themselves, and whereas Melito's theory is specifically Christian, derived ultimately from a Jewish tradition, and therefore different from any of those held by his contemporaries, it is nonetheless a theory formed partly out of the same suppositions about the nature of a sacred text. Ultimately there is the same attitude to the text's literal significance, it is of transitory and secondary importance. Perhaps Melito saw his own theory as being a Christian response to the Pergamenes, upholding against them the necessary historicity of events from which saving truth may be garnered as he upheld the supersession of these same events against the Jews.

So we may say that apart from reflecting contemporary interest both in the allegorical and etymological method and in the religious significance of ancient narratives, *Peri Pascha* form-critically reflects pagan writing as well, in that it leaves the subject in order to concern itself with questions of interpretative method. This digression may seem out of place, but it is in keeping with advice given to rhetoricians in the ancient world to digress.[162] Moreover one should note that Melito concludes his digression by returning to the subject in hand as the handbooks suggest.

In conclusion we may say that whereas Melito's exegetical method is traditional it is given shape by contemporary Hellenistic thinking. In particular we may note that PP34-45 may be formally understood in the light of pagan treatises on the subject of authoritative texts and

---

[161] See Hanson *Allegory and Event* 38-41
[162] On which see Wuellner "Greek Rhetoric"

their interpretation as a methodological post-script which would not
have seemed out of place.

After the proemium the first half of *Peri Pascha* falls into two clear
subsections, the story of the first Passover, told in vivid detail, and a
methodological post-script in which Melito outlines his typological
theory. These may be described as a historical *diegema* and a methodological post-script of the kind that was appended by literary critics. This latter excursus is unattested in the tradition which Melito
inherited and may be said to be entirely his own. The former part
shows again the way in which he received the tradition and made it
his own.

However, although we have gained an understanding of the religious tradition which gave rise to the second part of *Peri Pascha*, and
have managed to understand the entirety of the work in the light of
classical rhetoric, which was Melito's manner of giving expression to
the tradition he had received, we have not yet managed to identify
the means by which the necessity of declaring a narrative of the first
Passover came to Melito from the religious tradition. In order to do
this we should examine the manner in which Scripture was treated
within Judaism.

3.1.7 *Peri Pascha as Targum*

In our search for the genre of *Peri Pascha* we have noted that the first
half of the work treats of Scripture, but that it does not do so in the
manner of the synagogue homily. In order to locate it within the
tradition we must proceed to examine possible parallels with the Jewish methods of treating Scripture of which Melito might have been
aware. In order to undertake a form-critical classification using these
categories a degree of precision is needed. Daniélou, for instance, is
very liberal in his use of Jewish terms with regard to Christian literature.[163] Whilst such elasticity may have its uses, we must be far
stricter if we are to use them for the purposes of form criticism.
Nonetheless, given Melito's use of a Hebrew canon, and his links with
Jewish tradition, our search is a reasonable one to undertake.

The Torah, together with its associated *haftaroth* was read in the
synagogue in Hebrew. However, since Hebrew was not widely understood, a running translation would be given in Aramaic, the spoken
language of Palestine. These were known as *targums*,[164] the Aramaic

---

[163] Daniélou *Theology* passim
[164] We have adopted the English "targums" as the plural of targum for the sake of
simplicity and in accordance with widespread usage.

word for translations, and were made by the methurgeman. Bowker describes them as being midway between re-telling and translation;[165] this freedom of treatment was possible since the text had already been read in Hebrew and so there was no question of interfering with the text by using paraphrase in rendering it. We must enquire whether the first part of *Peri Pascha* is a Greek targum, given that it has a degree of freedom in its treatment of Scripture.

The most interesting thing about the targums is the amount of material extraneous to the text which is included. Le Déaut sums up the method which is being followed in the inclusion of this material by indicating that the Bible explains the Bible![166] Thus there is an overview of God's salvific action in history which enables a popularization of the Scripture to take place, additional texts to be adduced, expansions to be made, moralizations and practical applications to be added by way of making comprehensible what is obscure. Is this what Melito is doing?

Before answering this question we must see whether it is possible for the targumic form to have reached Christian Sardis. It is possible that Melito was aware of the form simply through his former connection to the synagogue. The use of Greek targums in connection with the reading of Hebrew scripture by Greek speaking synagogues has been alleged,[167], indeed, had the Hebrew scriptures been read at the Sardis synagogue they would probably have been incomprehensible to most. And yet the epigraphic evidence indicates that Hebrew continued to be used on a limited basis.[168] One may, moreover, note the almost talismanic significance attached to the use of foreign words and phrases in the Hellenistic world.[169] This would indicate that the use of a Greek targum in connection with a Hebrew reading at the Sardis synagogue is quite possible. However, if the first half of *Peri Pascha* is a targum that would be the result of the liturgical tradition of the Church there, and not an importation by Melito, nor the result of conscious imitation of the synagogue, as Wifstrand alleged.[170]

Thus if the first half of *Peri Pascha* is a targum, this would be the result of the targumic form having been passed to Melito through the Christian tradition. Daniélou alleges that there were indeed such things as "Jewish Christian targums" but in fact he seems to be con-

---

[165] Bowker *Targums* 8
[166] le Déaut *Nuit Pascale* 58
[167] By Zuntz "Opening Sentence" 308-310
[168] So see Trebilco *Jewish Communities* 41, 44
[169] Hull *Hellenistic Magic* 85-86
[170] Wifstrand "Homily" 217-219

cerned with translations of the Jewish Scriptures which reflect a
targumizing process, ie expansion, fusion and paraphrase.[171] This, for
instance, is the context in which he sees divergent texts, such as those
in the opening chapters of *Matthew* introduced by πληρωθῇ. He goes
on to collect complexes of texts which point towards the existence of
collections of *testimonia*, seeing divergences and fusions held in common by Barnabas, Justin, and Irenaeus. He shows that this method of
treating the Scriptures is widespread and already traditional by the
time of Justin. We shall not examine all his examples, but may note
that Melito shares in this complex in holding in common with
Barnabas and others certain divergences from the Septuagint text of
the prophets in his collection of testimonia concerning the passion,
whilst producing some of his own in addition.[172]

Daniélou's work is very thorough. The relevant questions, however, are whether this process is specifically Jewish Christian, and
therefore derived directly from Christianity's Jewish heritage, and in
what sense these are targums. The antiquity of the method is rather
demonstrated by the fact that it is already taking place in the New
Testament, and by the fact that the method itself does have certain
Jewish parallels:- it corresponds to the method outlined by le Déaut
by which texts are expanded and fused, in order to give an overview
of God's salvific activity in history.[173]

The suggestion that they are targums (regardless of the fact that
their method, broadly speaking, is targumic) is nonetheless militated
against by the widespread use of the Septuagint by Christians. What
one can positively say is that they are in some cases liturgical and so,
like the targums, bound up to the use of Scripture in worship. So it is
that *Ephesians* 4:8 quotes the text of *Psalm* 68:18 as ἔδωκεν δόματα τοῖς
ἀνθρώποις (cf Septuagint ἔλαβες). The manner of this quotation as
well as the alteration suggest a liturgical context. This is an alteration
with a recognizably Jewish Christian ancestry,[174] and so, like the
targums, would indicate that it is bound up to the use of Scripture in
worship. In the same manner *Barnabas* 2.10 alters and extends *Psalm*
51:17 to make it refer to the eucharist, without actually pointing out
this association.

For all this, however, targum is an inappropriate classification
since there is no evidence here of anything resembling a complete
Jewish Christian translation of the scriptures in order to supplement

---

[171] Daniélou *Theology* 88-115
[172] See Kraft "Barnabas' Isaiah Text" and Hall *Melito of Sardis* 32-35
[173] le Déaut *Nuit Pascale* 58
[174] In *Testament of Dan* 5.11

the Hebrew text. Rather the phenomena that Daniélou examines seem to be the product of Jewish Christian exegesis made entirely within the Christian context. Melito shares in this, not only in having a set of textual variants in common, but in his use of the word τύπος, shared with Justin and Barnabas.[175] But the texts collected by Daniélou are isolated examples, to claim that a targum existed would require more extensive citation of variant texts than we have here. Melito's use of a targum cannot be ruled out on the basis of Daniélou's failure to find such a thing as a Christian targum, but we must be clear that if he did use such a thing it is not a usage shared with Barnabas and Justin.

It is quite possible that Melito drew on a targumic tradition of *Exodus* 12 in the construction of his *diegema*, and indeed that this tradition was a Christian one; he refers to the Passover lamb as ἄμωμος καὶ ἄσπιλος, and in doing so does the same as the author of *I Peter* who at 1:19 refers to Christ as ἄμνος ἄμωμος καὶ ἄσπιλος. ἄμωμος is the usual rendition of תמים in the Septuagint version of *Leviticus*, *Exodus* 12 using τέλειος.[176] The second word is unattested by the Septuagint, and it is the common occurrence of the two in a similarly paschal context that makes the existence of a tradition probable. But a targumic tradition does not necessarily mean that a formal targum was in use.

Targumic methods were employed by John, and may thus be said to lie in Melito's tradition. Borgen for instance sees them at work in the Johannine prologue.[177] It is clear that there is a deliberate echo of the opening words of *Genesis* in the opening words of the Gospel; in the same way the themes of darkness and light and the word of God in creation are essential to both opening passages. On this basis Borgen sees the opening passage of *John* as a targumic treatment of the opening of *Genesis*. Further to this he sees 7-18 as corresponding to the first five verses as a meditation on the revelation of a later time corresponding to the meditation on the beginning of creation. The explanation is, he claims, arranged chiastically in that the themes are treated in the reverse order of their appearance. In this arrangement it reflects the Jerusalem targum of *Genesis* 3:24. The treatment of the opening of *Genesis* is indisputable as is the process of targum and comment in chiastic arrangement. Although in this case there may be a degree of overstatement since it is possible that parts of this pro-

---

[175] Justin *I Apol* 60; *Barnabas* 12
[176] So Selwyn *Peter* 145-146. He notes the connection with *Peri Pascha* but suggests that τέλειος is avoided on stylistic grounds
[177] Borgen "Observations" 288-295

logue belong to an earlier redaction, it is clear that Borgen has established the use of a targumic method by the evangelist.

Moreover, apart from targumic exegetical methods, it is possible to find John employing extant targums, and working with reference to a Hebrew text. So it is that Lindars sees rabbinic exegesis in play at *John* 1:51, in its allusion to *Genesis* 28:12 and 28:13.[178] The angels are going up and down upon the Son of Man, just as in *Targum Neofiti* and other targums the Hebrew is interpreted so that they go up and down on Jacob, as opposed to the ladder. This depends on a reading of a Hebrew text, but this is far from impossible, Freed believes that a Hebrew text has also been employed at *John* 13:18.[179] In addition to the use of a Hebrew text, and that of Hebrew exegetical methods, (and not simply those which would in time become rabbinic, Freed notes similarities with the manner in which texts are cited by the Qumran sectaries)[180], we may note affinities at several points between texts quoted as scriptural by John and the actual text of the targums. In this respect we may note with Freed *John* 6:31, 6:45 and 7:42.[181] Form-critically, however, the presentation of these methods is not straightforward but worked into the text of the Gospel.

In conclusion it would seem almost certain that targumic methods fed into the Christian tradition to which Melito was heir, but the question as to whether he would have known or recognised a formal targum, let alone created one, remains open, and to be decided on the basis of the text.

Apart from the question of historical possibility a necessary condition for the use of a Greek targum would have been a preliminary reading of the passage of *Exodus* in Hebrew. We have seen that this is a possible state of affairs at the synagogue in Sardis, and Zuntz has argued that this condition obtained in the church on the basis of the first line, ἡ μὲν γραφὴ τῆς ἑβραϊκῆς Ἐξόδου ἀνέγνωσται, which he would render as "The lesson from Exodus has been read in Hebrew."[182]

His contribution was one of the first to follow Bonner's publication of *Peri Pascha*, and issued as a result of Bonner's questions about the meaning of the opening lines of the work.[183] He began his argument by pointing out that the exodus of the first line referred to the scriptural book and not to the event. Bonner had in fact never denied this,

---

[178] Lindars *John* 122
[179] Freed *Old Testament Quotations* 91
[180] Freed *Old Testament Quotations* 118, 129-130
[181] Freed *Old Testament Quotations* 118, 119, 126
[182] Zuntz "Opening Sentence" 304
[183] Bonner "Two Problems"

but accepted Zuntz's clarification.[184] Zuntz pointed out that Melito always uses "Israel" when referring to the people, and not "Hebrews"; that γραφή with a genitive of an event is unparalleled, whereas a number of comparable parallels with ἡ γραφὴ τοῦ Ἐξόδου referring to a book are indeed extant, he quotes examples from *The Testaments of the Twelve Patriarchs*, Origen, Athanasius and Marcellus of Ancyra; that Ἑβραϊκῆς with a *nomen actionis* is likewise unparalleled; and that the scripture in question, *Exodus* 12, does not in any case deal with the exodus but with the preparations for the Passover. His conclusions in this regard have been accepted by everyone who has discussed this passage with the exception of Testuz who is somewhat hasty in his rejection of Zuntz on this point.[185] Zuntz's contention that Ἑβραϊκῆς refers to a preliminary reading of the text in Hebrew has, however, met with less agreement.

To be fair, his argument is an inductive one, and took off from the then agreed position that something had preceded the reading. The argument profited, moreover, from Zuntz's rendition of διασεσάφηται as "translated". These parts of the argument will be dealt with in the section concerning the actual liturgy of the Quartodecimans; but the argument over the word Ἑβραϊκῆς needs to be followed if a case for a targum as part of *Peri Pascha* is to be made, just as much as it does if the case made is for a preceding targum, and in this situation it lacks the inductive strength. The major hole in Zuntz's argument is that he is capable of producing no true parallel. That which he does produce, from Eusebius, reads ἐν τῇ Ἑβραϊκῇ βιβλίῳ τῶν Ψαλμῶν.[186] Perler points out that the difficulty here is rather reduced by the inclusion of the word βιβλίον in the title.[187] However, Zuntz is apparently unconcerned by the lack of a parallel, the situation, he says, is unique in the extant literature; it is "uncommon" but "not objectionable".[188]

It has, however, been found open to objection by a number. Bonner is followed by Gärtner in suggesting that a reading in the Syriac referring to the city of Jerusalem as ܐܘܪܫܠܡ might be rendered Ἑβραϊκῆς;[189] this would mean that the word in Melito's usage would be established as meaning "pertaining to the Jews". This reading, which Bonner had suggested in a footnote in his edition, has been borne out by Codex Bodmer, as Perler points out.[190] In any

---

[184] In "Supplementary Note" 317
[185] Testuz *Papyrus Bodmer XIII* 19
[186] Zuntz "Opening Sentence" 301
[187] Perler *Sur la Pâque* 132
[188] Zuntz "Opening Sentence" 302
[189] Bonner *Homily* 154 followed by Gärtner *John 6* 35
[190] Perler *Sur la Pâque* 132

case, how unique is this situation? The Hebrew language is referred to often enough as φωνὴ Ἑβραϊκῆς, just as Melito refers to the Αἰγυπτιακὴ φωνή of the Egyptian fathers of the slaughtered firstborn.[191] The usage by Melito of Ἑβραϊκή unqualified with φωνή, to mean "in Hebrew" looks increasingly unlikely, it would need very strong evidence indeed to confirm it. Zuntz claims that Ἑβραϊστί is too plain to accord with Melito's style, and that Melito would hardly qualify γραφή with a plain Ἑβραϊκή.[192] One might also add that no exactitude of expression is to be expected, Melito was not a "liturgiologist anxious to indicate to later generations an interesting aspect of Quartodeciman practice".[193] This argument can cut both ways; Hall uses it to ask why we should expect Melito to state the fact of a Hebrew reading at all. In support of his contention that Ἑβραϊκή Ἐξόδος means "Hebraic Exodus", he produces analogous expressions which mean precisely that.[194]

If there is no Hebrew reading preceding the delivery of *Peri Pascha*, as seems to be the case, then there is no obvious reason why a targum should follow it, unless a Hebrew reading had been the earliest tradition of the Christian community at Sardis, and a targumic treatment of the text continued to be given even after the tradition of reading the scriptures in Hebrew had ceased. There are points at which Melito's work seems sufficiently close to the text of *Exodus* to make this at least a possibility. And yet, however close it is at times, if we compare Melito's treatment of the text overall to that of the *Targum Neofiti* it will be readily noted that the considerable divergence of Melito is very different from the sobriety of the targum;[195] so much is this the case that whatever the origin of the use of a text at this point it is certainly not a targum as it stands at present. We have already noted the distortions which Melito makes in the order of the text in order to tell his own story, as well as his omissions.[196] The targum by

---

[191] PP29
[192] Zuntz "Opening Sentence" 302
[193] Hall "Melito *Peri Pascha* 1 and 2" 247
[194] Hall "Melito *Peri Pascha* 1 and 2" 247
[195] We have employed *Neofiti* here since le Déaut (*Nuit Pascale*; statement of conclusions on 63) would assign it a pre-Christian date, although this is controversial. Other targums are extant, but these, whilst preserving ancient tradition, are certainly later, and have been treated by later generations of scribes. Thus for the purpose of using the targums as comparative material for Melito's treatment of the Scriptures *Neofiti* is the most useful, as the earliest extant targum of *Exodus*. It is noteworthy however that the (early) Job targum from Qumran (11QtgJob) shows a similar sobriety. See Jongelin Labuschagne, van der Woude *Aramaic Texts*; the accuracy of the rendering is assessed on 7-8
[196] 3.1.1

contrast is sober in its rendition and close to the Hebrew text. Similar results obtain when Melito is compared to the Septuagint or to the Peshitta, itself an Aramaic targum in origin.[197] Melito may occasionally be closer to the Masoretic text, for instance in attributing the slaying to an angel rather than to the *memra* of The Lord, or in his version of verse 13 at which he states (in conformity with the Hebrew text) that God will strike Egypt, which the Targum renders as "I shall kill all the firstborn in the land of Egypt", but whatever the slight variations the overall shape of the Hebrew original may be discerned behind the targum in a way which is not possible in Melito's case. Both theologize, but the targum sees that the theology is wedded far more closely to the shape and form of the Hebrew text.

We have already noted that Melito's repetition of the command not to break any of the animal's bones appears close to the Septuagintal position, which indicates independence from the Masoretic Text, and yet divergences from the text of the Septuagint (for instance Melito employs the word ῥάβδος to describe the staff which is to be held, whereas the Septuagint uses βακτηρίον) indicate that Melito's text is distinct from the Septuagintal tradition also. Although this does not help us identify the form of Melito's "citation" it raises an interesting question concerning the provenance of his biblical text. The implication from this, as it was from the phrase ἄμωμος καὶ ἄσπιλος, would seem to be that Melito, in constructing his *diegema*, is employing a Greek translation of the Scriptures, possibly of Christian origin, but equally possibly, given Melito's Jewish origins, deriving from the Greek speaking diaspora; although given that it is no longer extant, it may be possible that this was properly a targum. And if Melito is using a targum, the possibility that in Melito's tradition a targum was read at this point, and that Melito has developed this tradition into something else, becomes correspondingly more likely. It may therefore be that in view of the knowledge of targumic traditions demonstrated by John that a targum in this place was the original practice of the Sardis community. It may also be that such Christian targums existed and were employed. Both of these suggestions are highly debatable, but if true they may give the key to Melito's claim to repeat the lesson of scripture here. However, whatever the truth of these issues, by the time of Melito such a development has been undergone that the targumic form is no longer recognizable; it has

---

[197] Isenberg "Jewish Palestinian Origins" shows this beyond doubt in that both a text type distinct either from the Masoretic Text or the Septuagint is displayed, and in that interpretative traditions are held in common between the Palestinian targums and the Peshitta

become something else entirely. Melito may demonstrate a knowledge of targumic traditions and share a method of exegesis based on the expansion of a text, but his διήγημα on the Pascha is not a targum in form.

Given the evidence that Melito's delivery of *Peri Pascha* followed on from Scripture and took the place that a targum in the synagogue might take, but noting that whatever the original tradition it has been extensively developed we are forced to enquire into the nature of the development. The targum within Judaism developed in time into the synagogue homily,[198] but we have already excluded this possibility. However, there are other possibilities which may be canvassed. In a later period of Judaism there was a development of liturgical poetry which may provide interesting and useful parallels into Melito's procedure here, and allied to the targumic method of exegesis there were processes of commentary subsumed under the heading of midrash. These processes must now be examined.

3.1.8 *Peri Pascha as a Liturgical Hymn*

Several times we have made reference to the article of Wellesz in which it was suggested that Melito had been directly influenced by Syriac styles.[199] We suggested that if there were a similarity then it was more likely that the two styles had diverged from the same root than that there had been a direct influence in either direction. Wellesz reached his conclusion on stylistic considerations alone, and the similarity which he saw between that of Melito and that of Ephrem. The grounds of this similarity were primarily the isosyllabism, and secondarily the parallelism of clauses. He also noted the recurring homoioteleuton, which may also now be seen as a mark of earlier Syriac poetry. These elements of the Greek were, as we have seen, faithfully imitated in the Syriac version. However, these stylistic traits were typical of the Asianist rhetorical style; it is a priori more probable that these are present in Melito's Greek work because of the influence of Hellenistic rhetoric and not as a result of any Hebrew or Syriac influence. The question of these similarities of Semitic and Hellenistic style is most recently studied by Brock, who concludes that they are entirely independent and separate developments.[200] In fact, Wellesz's whole approach is based on an opposition

---

[198] Moore *Judaism* 304
[199] "Melito's Homily"
[200] Brock "Syriac and Greek Hymnography"

of Hellenism and Semitism which has been shown to be an artificial construct.[201] Melito's highly artistic style in *Peri Pascha* is best explained in the light of the usage of his pagan contemporaries such as Polemo and Aelius Aristides, and reflects what was considered an appropriate style in a religious context.

However, we must also remember that *Peri Pascha* is a highly traditional work, deriving ultimately from a Hebrew tradition of liturgical observation of the Passover. We should therefore enquire whether its style had a foundation in the tradition as well as in the immediate context of second century Sardis, Melito's high rhetorical style finding an easy home in the tradition onto which he brought it to bear. The stylistic similarities between Asianist prose style and Hebrew versification, though independent in origin, nonetheless exist, and may be seen as the means by which the traditions were able to merge so easily.

At the *Targum Neofiti* of *Exodus* 12:42, as in other targums, there appears a long poem referring to the four nights of salvation, creation, *aqedah*, Passover and eschaton; all are nights of 14/15 Nisan, and all are dealt with in the text of *Peri Pascha* (though not in that half of the work with which we are dealing.) In the targum the text is suddenly left behind and the poem is appended. As a result of its inclusion in *Neofiti*, it is studied by le Déaut and dated to the first century.[202] Le Déaut comes to this conclusion on a number of grounds: the way in which its themes are reflected in the New Testament, the apparent ignorance of Christianity, (it would hardly be expected for a Jewish author with knowledge of Christianity to date the parousia to a time so pregnant with Christian expectation), the fact that this expectation has not been transferred to Rosh haShanah, the fact that reference to these themes in the *Midrash Rabbah* seems rather fuller and thus less primitive. Against this dating is the reference to the Messiah coming מרומה, "from Rome", but the text here may well be emended, for reasons other than convenience of dating, to read מרומא, "from on high". We may perhaps perceive here the ancestor of the piyyut.

The *piyyut* is a liturgical poem based on Scripture. The term is a Hebraicisation ultimately deriving from the Greek ποιητής. Originally thought to be mediaeval, the date of the form has been steadily pushed back with the discovery of piyyutim in the Cairo Genizah and the identification of the forms in the targums. Black suggested a date

---

[201] Classically by Hengel *Judaism and Hellenism*
[202] Le Déaut *Nuit Pascale* 339-371

not later than the fifth century,[203] Schirmann the second or third.[204] Whereas the flowering of the piyyut as a form is a phenomenon of a considerably later period we may suggest on the basis of the appearance of the poem of the four nights and its dating by le Déaut that the form has its origin in a tradition of liturgical hymnody of which this poem is an example. As such we may see that the tradition which gave rise to the *piyyut* is sufficiently early to have influenced the formation of Melito's tradition. It seems that these *piyyutim* originated in the exposition of scripture in the synagogue, and grew out of the targumic exposition. So it is that the poem of the four nights is found embedded in the targums at *Exodus* 12:42. Like earlier Syriac liturgical poetry these early *piyyutim* are marked by parallelism and suffix rhyme.

Brock is primarily concerned with a later period than ours, that of Romanos and his predecessors Ephrem and Basil of Seleucia. In this period it is clear that Greek and Syriac liturgical poetry underwent cross-influence; Brock notes also the underlying influence of Hebrew forms. It is further agreed that there was cross-influence between Syriac poetry and the Byzantine kontakion. Brock shows that the direction of influence is from the Syriac to the Greek, the kontakion deriving from a variety of Syriac forms;[205] this had been suggested long before.[206]

By contrast, in the period immediately preceding that of Melito, the period in which the liturgical tradition which he received was formed, we see that although the piyyut does not exist yet as an independent form there is poeticisation growing out of the targum, and that it is marked by isosyllabic structure with a variety of line lengths, and homoioteleutic suffix rhymes marking the *parallelismus membrorum*. This is what is meant by the tradition being fertile ground for the implantation of the Asianist rhetorical style. It is this form, taken over by Melito, which also provided the basis for Syriac liturgical poetry. However, not only does the style prepare the way, the liturgical position of this part of *Peri Pascha* is the same as that which would in the Jewish tradition be occupied by the *piyyut*, it follows on from and grows out of the reading from *Exodus*, not a targum but an extended reflection.

---

[203] Black *Aramaic Approach* 305. At 236-238 he assigns a pre-Christian date to the "four nights" on similar grounds to those offered by le Déaut
[204] See Schirmann "Hebrew Liturgical Poetry" for the arguments.
[205] Brock "Syriac and Greek Hymnography"
[206] Maas "Das Kontakion" and refs

Thus the hymn of the four nights for each night describes the event, sums it up in a citation of Scripture and comments on its implications. The events are each seen as fulfilment of the scriptures. (Here of course there is a theological difference, for Melito the events are fulfilled in Christ, not in themselves). This use of scripture is comparable to that of Melito, as is its prose-poetic form. It is also noteworthy that this hymn is said by the targum to have been written in a book of memorials (the word used is the Aramaic equivalent of *zikkaron*.) Le Déaut suggests that the significance of this is that the poem has a liturgical use, that its function is to remember and to cause God to remember, it is analogous to the *zikronoth* of Rosh haShanah, that it is in fact a remainder of a similar set of memorial prayers.[207]

This is significant not only in that we see that the hymn has a liturgical function beyond edification but in that it links the hymnic tradition within Judaism to Melito's overall function in *Peri Pascha* and moreover shows that this function is not restricted to the second half of the work.

The contrast between the process undergone at the time of Melito and that at the time of Romanos is particularly important in view of the comparisons which Perler sought to make between *Peri Pascha* and the kontakion.[208] We must say, however, that not only was the process different, the influence history exercised on the forms makes them distinct as well. Although the kontakion and the first half of *Peri Pascha* may be equally described as a "lyrische Predigt" the similarity stops there, the kontakion displaying acrostics worked into the text and a refrain, as well as a far more regular metrical structure.[209]

The Syriac style then influenced the Byzantine, the Syriac having its origins in the Hebrew, to which the further possibility must be added that an influence continued to be exercised.[210] Melito's situation was an entirely different one, an example of cross-fertilisation comparable to that which took place at the time of Romanos, but neither identical nor in any sense linked, except insofar as the tradition underlying his work was the same as that which underlay the Syriac tradition. Just as Syriac hymnographers digested the *piyyut* and

---

[207] Le Déaut *Nuit Pascale* 68
[208] Perler *Sur la Pâque* 24-29
[209] For the kontakion in general see especially Grosdidier *Romanos le Mélode*
[210] Yahalom "The Piyyut" 123-124 further suggests that "there must have been common contemporary factors in the eastern prayer house and its rhetorical and cultural background that led to common- Jewish and Christian- developments in its poetry"

made it their own, so Melito digests the ancestor of that form, in its liturgical context, and makes it his, a process made possible by the convergent styles.

Earlier in this chapter we suggested that the targum of Melito's community may have developed into something else. We may now see exactly what, that it was undergoing a similar process to that undergone within Judaism when the targum developed into the *piyyut*. The process through which Melito puts the scriptural text is moreover in keeping with Jewish models both stylistic and liturgical. We may add to this that the comparison with the kontakion attempted by Perler has a greater validity when applied to this half of *Peri Pascha* than when applied either to the second half or to the work as a whole, but that the relationship between the forms is rather more complicated than Perler sought to suggest. However, the task is not yet complete.

3.1.9 *Peri Pascha as Midrash*

We noted above the extraneous material which was introduced in the targums. This additional material is often known as midrashic material. It takes this name from the second type of interpretative material, midrash, or commentary. The word is often used to describe material related to, but extraneous from, the Old Testament scriptures, but properly speaking midrash means not simply the content, but the function and method of interpreting scripture.

A number of midrashim are extant, like the targums reflecting on occasion more ancient traditions than the dates of their own redaction.[211] They have different emphases, corresponding to different requirements. Among expository midrashim we may take as an example that on *Exodus* known as *Mekilta*. This is primarily halakhic, that is concerned with the publication of legal material based on the text. That known as *Rabbah* is exegetical, concerned purely to explain the content of the text, with particular regard to difficulties of interpretation or harmonisation with other passages, and from *Exodus* 12 on is cast into continuous prose rather than verse by verse exposition. Such are the expository midrashim. Then there are the homiletic midrashim known as *pesiqtoth*. These are concerned not so much with the exposition of a text as the textual exposition of festivals of the calendar. However, they too take off from a "base verse" and adduce

---

[211] This confidence is borrowed from Vermes *Scripture and Tradition*

interpretations by way of accruing material appropriate to the day.[212]

These extant midrashim are all rabbinic midrashim. The question of the extent to which earlier activity on the text can be called midrash is, however, an open one. Is it correct to limit the term to the later rabbinic midrashim, or might it be given a wider term of reference? Similar questions are raised about the appropriateness of employing rabbinic terminology to describe pre-rabbinic forms as were raised in the discussion of targum and piyyut. Porton sees the targums as a pre-rabbinic form of midrash.[213] As pre-rabbinic midrash he would also see retellings of the biblical text, and the *pesher* method of exegesis practised at Qumran, a method of interpretation not found among the rabbis.[214] Because of the different kinds of midrash and the different needs to which they were responding it is difficult to make a form-critical classification on this basis; there is, in fact, a genuine problem of definition. So Zeitlin for instance, would deny the term to anything except the rabbinic midrashim.[215] Wright would set the limits somewhat wider,[216] le Déaut wider still.[217] What we may state is that the midrashim have a purpose in common, to explain the text, rather than a shape; in using the term as a form-critical category it is therefore necessary to specify which type of midrash is meant. Perhaps it is more useful for our purpose to think in terms of genre rather than form, as we suggested might be the case.

However, having said this, part of a definition must include the fact that comments and explanation are at all times closely related to the individual texts which are subject to interpretation. As part of their treatment these texts are subject to close and precise examination. Midrash is more than commentary relating to large blocks of material. The question as to whether the first part of *Peri Pascha* may

---

[212] For information on the *pesiqtoth* see especially Neusner *Pesiqta de Rab Kahana* Introduction (169-248)

[213] Porton "Midrash"

[214] *Pesher* exegesis takes its name from the manner in which this kind of comment is introduced. A text is given, and then the interpretation introduced with the words פשרו על or פשר הדבר. It is really a particular form of midrash which seeks fulfilment of Biblical prophecies in present days, assuming that the text has an application beyond its immediate meaning, and that the interpreting community is the elect. Whilst it is a kind of midrashic activity it differs from the rabbinic midrashim treated above in that lengthy blocks of text are treated in this way, and in that authorities are not cited for the interpretations offered. It is clear on both formal and theological grounds that Melito does not employ this form in his treatment of the scriptures. See Nickelsburg *Jewish Literature* 126-128

[215] Zeitlin "Midrash"

[216] Wright "Literary Genre"

[217] le Déaut "A propos d'une définition"

be described as a midrash is therefore confused by a problem of definition.

In spite of the problems, Daniélou is quite happy to apply this term to Christian exegesis.[218] For instance he sees the section of *Barnabas* referring to the ritual for the Day of Atonement and the symbolism of the scapegoat as "a remnant of a Christian Midrash on the Day of Atonement".[219] What Daniélou in fact treats is a series of passages quoted by fathers as coming from Scripture which are not in fact to be found in the canonical texts but are rather to be seen as theologizing paraphrases. He is able to group them and so sees them as midrashim on the books to which they are related. Midrashic in tone they may be, in that they add details to the text in order to bring out a theological meaning, but this does not in itself make them midrashim. Nonetheless, they exhibit a great degree of attention to detail and appear to be the result of scholarly enquiry into the texts, indicating that there was from the earliest times a Christian tradition of scholarly enquiry into the texts of the Old Testament scriptures. This scholarly setting was the locus for the Jewish creation of midrash, for whereas the targums had a liturgical origin in the synagogue, the production of midrashim was principally a scholarly activity, related to the synagogue but not part of its worshipping function except insofar as the homilies were informed by the midrashic process. Did Melito share in this?

At a later time than that of Melito, the Jewish community at Sardis had a school,[220] although not only is the evidence from a different time from Melito, but in view of the extensive Hellenization of the Jews of Sardis, whether the methods would have been recognizable as

---

[218] Daniélou *Theology* 97-107

[219] Daniélou *Theology* 98. This is a questionable statement. The kind of midrash that Daniélou would appear to mean is along the lines of the *pesiqtoth*, and yet, although the *pesiqtoth* may well contain ancient material, greater evidence than that adduced by Daniélou would be needed to suggest that the later rabbinic form had its origins at this early stage. Additionally it would seem to imply that Christians kept this feast, but this would seem highly improbable given that this typology was attracted into the keeping of Pascha; since Barnabas associates the scapegoat with the passion, and moreover with the *aqedah*, the Passover connections of this passage would seem to be pressing. In Daniélou's favour we may cite Mann's reconstruction of synagogal homilies dating from this period made largely on the basis of the *pesiqtoth*, but this itself is highly controversial. Daniélou (99) in fact claims that the section in Barnabas concerning the scarlet and the thorns on the scapegoat is paralleled at PP79. However he is using Bonner's text and the point in question relies on a conjectural emendation by Bonner superseded by further textual discoveries.

[220] Kraabel *Judaism* 202

proto-rabbinic is questionable. More to the point, there is strong evidence that Melito concerned himself with close enquiry into Old Testament texts. There are then good grounds to ask whether the first part of *Peri Pascha* might be called midrash.

If what is meant is a midrash in the narrowest sense of the word, a rabbinic midrash, then the answer is clearly in the negative. Form-critically there is not the same attention to the detail of the text, not the same atomization of the meaning, not the same citation of authorities. Moreover, the intention is different. The rabbinic midrash seeks elucidation of the text either for its own sake, or for that of halakhah; *Peri Pascha* seeks to interpret the text in terms of its theory of typology, to show, in fact, that the text is superseded by the events of the new Passover.

However, a more general meaning to the term may be sought, on which basis it might be possible to classify this part of *Peri Pascha* as midrash. This general meaning might be derived from the basic root דרש "to enquire". The original enquiries were into the meaning of the prophets, but with the decline of prophecy and its replacement by an authoritative text the locus of the enquiry was transferred.[221] We stated above that in order for any writing to be considered midrash the underlying text had to be clear, as it is in this case. The potential vacuity of this definition would be avoided if comparative Jewish material which could reasonably be described as midrashic were supplied. Ideally the material would be pre-rabbinic, in order to avoid any charge of parallellomania.[222]

We saw above that Porton, who took a middle line in terms of the width or narrowness of what could reasonably be defined as midrash, described three types of pre-rabbinic midrash.[223] The first of these was targum. We have seen that *Peri Pascha* does not fit this description. Another was the *pesher* method of exegesis, but Melito does not employ this method. It is Porton's third category, which he termed "retellings", which holds out most hope for providing comparative material.

The first of these retellings which he mentions is the *Liber Antiquitatum Biblicarum*, which has been transmitted among the works of Philo, although it is clearly not by him. Preserved only in Latin, it reflects a Greek translation of a Hebrew (or Aramaic) original dating

---

[221] These points are made by Zeitlin "Midrash"

[222] A term coined by Sandmel "Parallellomania". It is the finding of Christian-Jewish parallels without regard for date or context

[223] Porton "Midrash"

from the period before the destruction of the temple.[224] Given, then, that we are dealing with a Jewish work, and one preceding the time of Melito, it is reasonable to seek parallels.

The *Liber Antiquitatum Biblicarum* is a retelling of biblical history from the time of Adam to the death of Saul. Obviously it is a longer work than Melito's *diegema*, and covers a wider expanse. In the process of telling its tale it passes by Melito's subject, the Passover lamb, in silence, going straight from the oppression under the new pharaoh to the crossing of the Red Sea, having paused to tell of the birth of Moses. Rather than discouraging us, however, this should encourage us, since it shows a similar liberty with the use of the biblical text. We noted above the great amount of *Exodus* 12 which Melito omitted. Melito particularly omits legal material; ps-Philo may have seen the whole of the chapter in this light.[225] Like Melito, moreover, at the times at which the text is being closely followed, it is possible to find citation alongside paraphrase alongside authorial expansion. When the author expands however, like Melito he leaves the text entirely behind, and we have a different product entirely. So examine the way in which ps-Philo tells the tale of the birth of Moses.[226] Beginning with a direct citation from the biblical text we are then suddenly thrust into the world of pious fable until, towards the end of the episode, the text is found again, citation alongside paraphrase. It is the same manner in which Melito takes off from a recognisable set of references to *Exodus* 12 to begin to tell his own tale of the angel's slaughter of the Egyptian first-born. Similar also is the manner in which theology is linked to narrative. Although the theologies are different, in the same manner the narrative presupposes a particular understanding and is seen as lending support to it.

Thus we see that Melito's *diegema* is comparable to an individual episode among those making up the *Liber Antiquitatum Biblicarum*; there is a similar approach to Scripture and a similar method of construction. We may also note that there is a similar vividness of detail. The *Liber Antiquitatum Biblicarum* may inform our approach to *Peri Pascha*, and in order to do this we should enquire first into its genre.

---

[224] The title of this work derives from the renaissance *Editio Princeps*. With regard to date and original language we accept the arguments of Harrington, Perrot and Bogaert *Pseudo-Philon* where the arguments and relevant bibliography can be found in more detail.

[225] ps-Philo does make reference at another point to the slaughter of the firstborn. It is evidently this in which he is interested, rather than the prescriptions for the Passover lamb.

[226] *LAB* 9

Cohn, first of the modern students of the work, notes midrashic parallels and refers to its "midrashic character".[227] Elsewhere he calls it a historic haggadah.[228] In this he is followed by Kisch.[229] This midrashic character in itself does not, however, make the work a midrash. Feldman also notes midrashic method, character and technique, as well as seeing a targumic tradition lying behind the work, but holds back from labelling the work as either.[230] He is impressed by the historical character of the writing, and seeks to draw parallels between ps-Philo and Josephus.[231] Whilst conscious of the greater amount of legendary material contained in *Liber Antiquitatum Biblicarum*, and the more consciously Hellenistic character of the work of Josephus, he nonetheless would see the work in the genre of history.

Perrot differs from him, seeing that whilst *Liber Antiquitatum Biblicarum* is a historical work, its author is not a self-conscious historian like Josephus.[232] As history it is history of a particular kind, "une histoire sainte". Seeking a Jewish genre, he agrees with previous commentators that the work cannot be described as a targum, since ps-Philo's liberty with the text is far too great. Moreover he sees that it is not a midrash, in the sense of a sustained commentary, the fruit of learned reading and reflection. He may equally have been talking of *Peri Pascha*. He goes on, however, to suggest that in the pre-rabbinic age we may employ the term with a greater liberty. Midrashim relate to the Scriptures either as "texte expliqué" or "texte continué". Whilst the former relates primarily to the biblical text, the latter relates primarily to the oral tradition of the sacred history of Israel, for which the source was not uniquely the written text, but the written text supplemented. In much the same way an oral law was erected to direct the application of Torah. As "texte continué" *Liber Antiquitatum Biblicarum* may be described as "midrash populaire". The midrashic material of the later rabbinic productions is derived from precisely this kind of effort.

In the same way, perhaps, *Peri Pascha* may be so described. If "texte continué" died out in Judaism, it may well have continued within Christianity, and may certainly have done so into the time of Melito. We therefore have a valuable clue to the form of the first half

---

[227] Cohn "Apocryphal work" 322
[228] Cohn "Apocryphal Work" 314
[229] Kisch *Pseudo-Philo's Liber* 18
[230] In James *Biblical Antiquities* LXVII
[231] Feldman in James *Biblical Antiquities* LVIII-LXVI
[232] Perrot in Harrington, Perrot, Bogaert *Pseudo-Philon* 22-28

of *Peri Pascha*. Our understanding of its function has to wait on our examination of that of ps-Philo's work.

However, *Liber Antiquitatum Biblicarum* is not an unique example. We may also examine the other "retelling" mentioned by Porton in this context, the *Genesis Apocryphon* found at Qumran, a work which has frequently attracted comparison with that of ps-Philo, though not with that of Melito.[233] It is an Aramaic work, in a fragmentary condition, dating, like ps-Philo, from either the first century BC or the early first century AD. Its extant fragments deal with the birth and the life of Noah and the Abraham story. What is particularly odd is the extent to which it is told in the first person. Like *Liber Antiquitatum Biblicarum* it is essentially an embellishment of the biblical text. The underlying text is at times recognisable, and there is no great distortion of the order of events, but there is extensive additional narrative.

On the grounds of the amount of narrative material extraneous to the biblical text it has been called a "collection of haggadic traditions."[234] This may be true, but does not answer completely the form-critical question. Because it has connections with extant midrashim and targums it has also been compared to these in terms of genre; Lehmann for instance calls the work "a midrashic targum."[235] Certainly "one gets the impression now and then that it is a targum".[236] In this respect it is reminiscent of that part of *Peri Pascha* which we are examining. Black at first described it as a "targum prototype", pointing out the manner in which it followed the chapter and verse of the biblical text.[237] Fitzmyer however points out, just as we did above in the case of Melito's work, that although in places or in isolated phrases there is a literal translation of the biblical text, the *Genesis Apocryphon* is more often paraphrase.[238] We may add to this assessment that, like *Peri Pascha*, the extent of the expansion goes beyond paraphrase. Fitzmyer compares the *Genesis Apocryphon* to the targums just as we did *Peri Pascha*, with similar result.

Black later revised his view of the targumic character of the work, and preferred the term "midrash".[239] However Fitzmyer is not prepared to allow this. He sees that "it is not simply a midrash, just as it

[233] Comparisons made by Feldman in James *Biblical Antiquities* LII-LIV and Perrot in Harrington, Perrot, Bogaert *Pseudo-Philon* 26
[234] Jongelin, Labuschagne and van der Woude *Aramaic Texts* 78
[235] Lehmann "I Q Genesis Apocryphon" 251
[236] So Jongelin, Labuschagne and van der Woude *Aramaic Texts* 78
[237] Black *Scrolls* 192-198
[238] Fitzmyer *Genesis Apocryphon* 36
[239] Black *Aramaic Approach* 40

is not simply a targum."[240] This may be so, but the term cannot therefore be excluded altogether. In this refusal he is working to the model of the rabbinic midrashim, a somewhat narrow definition of the term. Perrot believes that like *Liber Antiquitatum Biblicarum* it may be called midrash in the sense of texte continué.[241]

At this stage, however, to argue about whether this is or is not midrash is to miss the point of the argument. What is significant is the purpose and *Sitz im Leben* of these works. It is this which may shed some light on that of Melito. We may say that Melito's work is a midrash of sorts in the sense that *Liber Antiquitatum Biblicarum* and the *Genesis Apocryphon* are midrashim, but this does not greatly extend our understanding. We must divine the purpose behind these midrashim.

Cohn had claimed that the purpose of *Liber Antiquitatum Biblicarum* was simply one of edification.[242] Since this on its own does not fully explain the liberties which are taken with the biblical text, there have been a large number of suggestions made with regard to the purpose with which it was produced. On the other hand next to nothing has been suggested in this way with regard to the *Genesis Apocryphon*. The only suggestion with regard to the purpose of this document comes from le Déaut, who, in the light of the great departures in these works from the biblical texts, in contrast to the later targums, suggested that these were non-liturgical targums for private reading.[243]

Even granted that they come from entirely different schools, if these works are form-critically identical we should expect a degree of functional identity. And if the parallels adduced with *Peri Pascha* have any validity, the fact that this work is *prima facie* liturgical, whether homiletic or otherwise, and certainly intended for public use, must militate against le Déaut's suggestion. As regards *Liber Antiquitatum Biblicarum*, most of the suggestions made see the work as polemical, ranged for or against the Samaritans for instance. These are all treated by Feldmann who finds them all in some respect wanting.[244] Perrot sums this up by stating that the work is neither a pamphlet, nor a theological treatise. Its purpose *is* simply edification. This said, however, it is still necessary to ask why it was produced, and Perrot suggests the simple solution that it is a haggadic collection made for the benefit of "targumists and homelists"; in this it reflects the needs

---

[240] Fitzmyer *Genesis Apocryphon* 9
[241] Perrot in Perrot in Harrington, Perrot, Bogaert *Pseudo-Philon* 22-28
[242] Cohn "Apocryphal Work" 328
[243] le Déaut (Review)
[244] Feldman in James *Biblical Antiquities* XXXIII-XLVII

of the synagogue before the destruction of the temple. It echoes these homilies, but falls short of being a collection of them.[245]

Perrot shows that this "liturgical" thesis explains a number of things, for instance the pre-eminence of certain chapters, the manner in which it is constructed around themes, the stress on liturgical matters such as the order of feasts, the primary reference to and different use of the Torah, as well as certain omissions and links which might be explained by reference to the (later) lectionary system. Despite the links with the haggadic tradition reported by Josephus the form is different.[246] If *Liber Antiquitatum Biblicarum* reflects first-century haggadic homilies, then this, in view of the similarity of shape, explains the form of PP11-33. It is a haggadic homily, perhaps growing out of what in the loosest sense may be called a targum. In Melito's church the scriptures were no longer read in Hebrew, but the tradition remained. It is not circular to state that the liturgical context of Melito's work lends support to Perrot's theory concerning ps-Philo. Whether this argument may be extended to the *Genesis Apocryphon* it is for someone more competent to say; however, this would seem to be likely.

It may seem that we have come full-circle in this chapter, beginning with the hypothesis that the first half of *Peri Pascha* was a homily, rejecting it, and then taking it up again. However, in the process we have in fact clarified a great deal. Our understanding of what it might mean to call this half of *Peri Pascha* a homily is greatly increased. It is most particularly a haggadic homily, and not expository, and is liturgical to a higher degree than an expository homily; as such it is more comparable to the *piyyut* than the rabbinic synagogue homily. Interestingly the piyyut is a genre which combines homiletic aims with liturgical procedure. We may see that these forms co-exist in *Peri Pascha*. They each grew out of the targum, and this appears to be what is happening at Sardis. When commentators have referred to *Peri Pascha* as a homily they have intended something that would be recognised in the twentieth century as such; insofar as any part of *Peri Pascha* is a homily, it is not a type that would be recognised today.

3.1.10 *Conclusion*

At the end of our exhaustive examination of the possible genres of *Peri Pascha* we are in a position to venture certain conclusions. Firstly we have observed that *Peri Pascha* is divisible. The nature of that

---

[245] Perrot in Harrington, Perrot, Bogaert *Pseudo-Philon* 27-28
[246] The links are brought out by Feldman in James *Biblical Antiquities* LVIII-LXI

division and the relationship between those two parts needs to be explored.

Secondly we have found it necessary to posit a distinction between Melito's Jewish Christian tradition and the Hellenistic media´ with which he gives it expression. Observing this distinction we were able to note that the first part of *Peri Pascha* functions as a rhetorical historical *diegema*, with a digression, and simultaneously as a historical haggadah. The liturgical significance of this needs to be explored in order that our overall aim of situating *Peri Pascha* within the Quartodeciman Pascha may be achieved. The second part of *Peri Pascha* is indeed a haggadah, the position which we had set out to demonstrate in the beginning and at the same time it may be recognised as a prose hymn, the *kataskeue* of the earlier *diegema*. Again, the manner in which this fits into the Quartodeciman Pascha must be explored. It is to these remaining questions that we turn in the second part of this chapter.

3.2 The Form and Function of Peri Pascha

We have concluded our examination of the genre of *Peri Pascha* but it remains to pull the results of the examination together, in order that an overall view of the work may be gained. This will enable us to see that the work is a unity and that both its combination of forms and its language betray a liturgical origin.

3.2.1 *The Forms of Peri Pascha*

On the basis of the foregoing argument we may now note that *Peri Pascha* as it stands is a single piece of oratory constructed out of a number of discrete forms.

The major division in the work is to be found at PP46, where Melito announces that having delivered the *diegema* of the Pascha, he will now go on to the *kataskeue*. We have noted that these are distinct rhetorical categories, and that therefore a division in the work might be made at this point. This division accords with the suggestion of Hall that the work should be divided into two, the first half being seen as a synagogue homily, the second as the Passover haggadah.[247] We have seen that the first part of the work is in a sense a homily, though not a synagogue lecture, and that the second half indeed corresponds

---

[247] Hall "Melito in the Light of the Passover Haggadah"

to the haggadah. At the same time we might say that the first half is a rhetorical history, with a methodological post-script, and that the second half is a prose hymn. In either event a two-fold division may be upheld on internal grounds.

Apart from the major division of *Peri Pascha* to be found at 46, there are other divisions to be found in the work. In particular one should note the doxologies which are to be found at 10 and 65. These surely have a role in the division of the work, since the major twofold division is marked in this way. Thus, on the basis of the doxologies and the previous work of classification we may divide the work as follows:

PP 1-45: Diegema of the Pascha

PP 1-10 Proemium
PP 11-45 *Diegema* of the Passover including at PP34-43 a digression on literary method.

PP 46-105: Epideictic Prose Hymn

PP 46-65 *Kataskeue* of redemption
PP 66-105 Peroratio, including *egkomion* and *psogos*

Here, where possible, we have employed the categories which Melito himself employs. These are the categories of a Hellenistic rhetorician. Melito does not refer to his own digression, and so we have not labelled it; one should note that it is purely a digression, and not bound up to the structure of the work in that is not separated in any way through a doxology; it is attached to the *diegema*. As consisting of proemium followed by *diegema* followed by *kataskeue* as the first element in proof,[248] we may see that *Peri Pascha* obeys the canons of classical rhetoric as a whole; it is on this basis that we have labelled the concluding hymn as *peroratio*. This observation may receive further force from noting the location of the digression. Quintilian tells us that is the practice of the schools of declamation to insert a digression of some kind at the end of the *narratio*, before proceeding to *probatio*, and to link this digression to the *narratio*.[249] This is precisely what Melito has done.

However the work may also be viewed, on the basis of the same two-fold division as a haggadic midrash followed by a Passover haggadah. That there should be this concatenation of Jewish and Hellenistic forms should not surprise us. This is only what one would

---

[248] So Quintilian at *Institutio Oratoria* 4.3.1
[249] *Institutio Oratoria* 4.3. Quintilian does not think that the παρέκβασις (which he defines as the handling of a theme at a point which digresses from logical order) need be limited to this point in the speech.

expect from a Christian whose tradition is rooted in the Johannine tradition.

Smalley concludes his investigation of the Hellenic background to *John* thus: "Consideration of a possible Greek background for the fourth evangelist and his tradition has led us to the conclusion that neither seems to be influenced by Hellenism beyond that which belonged to normative Judaism at the time."[250] Even allowing for a degree of apologetic motivation in the writing of Smalley this is nonetheless a reasonable summary of the view of the mainstream of Johannine scholarship, that *John* is a work deriving more or less directly from the Palestinian Aramaic Christian tradition which has undergone a degree of Hellenizing influence consonant with such an origin. Such an origin is betrayed by frequent Semitisms in the text,[251] the manner in which John uses the Old Testament[252] and an apparent acquaintance with the topography of Palestine.[253] This does not enable us, however, to write off any trace of Hellenistic influence.

Hellenistic influence was available initially within Palestine itself. We know of the "Hellenists" of *Acts*, the verb Ἑλληνίζειν implying that they did more than speak Greek but had adopted Greek manners and ideas as well. Significantly, Cullmann argues that it is precisely within this circle of Hellenists that Johannine Christianity had its origin.[254] He compares the ideas on the supersession of the temple in *John* with those in Stephen's speech in *Acts* and finds a great degree of similarity. He also discerns a common interest in the mission of the Church outside of Israel itself. He does not see it necessary to look for further Hellenistic influence, however, not holding the view that the Gospel was written at Ephesus. But he cannot trace the Johannine circle any further than Syria, and sees no further distinctive trace of it in the church. Since Melito seems to be an example of distinctive Johannine Christianity at a date later than the end of the first century, we cannot follow him here. On the other hand Kossen shows quite clearly the influence of an Asian milieu mingling with an earlier Hellenistic Judaism.[255] He notes that it is Andrew and Philip, the disciples who bear Greek names who are approached by the Greeks. Philip appears in the same letter of Polycrates from which we know of Melito, and Andrew appears, also in an Asian context, in a record of

---

[250] Smalley *John* 58
[251] So, most cautiously, Black *Aramaic Approach*, conclusions on 272-273
[252] See 3.1.7 above and refs ad loc
[253] So, cautiously again, Barrett *John and Judaism* 36
[254] Cullmann *Johannine Circle* 39-52
[255] Kossen "Who were the Greeks"

Papias of Hierapolis.[256] These apostles are given a prominence in
John which they do not receive elsewhere. Kossen sees the evangeli-
sation of the gentiles as the fruit which will be borne of the death of
Jesus, for the moment they cannot see Jesus directly. From this he
deduces that the Asian context is one that suits the scenario admira-
bly, the Asian mission is the situation in which the Greeks are
brought to Jesus.

This does not mean a necessary Hellenistic influence, a confluence
is probably a better way of describing the phenomenon. Hengel suggests that the message of the Hellenists took root particularly because
of a co-incidence between the aspirations of Greek thought and the
message of Jesus.[257] What does happen, as with Melito, is that a faith
with Jewish origins becomes expressed in a Hellenistic manner, being
already susceptible of such an understanding and expression. This
Hellenistic expression in turn makes the kerygma more acceptable yet
to the Greek mind. One example may suffice. In 1.2.2 we traced
Melito's typology to John, in the sixth chapter of whose Gospel we
find the manna of *Exodus* 16 being interpreted in a rabbinic manner
to make a Christian point. This process of typology can be understood in a variety of ways. Whereas the Jew would recognise a type of
exegesis relating to the prophetic eschatology,[258], the Platonist on
hearing ἀληθινός would tend to think of the true world of the
forms.[259] One who stood in both thought-worlds, but who did not
make the distinction, would understand it in both ways at once, and
would see no contradiction. Thus Melito's explanation in terms of the
sculptor's model is susceptible both of a temporal understanding, the
Church has arisen and supplanted Israel, and a metaphysical understanding, the Church is superior and more heavenly than Israel.

This is the dual tradition from which Melito derives; we believe
that we have shown that it is a tradition in which he continues to
stand, a Hellenistic Jewish Christian in a strongly Hellenistic milieu.
So it is that he is in receipt of the traditional etymologies of Hebrew
words, *Pascha* and Israel, which have been constructed on Greek
lines. Insofar as he shares them with Philo they are part of the *koine* of
Hellenistic Judaism. In time, this process of etymologizing on the
basis of homophonous roots was received entirely into the Jewish
tradition as a hermeneutic rule.[260]

---

[256] Recorded at *HE* 3.39
[257] Hengel *Earliest Christianity* 72-73
[258] Gärtner *John 6* 20-25
[259] This is the manner in which Dodd *Interpretation* 72, thought that John, following
Philo, understands it.
[260] Liebermann *Hellenism* 68

On the basis of our classification of *Peri Pascha*, and on the basis of our understanding of the dual cultural world which Melito inhabited, we may sketch a hypothesis. That Melito is in receipt of the traditional paschal observance of his community, a part of which was a haggadah said over the table of which the elements were generally understood. It need not have been called that (no Greek translation of the term survives, נגד is rendered with compounds of ἀγγέλειν by the Septuagint, including at *Exodus* 13:8 which is taken as the biblical basis for the haggadah); we shall suggest below that it might have been called a μνημόσυνον, or alternatively an ἀνάμνησις.

It falls on Melito to declare the haggadah, which he duly prepares. As a sophist, he understands the task of delivering the haggadah as delivering a piece of epideictic oratory on a set theme suitable to the religious context. This cross-cultural understanding is exhibited within Judaism itself. Stein has shown how the symposiastic form of literature has influenced the Passover observance of Judaism, in the forms of the speeches made, in the shape of the seder and even in what is eaten.[261] So the *kiddush* and *hallel* mirror the prayers and hymns of the Greek symposium; the reclining and the washing of hands are Greek customs; the *nishmath* elegy is in the shape of a *logos basilikos*, itself a sub-species of epideictic; the embellishment of plagues is in the order of what we might expect from a speech in the genus of epideictic; lettuce and haroseth are hors d'oevres known to the Hellenistic sympotic writers.

Stein believes all this to have taken place after the fall of the temple. The date however is not relevant, it is a development which took place in Judaism, either before the fall of the Temple or afterwards. And if it took place within Judaism then it becomes all the easier to see how within Christianity Melito can understand what he is doing in the same terms. It becomes equally difficult to follow McDonald when he argues against the understanding of *Peri Pascha* as a haggadah on the basis that Melito is a Hellenist, and that this excludes the possibility that he uses forms of Jewish origin.[262]

However, before this hypothesis can be pursued through an examination of the Quartodeciman paschal rite, it remains to defend the unity of the extant *Peri Pascha* and to show that there are sufficient grounds for seeing that it is at least in part a liturgical document.

---

[261] Stein "Influence" especially 25-28
[262] McDonald "Comments"

3.2.2 *The Division of Peri Pascha*

In seeing *Peri Pascha* as essentially two-fold we have adopted the suggestion of Hall that the work divides fundamentally into two.[263] Hall's twofold division of the work, and its accompanying explanation, has the immense virtue of simplicity since it neatly accords with known Jewish practice, the division between pre-Passover teaching and domestic Passover ritual. There is moreover some external evidence for such a division. However, we intend to show that this external evidence is weak.

Hall first of all he notes that the Georgian scribal tradition circulated the work in its two parts entirely separately. He does not speculate on how far back in the history of the text this division goes.[264] That it may be ancient is illustrated from the Chester-Beatty Codex. At this point Bonner describes "a paragraph sign, beginning in the margin with a diplê...continued as a single line under αἰῶνας ἀμήν, then turned upward at a right angle; then two parallel strokes drawn from this vertical through about three letter-spaces to the right."[265] This phenomenon is especially noted by Hansen who makes it part of the basis for his insertion of a major division at this point.[266] Hansen claims it as unique, but he is no papyrologist and moreover cites no authority for this assertion. The end of a book is usually shown by a line with a diplê at either end, and this indeed is the case in this codex, where Enoch is separated from Melito. Thus, whatever this division is, it is not a division into books. Perhaps it is a section division.[267] The scribal markings in this codex are indeed eccentric, in PP82 Bonner notes that "after κόσμον a long paragraph sign (a diplê with a long stroke continued from its apex) fills the greater part of the remainder of the line. The O at the beginning of the next line is larger than usual and set to the left of the usual margin."[268] And yet this marking takes place not at a point which might be considered a major juncture in the text but in fact disrupts a paragraph in a most improbable place. It would seem that not too much can be read into the scribal markings in this codex. The division of the work at PP46

---

[263] Hall "Melito in the Light of the Paschal Haggadah" 36-37

[264] Hall "Melito in the Light of the Passover Haggadah" 41-42

[265] Bonner *Homily* 115. See also the facsimile in Kenyon *Chester Beatty Biblical Papyri* 8

[266] Hansen *Sitz* 68-70

[267] That this, and the other division in this copy of *Peri Pascha*, is a section division is a suggestion of Prof. J.N. Birdsall. He further suggests that these were inserted on scribal initiative

[268] Bonner *Homily* 145

evinced by Chester-Beatty is also to be found in the earlier Papyrus Bodmer. At this point what Testuz calls "an arrow-like marking" has been made in the margin. However, these markings are frequent in the papyrus and are to be found at points which, as Testuz points out, appear to bear little relation to the logic or the sense of the document.[269] On the basis of the manuscript evidence it would indeed seem that *Peri Pascha* was divided at this point from an early date but that it was never divided into books at this point. If it was divided here, it was divided into sections within the one book.

As a second piece of external evidence Hall sees that a similar shape is evinced by the *In Sanctum Pascha* of ps-Hippolytus. It too may be divided on internal grounds into two parts, the first an explanation of the text of *Exodus* 12, the second a more general expansion of the subject into the saving acts of Christ.[270] Although ps-Hippolytus has undergone further development, away from its Jewish origins, and become a more purely Christian work, the shape is nonetheless comparable, as we shall note in a moment.

Further evidence of the division is produced by Eusebius, who in his list of Melito's works refers to "the two books on the Pascha".[271] Hall takes this as implying that Eusebius, or rather his source, knew the work in two separate parts.[272] The difficulties produced by Eusebius' witness have already been referred to. We may recall that they led to Huber denying that Melito was a Quartodeciman, in part to Nautin's denial of the authenticity of the work, and to Hyldahl's denial of the attribution of the work to Melito.[273] Apart from the fact that Eusebius describes the work as being in two books there is the additional difficulty that he writes of the work that Melito Ἐν μὲν οὖν τῷ Περὶ τοῦ Πάσχα τὸν χρόνον καθ᾿ ὅν συνέταττεν, ἀρχόμενος σημαίνει ἐν τούτοις Ἐπὶ Σερουιλλίου Παύλου ἀνθυπάτου τῆς Ἀσίας ᾧ Σάγαρις καιρῷ ἐμαρτύρησιν, ἐγένετο ζήτησις πολλὴ ἐν Λαοδικείᾳ περὶ τοῦ πάσχα, ἐμπεσόντος κατὰ καιρὸν ἐν ἐκείναις ταῖς ἡμέραις, καὶ ἐγράφη ταῦτα. τούτου δὲ τοῦ λόγου μέμνηται Κλήμης ὁ Ἀλεξανδρεὺς ἐν ἰδίῳ περὶ τοῦ πάσχα λόγῳ, ὃν ὡς ἐξ αἰτίας τῆς τοῦ Μελίτωνος γραφῆς φησιν ἑαυτὸν συντάξαι.[274] This may be read as implying that the work was of a polemical nature, since Clement had seen fit to respond. The contro-

---

[269] Testuz *Papyrus Bodmer XIII* 15. These look to me like *diplai obelismenai*, which according to Turner *Greek Manuscripts* 12 were used to mark paragraphs

[270] Hall "Melito in the Light of the Passover Haggadah" 42-45; Visonà *Pseudo Ippolito* 49 also notes the same basic twofold shape.

[271] *HE* 4.26

[272] Hall "Melito in the Light of the Passover Haggadah" 42

[273] On these see 1.1.1

[274] *HE* 4.26, Fragment 4 in Hall *Melito of Sardis*

versial subject is, however, uncertain. Hansen, in view of the
martyrdoms around that time suggests a controversy over martyrdom.[275] However, our work is not controversial, and is not about
martyrdom. Moreover the citation from Melito's work is nowhere
found in the extant *Peri Pascha*.

This last problem may be easily dealt with. Perler provides extensive evidence for the addition by scribes of chronological notes at the
head of manuscripts.[276] It is this which we appear to have here. The
clinching proof of this lies in Eusebius' last words, "καὶ ἐγράφη ταῦτα,
implying that the text is to follow. The reference to Clement is unclear. There is a citation from Clement's work in the *Chronicon Paschale*
which would indicate that Clement's subject is chronology, since
Clement is here concerned to expound the Johannine passion chronology, but whether this is the basis of Clement's difference with
Melito is not at all clear. The biggest difficulty is that the *Peri Pascha* to
which Eusebius refers and to which Clement responds would appear
to be a *Streitschrift*, not simply because Clement replies but because it
would appear to be connected with the debate at Laodicea. However,
to say that one has written a work ἐξ αἰτίας another does not necessarily mean a direct response to a polemical work, it could equally
mean a work inspired by another,[277] or that some particular aspect of
a non-polemical work had caused offence. Hall, with good reason
given their slightly different theories of typology, suggests that Clement is replying to Melito's use of the Old Testament.[278]

There are good grounds to show that the *Peri Pascha* mentioned by
Eusebius was not a polemical work. First the connection with the
dispute at Laodicea is tenuous, deriving from the surmise of the later
scribe who produced the chronological introduction. Secondly we
may note that in the fragment preserved in the *Chronicon Paschale*
Clement speaks of Our Lord explaining to the disciples τοῦ τύπου τὸ
μυστήριον. This language has clear echoes of Melito, and implies that
Clement was inspired rather than enraged by the work he had read,
and that the work moreover is that which we possess. Elsewhere in his

---

[275] Hansen *Sitz im Leben* 167
[276] Perler *Sur la Pâque* 19-20. Interestingly Bauer *Orthodoxy and Heresy* 79-80 had
suggested that this might be the case even before the discovery of the Greek *Peri
Pascha* on the basis of pure common sense. In a time of persecution and hardship
Melito would hardly have launched into an argument concerning chronology which
such insensitivity.
[277] So Mara *Évangile* 85 holds that Clement had written "sous l'impulsion et
l'inspiration du livre du Meliton"!
[278] Hall *Melito of Sardis* xxi

work Eusebius implies that Clement cites Melito with approval.[279] Again this implies that his work was motivated by approval of that of Melito rather than by an urge to oppose. Finally we should note with Bonner the similarity, as well as the differences, between the approaches of Clement and Melito to the idea of an artist's model providing the basis for a typological theory.[280]

The fact is that Eusebius is simply not a reliable witness. The information he has concerning *Peri Pascha* may derive entirely from Clement or indeed from a traditional list.[281] That he is working from a list and has not actually consulted the works of which he is writing is supported by the fact that he goes on to quote from a work, the *Eklogai*, which are not in fact contained in the list that he had previously employed. This unreliability does not justify us denying the authenticity or authorship of the work. The underlying catalogue however may well be reliable; this however points not to a work in two parts but to two discrete books. If this is the case then the work we possess is the first of these books; there is no reason why it should not fit on a single roll. It is of course possible that the *Peri Pascha* which we possess was not a member of the list which Eusebius employed, but in view of the identity of headings, the widespread distribution of our work, and the fact that *Peri Pascha* would appear to be the work to which Clement refers, this is unlikely. There is no title in Eusebius' list which might be *Peri Pascha* under another name.

The internal evidence for Hall's proposed division of the work, and thus for his description of the second part of *Peri Pascha* as fulfilling "the general conditions ... appropriate for a Passover haggadah" is good. However the external evidence is weak. The division in the codex is a division into sections, whereas the work known to Eusebius was in two distinct books. There are moreover good grounds to reject Hall's reasoning behind his division of the work, namely that the first half is a synagogal exposition of *Exodus* 12..

Firstly, at PP46 Melito states τὸ μὲν οὖν διήγημα τοῦ τύπου ἀκηκόατε... the *diegema* of course being what we have recognised as the first half, that which Hall suggests is a homily for the preceding Sabbath. PP46, however, falls at the beginning of the second half, which according to this theory would fall on the eve of Passover.

---

[279] *HE* 6.13; Casel "Art und Sinn" 9 notes that Melito, for Clement, is an authority
[280] Bonner *Homily* 69. It is particularly interesting that Bonner should note this since he was under the impression that the *Peri Pascha* known to Clement was an entirely different work than that which now bears that name. Indeed he warns us against the confusion!
[281] So Bauer *Orthodoxy and Heresy* 153-154

Although no indication of the time at which this would have been heard, such as that at PP11, is given, it would be stretching the memories of the hearers somewhat to expect them to recall the previous Sabbath in such detail. It would moreover be stretching the use of the perfect tense somewhat. If the reference was to a previous day then we would expect to hear ἠκούσατε, but the manuscripts are quite clear. The absence of an indication of time makes it all the more probable that there had been no time lapse between the two halves. This statement at PP46 corresponds to a suggestion of Quintilian that the orator may wish to break up the narratio with a phrase such as audistis quae ante acta sunt, accipite nunc quae insequuntur.[282] Secondly we should recall that Melito states that following on from the *diegema* he will now give us the *kataskeue* of the mystery. ·Surely these related terms indicate that the activities described belong more closely together than would be the case if two separate and distinct activities were separated by at least a day. The whole of *Peri Pascha* does, after all, satisfy the conditions for a single piece of declamation. It is divided by doxologies marking off each element in the rhetorical structure, and this is the internal ground for division, but the structure of *proemium, diegema, kataskeue* and peroration are each single parts of an epideictic whole. Thirdly it should be noted that PP1-46 simply does not correspond to the shape of a synagogue homily![283]

Thus on the grounds of both external and internal evidence we may see that the division between the two halves was not as great as Hall maintained. In this light his rejected suggestion begins to appear more probable, that among Christians the reading and exposition of Passover Torah was a part of the Passover Eve celebration.[284] In other words, Hall is correct in dividing the work, but incorrect in making the division a division between two activities on different days. This in turn makes it unlikely that the two halves of *Peri Pascha* are the two books to which Eusebius refers. However, if the first half of *Peri Pascha* is not a synagogue homily for a preceding Sabbath the reason for the reading of *Exodus* 12 on the occasion of the paschal celebration itself still needs to be adduced. We may begin by taking up Hall's rejected suggestion.

Hall suggests that the laws concerning Passover were taught in the temple in the days leading up to the feast is clear. This reading of the Passover law would include this passage of *Exodus*. He suggests that

---

[282] *Instituto Oratoria* 4.2.50
[283] As was argued at 3.1.1 above.
[284] Hall "Melito in the Light of the Passover Haggadah" 35-36

after the destruction of the temple, since it became impossible to keep this ritual law, the reading of these passages of Torah on Passover eve became a meritorious substitute for their actual keeping. However, against this he notes that there is no Jewish evidence for such a practice. He suggests moreover that it would be more appropriate for the synagogue to be the place for this exposition than the home on Passover eve. If, therefore, such a transference took place then it would more probably have taken place among Christians, who met both as synagogue and family, there being no distinction between the ecclesial and the domestic.

This suggestion is both more complex and laden with supposition. The process by which this came about, however, need not have been related to the destruction of the temple. In Johannine circles the worship of the temple was repudiated in any case, and the regulations may thus have undergone precisely such a typological explanation as is found in *Peri Pascha*. Moreover, we may note that we may even have a pre-Passover homily in *John* 6.[285] This would indicate that the custom of explaining Passover lections on the Sabbaths preceding Passover continued among Jewish Christians, and that there is some other reason than the destruction of the Temple by which *Exodus* 12 became attached to the Passover Eve celebrations. This we may seek in time, but the shape of *Peri Pascha* at least may be explained with reference to the homiletic explanation of *Exodus* 12 in the relatively free manner of the synagogue before the fall of the Temple, an extended midrash, become further developed under the influence of stoic theory concerning the interpretation of texts and rhetorical practice concerning the delivery of history.

We have accounted for parallels with most of the Jewish haggadah, but not for the introductory midrash, that on *Deuteronomy* 6:21ff. Is it possible that the treatment of *Exodus* 12, following on from the reading of scripture, has been substituted for this? It is equally possible that the reading and treatment of *Exodus* 12 is a purely Christian addition and that, in view of the fluidity of shape the initial midrash was felt not to be an integral part of the rite. We should expect a fair degree of variety in Passover haggadah and ritual in the Judaism prior to the destruction of the temple and this would readily be transmitted to Christianity.[286] We do not seek to decide about the process by which *Exodus* 12 becomes part of the Christian rite, but may seek to explain why it should have come to have significance for Christians.

---

[285] See 3.1.1
[286] So Daube "Earliest Structures"

Both Jewish and Quartodeciman paschal celebrations were commemorative.[287] However, the Quartodecimans did not simply remember the first Passover with its subsequent exodus from Egypt into
the promised land but commemorated these events according to their
typological understanding of Pascha as human release from sin and
into eternal life as achieved by Jesus, the true paschal lamb. It is
perhaps for this typological reason that *Exodus* 12 became the lection
used by the Quartodecimans. The evidence of ps-Hippolytus is sufficient to show that this was not a local peculiarity of Sardis but something common to Quartodeciman congregations, and presumably
originating in the paschal practice of the earliest Christians in Asia
Minor. As these congregations saw the Passover primarily through
Johannine eyes, the slaughter of the lambs being superseded by the
death of the Lord of whom no bone was broken, this chapter would
suggest itself entirely naturally to them as one expressing this mystery,
containing additionally the command to treat the feast as a μνημόσυνον, and thus containing all that was central to their celebration. All
this accords with the idea of remembrance in the Johannine theological community being a means of understanding the Old Testament.
In the context of remembering the events of the death and resurrection of the Lord they remember this scripture, and in remembering
understand it. Note that whatever practice had been taken over from
Judaism, it is the reality and not the shadow which is the primary
focus of remembrance. As in *John*, it is not the Old Testament which
lends typological shape to the Gospel, but the Gospel, the events of
the life and death of Jesus, which make (typological) understanding of
the Old Testament possible. Thus the abolition of the temple has
nothing to do with the transference of a pre-Passover lection to Passover eve as a meritorious substitute for the keeping of the law; there is
already a more than meritorious substitute for the paschal lamb.
Rather the use of this lection is dictated by the mystery, the remembrance of which enables the Christians of Asia Minor to call to mind
and understand this Scripture.

Thus although we may agree with Hall that *Peri Pascha*, broadly
speaking, falls into two parts hinging at PP46 and marked by a doxology, we may further note that each part is subdivided with concluding doxologies, the first at PP10, with a digression starting at PP34,
and the second at PP65. Furthermore there are no grounds for dividing up *Peri Pascha* into separate works entirely, since it hangs together
in terms of sense and because the entire work was delivered on one
single occasion. This is of vital significance in our attempt to discern

---

[287] As argued at 2.2 above

its role in the Quartodeciman Pascha. *Exodus* 12 was read as a summary of the meaning of the feast, and as a preliminary midrash before the seder properly began.

Apart from that of Hall, two suggestions have been made concerning the identity of the second book. The first is that of Perler,[288] with which we shall deal below. The second is that of Pseftogas, who claimed that *Peri Pascha* is the second part of a double work of which the first part is the work now known as the *In Sanctum Pascha* of ps-Hippolytus.[289] Although *In Sanctum Pascha* is a work from a similar Quartodeciman background in second century Asia Minor showing similar stylistic traits and holding liturgical and catechetical formulae in common it is not a work derived directly from *Peri Pascha* or even from a common source; there is no literary dependence, and such common traits as the two works hold may be assigned to background. It is easiest to see *In Sanctum Pascha* as a probably later production than *Peri Pascha*; the comparison that we shall make here may help us see how the practice of the Quartodecimans developed, and enable us to see to what extent Melito's originality has had a hand in *Peri Pascha* as we possess it.[290]

Having reached our conclusions concerning the structure of *Peri Pascha* on the basis of the text of *Peri Pascha* alone we may compare the work thus analysed to the *In Sanctum Pascha* of ps-Hippolytus, with the aim of seeing whether that work displays anything comparable in terms of structure, or whether it is indeed the second part of a double work. Cantalamessa divides the work into three main parts, which he calls praeconium, exegesis and homily.[291] The first sums up the themes of the work; the second is a close exegesis of *Exodus* 12, quoting the text in full and then dividing it up into verses for consideration; the third is a more general treatment of the theme. The difference between this and *Peri Pascha* is immediately clear. When Melito gives his exegesis of *Exodus* the text is not repeated, nor is it broken down verse by verse, rather he gives us what he calls a *diegema* based on the text. On the other hand, the beginning of this *diegema* looks like a citation of the text, and is indeed claimed to be such by Melito. Thus the citation of the text preliminary to exegesis is obviously part of the tradition, ps-Hippolytus however has a less free approach towards the text. This appearance of the text in *In Sanctum Pascha* is not

---

[288] Perler *Hymnus*

[289] Pseftogas Μελίτωνος Σαρδέων Περὶ τὸ Πάσχα δύο

[290] On *In Sanctum Pascha* in general and with regard to its background and relationship to *Peri Pascha* see Cantalamessa *Omelia* 45-65 and Visonà *Pseudo Ippolyto* 39-78

[291] Cantalamessa *Omelia* 430

the reading but a repetition for the purpose of παραβολή and παράθεσις[292] similar to that appearing in Melito's work.

Once this apparent difference has been seen as not a difference but a similarity, the overall similarity of outline between the works becomes clear. Melito begins by summing up his theme and then goes on to exegesis, having cited part of the text. The major haggadic part of the work, 46ff, corresponds to what Cantalamessa has called the homiletic section. There, as in *Peri Pascha*, the plan of salvation is described. This similarity of outline accords with Visonà's analysis of *In Sanctum Pascha*,[293] but not, however, with that of Cantalamessa.[294] Rather he sees the whole of *Peri Pascha* as corresponding to what he calls the homiletic section of *In Sanctum Pascha*. The praeconium and exegesis he sees as having already been delivered before the extant *Peri Pascha* begins, perceiving a reference to this interposed material in the opening lines of the work.

We shall examine the opening lines to see what preceded *Peri Pascha* in the next section, where we shall find that it is improbable that such exegetical activity had already taken place, a position with which Visonà agrees.[295] Additionally, Cantalamessa takes no account of the divisions which we have found within Melito's work, seeing it as an undifferentiated work, which it is not. Apart from this the comparison that we have produced here has the virtue of simplicity. This is the twofold division in *In Sanctum Pascha* which Hall had indicated as additional evidence for his division of *Peri Pascha*.[296] The comparison between the two works is therefore as follows (our terms are used for *Peri Pascha*, those of Cantalamessa for *In Sanctum Pascha*.)

PP: Paras	IP: Chapters
1-10: Proemium	1-3: Praeconium
11-33: Diegema	4-42: Exegesis
(34-45: Digression)	
46-105: Haggadah	43-63: Homily

Firstly we may note that the digression in *Peri Pascha* which we claimed as the result not of Melito's tradition but of his originality is precisely that section which is not paralleled in the work of ps-Hippolytus. Secondly we may note that the whole of *In Sanctum Pascha*

---

[292] *In Sanctum Pascha* 5.2
[293] Visonà *Pseudo-Ippolyto* 47-55
[294] Cantalamessa *Omelia* 434-436
[295] Visonà *Pseudo-Ippolyto* 49-55
[296] Hall "Melito in the Light of the Passover Haggadah" 42-45

is in a loose sense homiletic; this applies not only to the section which Cantalamessa sees as being a homily but also to the highly didactic exegetical section and indeed the praeconium, which is itself a member of the species homily. Cantalamessa sees this total unity and claims it as forming a paschal "liturgy of the word".[297] There is some basis for this in the text, since at ps-Hippolytus speaks of receiving the nourishment of the word and of eating the λογικὸν πάσχα.[298] This fundamental similarity of outline is recognised by Pseftogas, though oddly this becomes for him evidence for their single authorship and identity. However, if *In Sanctum Pascha* possesses a shape comparable to that of *Peri Pascha* this is surely an argument against their being parts of the same double work. Further to this there is the matter of the distinction in style between the two works.

Thus if Eusebius' witness concerning *Peri Pascha* in two books is to be upheld then the only remaining possibility is the theory of Perler that the second book mentioned by Eusebius is a liturgy preserved in fragmentary form as Fragment 17.[299] Since the first part of *Peri Pascha* (namely, according to his theory, that which is extant) is itself liturgical, as we hope to show, then to explain the report concerning two books on this basis is feasible. Firstly, however the liturgical basis of the extant *Peri Pascha* needs to be demonstrated. This we shall do after showing that the form of *Peri Pascha* which we have uncovered is patient of a liturgical function.

3.2.3 *The Function of Peri Pascha*

Having determined the forms and genre of *Peri Pascha* we must turn to establish the functions which would be determined by this form. Form is not merely an external thing, but implies a function.

We have concluded that whereas *Peri Pascha* is a single work, it is made up of a complex of forms carefully divided from one another with doxologies. The reason for this phenomenon of discrete parts being joined together may well be liturgical; a hymn at least is a liturgical unit, and we have shown that part at least of *Peri Pascha* may be classified as such. So we may perhaps describe the parts of *Peri Pascha* as discrete parts of a single liturgy. This in turn opens up the search for a liturgical basis which would hold the different elements together. A Jewish liturgical context is provided by the parallels with the Passover haggadah demonstrated by Hall. However, it is not so

---

[297] Cantalamessa *Omelia* 450
[298] *IP* 4
[299] Perler *Hymnus*

simple to see the way in which a piece of epideictic oratory may be
described as liturgical.

Epideictic oratory had been one of the three types recognised by
Aristotle, together with forensic and political oratory.[300] It has been
frequently suggested that in an imperial culture the latter two found
little opportunity for use, and so the epideictic became supreme, an
art form in itself, that a system of education intended to prepare
young men for a life in which an ability to speak was an essential life-
skill became a "pure" science.[301] However, this was not really so.
Litigation continued unabated despite the Empire, and there is ample
of evidence of sophists appearing in court, either for themselves or for
clients. Moreover local politics did not cease, despite the presence of
an emperor in Rome. Under the protection of the Empire political
life may have taken on a different complexion, but that did not mean
that it ceased altogether.[302] We shall see below that sophists found
functions in the imperial city, but that they were not restricted to
those which rhetoric had originally served. This indicates to us that
the development of the *melete* was certainly related to social move-
ments in the Empire, but that it derived from the popularity of the
medium, from the rewards that might accrue to the successful sophist;
the change in the nature of political life was only a single factor in a
more complicated development, a development which may be known
as the second sophistic.

The term "second sophistic" is one coined by Philostratus. He uses
it to distinguish the sophistic movement of his day from that of the
time of Gorgias, and states that it is different by virtue of the fact that
it treats historical rather than philosophical themes.[303] Bowersock
examines this thesis and finds that it is not themes which are distinctively different but the social status of the sophists and the diffusion of
their functions through society.[304] An interesting list of sophistic du-
ties is given by Aelius Aristides, noting the things that philosophers, in
contrast to sophists, do not do. "They neither declaim, nor create nor
discover beautiful literary art, they do not adorn the state festivals,
they do not honour the gods, they do not advise cities, do not console
the grieving, nor settle civil strife, they educate neither the young nor

---

[300] Aristotle *Rhetorica* I 3 9
[301] So Marrou *Education* 195. Note also the comments of Hinks "Tria Genera"
[302] For the decline of political life under Roman rule see Jones *Greek City* 170-192.
However Anderson *Second Sophistic* 7-8 gives us some insight into the fact that this
decline was not necessarily perceived as such by its contemporaries.
[303] *VS* I 482
[304] Bowersock *Greek Sophists* 9-27

anyone else, and they think nothing for beauty in their speech."[305]
Again, it is a social movement, relating to the status which may accrue to the sophist.

The sophists' rhetorical speciality was epideictic oratory, and this gave rise to public displays, including rhetorical contests at the festivals on set themes. This implies that epideictic oratory was a popular as well as a "high" culture. As Boulanger says, "en deuxième siècle la sophistique est partout."[306] Wright describes the high importance in which contemporary sophists were held at the time by pointing out that they were exalted to civic office and enjoyed imperial favour.[307] Cities would endow chairs of rhetoric and at least Ephesus had a municipal library. Bowersock describes the characteristic of the second sophistic as "the union of literary, political and economic influence."[308] In view of this it is hardly surprising that Melito should demonstrate rhetorical traits in his work.

Wifstrand has suggested that the influence on Melito derives directly from the Hellenistic synagogue where the second sophistic had taken root,[309] but against this has to be held the fact that commerce between synagogue and Church could not have been all that great given Melito's view of Judaism. Rather, what we would suggest here is that there is a more direct link between Melito and the sophists of his age, and that Melito, like ps-Hippolytus who also betrays the influence of the second sophistic,[310] has undergone a process similar to that which took place in the Hellenistic synagogue. Sophists could perform liturgical functions and rhetoric could be liturgical, and it is for this reason that Melito acts as a sophist.

To this the clues are sparse but nonetheless present. There is a significant story preserved by Philostratus of Polemo, the famous sophist of Smyrna noted for his exaggerated Asianism, a friend of Hadrian who is known to have visited Sardis.[311] At the dedication of the temple of Olympian Zeus by Hadrian in around 130 he is called upon ἐφυμνῆσαι τῇ θυσίᾳ. This he does, he διελέχθη and declares moreover that it is with divine impulse that he speaks.[312] This is significant because it demonstrates that a sophist in the second century is not out of place taking a leading part in a religious ceremony

---

[305] Aelius Aristides *Oratio* III, 672
[306] Boulanger *Aelius Aristide* 50
[307] Wright *Philostratus and Eunapius* xv-xviii
[308] Bowersock *Greek Sophists* 27
[309] Wifstrand "Homily" 217-219
[310] So Cantalamessa *Omelia* 335-367
[311] So Bowersock *Greek Sophists* 123
[312] *VS* I 25 533

and because it is equally not out of place for one of these to claim
divine inspiration for his speech. Nor is this story of Polemo an isolated instance. Scopelian, another Smyrnian of Asianist style, was
high priest of Asia;[313] Antiochus, as well as Polemo[314] frequented the
temple of Asclepius as indeed did Aelius Aristides, who produced the
ἱεροὶ λόγοι concerning the revelations he received from Asclepius.
One must also note the lyric nomes produced by Hippodromus[315]
and the fact that Heracleides was also a priest.[316] Quintilian tells us of
the sacred contest, at which the oratorical praise of Capitoline
Iuppiter played a major part.[317] Apart from the story of Polemo
however we must especially note that Apollonius was hierophant of
Demeter. Philostratus seems to imply that this is a position generally
held by a sophist, by telling of other sophists who were noted as
hierophants.[318] Thus we may see that at a time contemporary with
Melito there are distinct religious functions in paganism associated
with the practice of rhetoric which have to do particularly with the
expression on behalf of the congregation of devotion to the gods and
communication on behalf of the deity. Whereas it would be prema-
ture to state that this is what Melito is doing at the Pascha, we may
nonetheless note that given the extent to which rhetorical functions
met liturgical needs, *Peri Pascha* as an epideixis may be seen as per-
forming a liturgical function, and that Melito at the seder may well
have perceived himself as a sophist in the light of the sophistic functions of the festivals.

In our analysis of genre we have noted that the first half is fundamentally a *diegema*, and that the second part is described as a *kataskeue*;
both are hymnic in tone and form. As these together make the up the
epideixis, so the whole may described as having a liturgical function.
Moreover there are the links with the process of remembrance to
bear in mind, both those of the retelling of scripture by bringing to
mind a *phantasia* of an event, and the links with the Johannine understanding of remembrance, by which events bring forth understanding
of scripture.

However, there has been criticism of previous attempts to perceive
Peri Pascha as a liturgy, in particular the critique of Hall offered by

---

[313] *VS* I 21 515
[314] *VS* II 4 568
[315] *VS* II 26 613
[316] *VS* II 27 620
[317] *Instituto Oratorica* 3.7.4
[318] *VS* II 20 600-601. To these examples from Philostratus we must add those
reported by Anderson *Second Sophistic* 200-203. He suggests that the religious roles of
sophists derived from their functions at the festivals

McDonald.[319] He argued against the classification on the grounds that Melito was a thorough Hellenist whereas the haggadah was a thoroughly Jewish form. This has already been shown to be an invalid argument, as has his accusation of a lack of any purpose in the context of Melito's paschal observance. His suggestion that the *diatribe* lies behind *Peri Pascha* has also been shown to be worthless. One significant part of his argument, however, remains to be dealt with. Cross had claimed that if *Peri Pascha* was a haggadah it was not therefore a homily.[320] McDonald argued that even if it were a haggadah (not that he believed for a moment that it was) this did not preclude its homiletic character. The two were false antitheses.

The basis of his argument is the work of Finkelstein which shows that the origins of the haggadah were homiletic.[321] This argument does not, however, take note of the subsequent development of the haggadah, and is thereby somewhat limited. Although the basis of the haggadah is a midrash, it became ritualized. Although the suggestion that the antitheses are false is interesting, by nature of what are effectively the homiletic origins of the haggadah, we must note the possibility of a distinction between ritual and homiletic haggadah to which Cantalamessa points us.[322] However, in order better to understand the relationship between haggadah and homily the roots of Melito's haggadic tradition, both Hellenistic and Jewish, must be noticed.

In the first instance it is clear that Jews contemporary with Melito kept the Passover in a liturgical manner. At PP80 Melito contrasts the behaviour of the Jews at the festival with the sufferings of the Lord: they recline, make music, feast, and dance. Van Unnik finds this last act particularly interesting and links it to the dance of Jesus in the *Acta Johannis*.[323] He suggests that it is based on the behaviour of Jews known to Melito and to the author of the *Acta*. Given the links already established between Melito and the *Acta* as Johannine trajectories and given that the dance is performed by Jesus himself, we may in fact suggest that Jews and Quartodecimans alike celebrated the Passover with dancing as well as music and hymn-singing, and that this was a tradition passed to Melito through his Jewish predecessors. Of course this does not necessarily mean that Quartodecimans and Jews are celebrating identical rites at identical times, but there are definite Jewish antecedents for a liturgy connected with Passover which Melito may reasonably be said to have followed.

---

[319] McDonald "Comments"
[320] Cross *Early Christian Writers* 107
[321] Finkelstein "Oldest Midrash" and "Pre-Maccabean Documents"
[322] Cantalamessa *Omelia* 439-447
[323] van Unnik "Note"

In Melito's Hellenistic contemporaries we may also see a co-incidence of homiletic delivery and liturgical action. We were able to see
the similarities between *Peri Pascha* and the *Hymn to Zeus* of Aelius
Aristides, a hymn which involved a recounting of the deeds of the
god. Although the *Sitz* for this hymn was the fulfilment of a private
vow, there is ample evidence that the sophists operated at the festivals. Here we may recall again the manner in which Polemo graced
the dedication of the Temple of Zeus by Hadrian. Rhetoric was
bound up to liturgical functions.

Thus to say that a work is homiletic does not mean that it is barely
and simply homiletic, rather this part of its character may intimately
be bound up to liturgy. On the basis of both Jewish and Hellenistic
parallels it is most improbable that *Peri Pascha* was barely and simply
recited;[324] more probably it was delivered in ecphonetic style. Does
this then make it a liturgical homily? This is much the understanding
to which Perler comes.[325] He notes similarities in expression and
content between *Peri Pascha* and the various paschal praeconia of the
Latin rites. A similar effort was made by Tsakonas who sought in *Peri
Pascha* the literary ancestry of the Byzantine Holy Week hymns, but
the verbal parallels he cites are slender indeed.[326] Chrestos likewise
seeks parallels between *Peri Pascha* and the Byzantine liturgy, but
overstates his case.[327] Nonetheless he recognises the hymnic character
of the piece, and suggests a liturgical *Sitz im Leben*, which is valuable.
Whilst Perler's arguments, like those of Tsakonas and Chrestos, may
be overstated in places, for instance the fact that there is content held
in common is only what would be expected and can hardly be the
basis for a formal parallel, his basic point is worthy of consideration.
It is that the rhetorical treatment of the haggadah in the early Church
has given rise to what he describes as "une homélie d'un genre
particulier". It becomes a praeconium in the Latin rite, a kontakion
in the Byzantine.

In examining the developments in the haggadah which, according
to Perler, gave rise to the praeconium and the kontakion by virtue of
being treated in either a Greek or Latin method, we should also call
to mind the comments of Wellesz about the link between Romanos'
kontakia and Ephrem's hymns.[328] Wellesz had claimed that Melito

---

[324] On Jewish cantillation see Foley *Foundations* 64-65; as evidence for cantillation
within the Asianist rhetorical style we may note the story of Dionysius of Miletus at
VS 1.20.413 who is criticised for delivering his declamations ξὺν ᾠδῇ

[325] Perler *Sur la Pâque* 24-29

[326] Tsakonas "Usage"

[327] Chrestos "ἔργον"

[328] Wellesz "Melito's Homily" 46-47

was the point at which Greek and Syriac styles had converged, we
suggested that it was rather the case that they simply diverged from
the same origin. The question then becomes one of the extent to
which all of these are liturgical, the Syriac as well as the Greek and
the Latin. The differences between these genres must, also, however,
be taken into account. "Une homélie d'un genre particulier" is a fair
description of the kontakion, which dealt with the reading at matins,
but does this apply to *Peri Pascha*? It certainly does not apply to the
Syriac *madrasha*. Again, the praeconium of the Latin rite has a different function from the kontakion, a term which may perhaps be appli-
cable to the first half. Perler is labouring under the impression that
the whole of *Peri Pascha* is designed as an exposition of *Exodus* 12 and
may thus have been misled into seeking an exegetical content for the
whole. The point is that all these subsequent developments are to
some extent liturgical. Should the same not be true of *Peri Pascha*, the
oldest extant Christian version? For although Melito invites his audience to learn from him (μάθετε, PP46) his tone is not didactic, he is
doing more than explain.

Both Jews and Quartodecimans kept Passover in a liturgical manner, and among the pagans rhetoric had a liturgical function. Since
Peri Pascha is bound up to the ritual of Passover, and because of its
prose-hymnic style,[329] the second half at least we should claim as
being primarily liturgical, in spite of its links with later homiletic
forms, such as the kontakion, and earlier, such as the primitive
haggadah. In the light of this the second half may best be called a
haggadah/epideixis, recognising that this classification embraces a
degree of liturgical action; the first may be called a homily, with the
recognition that it is bound up more closely to the overall liturgical
function of the seder than the modern homily, or the Jewish synagogue homily. The function of the whole is the praise of God, as
Salzmann notes.[330]

This is the context in which to see the specific liturgical parallels
and forms which may be found in the work, including those parallels
which Perler has himself uncovered. We should also note the parallels
discovered by Bonner between *Peri Pascha* and the *Apostolic Constitutions*.[331] These are found particularly between PP82 and 85. He first
notes similarities between PP82 ὁ τὸ φῶς ἐπανθίσας etc. and *Apostolic
Constitutions* 8.12.6ff, that part of the work containing the eucharistic

---

[329] It is Grotz (Review) who claims that the prose-hymnic form suits a liturgical
setting better than a homiletic
[330] Salzmann *Lehren und Ermahnen* 270
[331] Bonner *Homily* 144-145, 147

prayer, this part in particular dealing with the creation. Subsequently at PP84 he sees similarities with *Apostolic Constitutions* 6.20.6, chiefly on the basis of the rare word μαvvαδοτέω, but notes also the possibility that 8.12.26 (still part of the eucharistic prayer) lies behind it. All this leads him to postulate a common liturgical source behind Melito and the *Apostolic Constitutions*.

Hall suggests that the parallels are exaggerated and that the common source is simply biblical.[332] However, given the fact that this is a development from the haggadah, and more particularly that this section has parallels with the *dayyenu*, and is therefore liturgical in context, the similarities both of content and of context begin to be more pressing than would be the case with parallels of content alone. Not only is this the case, but a further parallel may be adduced from Athenagoras.[333] The context of liturgical Passover keeping and the haggadic form make it clear that we do not have liturgical portions grafted into a different form, such as the citations from the liturgy which may be found in the letters of the New Testament.

It is odd that Bonner felt obliged to bring *Apostolic Constitutions* 6 into the argument, rather than simply suggesting a more direct parallel between PP84 and *Apostolic Constitutions* 8.12.6-27, which is from a different source than Book 6.[334] This makes the most pressing case simply by virtue of its simplicity; he may have been dissuaded by the paragraph marker in PP82 described above. The other liturgical parallel noted by Bonner is that between PP102 and the *Apostolic Tradition* of Hippolytus 4.8,[335] again part of the eucharistic prayer (interestingly this is an acknowledged source of the liturgical section in *Apostolic Constitutions* 8 from which the earlier parallels were adduced.)[336] Bonner suggests that an ancient hymn lies behind both passages, and in this is followed by Hall.[337]

Similar examples of the interplay of the liturgical and the homiletic may be observed in the fourth Gospel. It would seem that parts of the Johannine liturgy may be discerned at times behind the discourses. Whilst arguing that the background for John's discourses is fundamentally non-rabbinic Judaism, Schulz produces an interesting Mandaean liturgical parallel to the "I am" saying at John 6:35.[338]

---

[332] Hall *Melito of Sardis* 45, 47
[333] *Legatio* 13. The parallels are noted by Barnard *Athenagoras* 153
[334] O'Leary *Apostolical Constitutions* 59; Fenwick *Missing Oblation* 16
[335] Bonner *Homily on the Passion* 23-24
[336] Jasper and Cuming *Prayers of the Eucharist* 100
[337] Hall *Melito of Sardis* 59
[338] Schulz *Komposition* 96-97

This need not be seen as an isolated incidence if one takes account of the pattern of the "I am" sayings which Schulz describes,

a) I am
b) Image/
c) invitation.
d) Promise[339]

So compare *John* 6:35 to PP103:

a) I am	c) Come you families of nations
b) the bread of life	d) receive forgiveness of sins
c) Whoever comes to me,	a) I am
d) will never hunger.	b) your release

Here we see the same pattern, albeit inverted, in a passage of which the liturgical context has already been shown. This leads one to ask whether the expository homily explains the shape of *all* the discourses of the Gospel, or whether, for instance, the Last Supper discourses are shaped rather by a liturgical homily, like the Passover haggadah. The less prosaic nature of some of the discourses might indicate this. In *John*, as in *Peri Pascha* we have an interplay of liturgical action an homiletic explanation.

Thus far then we have established the genre and make-up of the various parts into which *Peri Pascha* falls. However, before we are ready to examine the liturgical observance of the Quartodecimans at Sardis and to see how *Peri Pascha* may illuminate our understanding of this we should recall that a genre implies a purpose and a function. Most significantly, the fact that the second half of the work may be seen as a Christian paschal haggadah implies that like the Jewish (ritual) haggadah its purpose is commemoration, it is to be as a זכרון/μνημόσυνον. If this is the key to the interpretation of *Peri Pascha* then this is the key also to the import of the entire Quartodeciman celebration, as it is for the Jews. It is thus in accordance with the command of *Exodus* 12 to treat the feast as a μνημόσυνον, a command which Melito repeats in his treatment of this chapter. Further confirmation that commemoration lay at the heart of the Quartodeciman observance of Pascha is given by Theodoret. The Quartodecimans, he states, πανηγυρίζονται τὴν μνήμην τοῦ πάθους.[340] In Greek categories the liturgy was understood as being basically a festal oration, but at the heart of this was an act of liturgical remembrance originating in the Jewish paschal tradition. Hence it is their memory which the Quartodecimans celebrated in this manner. Commemoration how-

---

[339] Schulz *Komposition* 87
[340] *Haer. Fab. Comp.* 3.4.

ever is not unknown to the wider Hellenistic world, and was seen as
a possible function of epideictic oratory. Quintilian thus informs us
that the acta of Gods, when being praised, are commemoranda.[341]

The manner in which this command was kept is the matter of the
next Section, but we may now suggest that the whole of *Peri Pascha*, in
the context of the table and with its preceding lection, was part of this
process of ritual commemoration. So it is that the act of remembering
extends not only to the second half of *Peri Pascha*, the haggadah
proper, but to the entire work. Whilst Melito's use of the term
διήγημα is motivated by the language of the rhetorical schools, we
may note with Perler that the word διηγοῦμαι is used in the
Septuagint to translate סָפַר, the telling of the works and commands
of God preparatory to praise.[342] Perler suggests that the term is employed in order that the command of *Exodus* to remember might be
seen to be fulfilled. We may add that this proclamation is the result
and the cause of the events of the first Pascha being remembered. We
may also recall that the *piyyut* form might be a means of liturgical
commemoration and that the means by which Melito constructs his
diegema, making full use of figures of sound, may be seen as a means of
making this event present for his audience; we may now see the
reasons lying behind this. Each half of *Peri Pascha* expresses a different
facet of the mystery commemorated, its typological expression in the
words of the Old Testament and the truth of its fulfilment in Christ,
the τύπος and the κατασκευή of the mystery, both of which are subjects to be commemorated. Remembering them becomes a means of
participating in these mysteries and receiving their benefits, since by
remembering them Melito and his listeners come to be present in
them, in the protected Israel and in the exalted Christ.

It is in this way then that we see how it is possible for something
originating as a homily and still reading as such, may in context in
fact be a liturgical act. Thus we may state that like the Jewish
haggadah it is a liturgical text deriving from homiletic origins, which
has become ritualized in the context of a commemorative liturgy; for
not only do we now see that the two halves of the work are related in
terms of form, we may now note that their functions appear to be
identical also, namely liturgical commemoration. In the case of
Melito the process of "liturgization" seems to have taken place under
the influence of the *melete* as well as that of the table rite of Pascha.
This basic similarity between the parts, and the realisation that both
are bound up to the process of commemoration not only enables us

---

[341] *Institutio Oratoria* 3.7.8
[342] Perler *Sur la Pâque* 143

to realise the liturgical nature of the first half in a new way, but also, by enabling us to see the influence of midrash on the second half, explains the closeness of parts of *Peri Pascha* 46ff to the corresponding parts of *Genesis*.

This thesis of liturgization would, however, appear to be contradicted by the evidence of *In Sanctum Pascha*. The first part of this work, with its atomization of the text, would appear to be didactic and exegetical in intent. There are two possible ways to explain this difference. Either Melito has created something not of the tradition, seeing the exegetical task put upon him by the tradition as one of creating a *diegema* along Hellenistic lines, and so creating something which was not held within the tradition, or the form has developed by the time that ps-Hippolytus comes to write in such a way that the form is more directly homiletic. If the first of these possibilities is correct then the links and similarities which we have shown between Melito and the works deriving from the Jewish tradition such as the *Genesis Apocryphon* and the *Liber Antiquitatum Biblicarum* must be merely fortuitous and coincidental. These links however are so clear once perceived that this in itself makes it more probable that it is ps-Hippolytus who has developed rather than Melito.

Basing his argument chiefly on ps-Hippolytus Cantalamessa seeks to show that the Christian tradition of paschal homiletic developed from the haggadah not directly but by way of the New Testament.[343] He distinguishes between the liturgical or ritual haggadah and the homiletic haggadah, and claims that *In Sanctum Pascha* and *Peri Pascha* are both members of this second genus.[344] His argument is based primarily on the different understandings of *Pascha* in the Christian and Jewish rites. Whereas the Jews understood *Pascha* as "passing over" the Christians saw this in terms of Christian typology as the suffering of Christ. Hence the fact that the Christians treated primarily *Exodus* 12, the preparation of the lamb, rather than the actual escape from Egypt. He also notes Melito's vituperation against the Jews, and suggests that one who felt such would hardly borrow a rabbinic rite. Finally he notes the lack of eschatological expectation in the Christian documents in contrast to the eager expectation of the Jews. The basic argument is that the Christians had employed their typological reading of Scripture to put a distance between themselves and the Jews and that this typological reading was the basis of their paschal homiletic.

---

[343] Cantalamessa *Omelia* 444-448
[344] *Omelia* 439-443

However, there is no clear reason here why *Peri Pascha* should not be seen as a ritual haggadah. Although the understandings of *Pascha* are different, we have already seen that Gamaliel's explanation as "passing over" is a later justification[345] and that in concentrating on the Passover lamb Melito is in receipt of a pre-rabbinic tradition. We have never claimed that Melito borrowed a rabbinic rite, but that his tradition was the same as that which lay behind the rabbis. The treatment of *Exodus* 12 is indeed a mark of distinction between Jews and Christians, but is not the same as a distinction between ritual and homily. Likewise there are different understandings of eschatology, as one might expect, but this does not constitute the basis of a distinction between different kinds of haggadah.

It may well be fair to claim *In Sanctum Pascha* as a homiletic haggadah, influenced by the New Testament and indirectly related to the Jewish prototype, but the same claim cannot be made for the work of Melito. *In Sanctum Pascha* shows considerably more acquaintance with the written New Testament than does *Peri Pascha*, and there perhaps is the key. Under the influence of the New Testament and such homiletic writings based on the Passover literature as *I Corinthians* 5:6-8, *I Corinthians* 10:1ff, *I Peter* and indeed *John* 6, all of which are cited, the circle which produced *In Sanctum Pascha* moved away from the ritual haggadah. This affected both parts of the haggadah, the treatment of *Exodus* 12 and the story of salvation. In *In Sanctum Pascha* they are both far more didactic, Melito reflecting a far more primitive situation in which ritual haggadah is the primary note, this evidenced by the extensive Jewish parallels which we have been able to show. Whether this in turn makes the second half of *In Sanctum Pascha* a homily in the strict sense, as Cantalamessa would appear to claim, is of course another question; however, this would appear to be likely.

For *Peri Pascha* on the other hand we may safely continue to uphold our claim that we have here a ritual haggadah akin to the Jewish model. This is the only possible conclusion in view of the liturgical parallels and variety of forms that we have found within the work, and in view of the commemorative function of the work. The text lying behind the ritual might have had a homiletic origin, but it had developed already into a liturgical text by the time that it was passed to Christianity. This process reversed itself in time, under the influence of the New Testament, but this reversal had not taken place at the time of Melito.[346]

---

[345] 2.1.4 above

[346] We will examine this process further with regard to *In Sanctum Pascha* at 4.2.6 below

Since the fundamental similarity between the two halves of *Peri Pascha* must continue to be upheld we should seek to see the function of both parts of the work within the seder/liturgy itself. Thus we may advance once again the hypothesis suggested above: that the church of Sardis was of immediately Johannine Palestinian origin and that the keeping of Pascha which it had inherited from that tradition involved a table rite, including the haggadah. Melito, who had received an oratorical training, was, in common with the rest of the community, unable to distinguish *epideixis* and haggadah. Thus, when he comes to deliver the haggadah, it is epideictic in form and inspiration. We, however, understanding his background in a way he could not, are able to see his action in other terms besides. The details and nature of this act, however, are the substance of the next Chapter, in which, on the basis of the work we have now done we shall endeavour to reconstruct the paschal observance of the Quartodecimans at Sardis.

CHAPTER FOUR

PERI PASCHA AND
THE QUARTODECIMAN PASCHAL LITURGY

Although the Quartodecimans have been subject to scholarly enquiry since the seventeenth century we do not concern ourselves with the earlier work in this monograph but take as our starting point in this discussion the work of Schmidt in 1919.[1] His was the first attempt to discuss the paschal liturgy of the Quartodecimans on the basis of a document of Quartodeciman provenance, the then newly discovered *Epistula Apostolorum*. Whilst others contributed to the argument it was Lohse who first produced a reconstruction,[2] largely following Schmidt but with the advantage that Bonner's edition of *Peri Pascha* enabled him to include the evidence presented by Melito. There have been further contributions from Perler,[3] Hansen,[4] Cantalamessa[5] and Rouwhorst.[6]

This is therefore not the first attempt to reconstruct the Quartodeciman paschal liturgy. What is new and unique in this attempt is the fact that after our form-critical examination of the work we are now able to draw upon the evidence provided by *Peri Pascha* in a new way. Heretofore it has been assumed that Melito's work is uniform in nature and is simply a homily on *Exodus* 12. *Peri Pascha*'s place in the liturgy was assumed therefore to be as part of some kind of "liturgy of the word".[7] Now that we begin to see *Peri Pascha* as a liturgy almost in its own right, that it may in part be described as a haggadah, and that there are internal divisions within the work, the task becomes one of seeing how this accords with the other evidence we possess of the liturgical observance, enabling us to check the veracity of previous

---

[1] Schmidt *Gespräche Jesu*. A useful review of the earlier period of scholarship is provided by Lohse *Passafest* 20-40, as noted at 1.2.2 above

[2] Lohse *Passafest* 62-89

[3] Perler *Hymnus*

[4] Hansen *Sitz*

[5] Cantalamessa *Pasqua della Salvezza*

[6] Rouwhorst "Quartodeciman Passover"

[7] Firstly by Lohse *Passafest*, and subsequently universally, with only slight variations of emphasis. Various individuals, such as Wood (Review) and Chrestos "ἔργον" have suggested liturgical dimensions to the work, but not as part of any ordered exploration of the liturgy as a whole.

reconstructions against this new evidence, and filling in details of that observance. It is hoped in this chapter to show that *Peri Pascha* itself is the liturgical text of the seder, on the basis that it is formally a haggadah, and so like the Jewish haggadah belongs in a liturgical setting, on the basis that it is commemorative in intent, as is the paschal liturgy as a whole, and since its shape is dictated by liturgical needs. An examination of the external evidence for the Quartodeciman liturgy will, it is hoped, demonstrate that there is a place for *Peri Pascha* understood in this way.

4.1 THE BACKGROUND AND SETTING OF THE QUARTODECIMAN PASCHAL LITURGY

Before we begin our reconstruction it is necessary to examine certain questions which, whilst not directly pertinent to the task which we have set ourselves, may affect it in some way. These are questions concerning the background to the Quartodeciman commemoration and the paschal disputes of the second century, and in particular the role of Scripture in these disputes. It is primarily these issues which have been for so long subjects of controversy and the discussion of which was transformed by the *Epistula Apostolorum*. The attempt to distinguish and to answer these *Vorfragen* thus forms the first part of this chapter; we shall see more of the Quartodeciman background to *Peri Pascha*, and indeed see whether *Peri Pascha* casts any new light on these old questions. The posing of the questions may equally illuminate some aspects of Melito's work.

4.1.1 *The Subject of the Quartodeciman Commemoration*

We have stated that the function of the Quartodeciman celebration was one of remembrance without stating explicitly what the Quartodecimans remembered. Obviously they remembered the first Passover, as is clear from the reading of *Exodus* 12 and the graphic description of the slaughter of the Egyptian first-born. Typologically interpreted this is seen as the suffering of Christ, present in the lamb and protecting believers.

Further evidence for this understanding of pascha centring on the suffering of Christ may be gathered from Melito's statement that pascha gets its name from πάσχειν, and in particular from the suffering undergone by Christ. This was part of the Quartodeciman tradition, and not an insight of Melito alone, since by the time Melito wrote the "paschal pun" was already traditional. For although in Mohrmann's study of the question Melito is cited as the earliest example[8] there are hints of the paschal pun in Irenaeus and Justin Martyr[9], and so we must say that it is coming into common usage at the time of Melito; it is moreover found in ps-Hippolytus[10] and may therefore be said to have become an established part of the Quarto-deciman tradition. Interestingly Daniélou sees hints of it in Philo, where Philo states that the crossing over which constitutes the Pascha may be seen as a passage from πάθη.[11] Mohrmann disputes this, and indeed she is correct in stating that διάβασις (or διαβατήρια) is Philo's interpretation of פֶּסַח, both here and elsewhere.[12] She therefore suggests that these passages of Philo should be interpreted as word-play rather than serious etymology. She sees that the stoic theory of passions is being brought into play. This presupposes that the ancients distinguished between serious etymology and word-play. The stoic theory of passions is most certainly in play since the διάβασις, according to Philo, is from πάθη; that is why Philo may be appearing to perpetrate the paschal pun without meaning to. And yet we may ask why it has occurred to Philo that the διάβασις should be from πάθη and not from ὁρμαί, for instance, or τὰ παρὰ φύσιν. How did πάθη suggest themselves?

The answer is that stoic methods of exegesis are also in play, by which points are built upon the similarity of words. So of Cleanthes we hear that he treated Homer's use of the word μῶλυ, stating that reason is meant because it is through reason that μωλύνται αἱ ὁρμαὶ καὶ τὰ πάθη.[13] This is not intended to suggest that Melito knew Philo, but that we are dealing with a commonplace. As Mohrmann shows, in time the pun becomes so common, in writers who could hardly have known Melito, that there must be a further, unattested tradition.

Cantalamessa also notes that Melito uses traditional materials, using this to explain material common to ps-Hippolytus and Melito.[14] The materials are liturgical and catechetical, they are notable in that they fall into stereotyped formulae and are therefore memorable. As liturgical material Cantalamessa notes the doxologies to Christ. The constant antitheses between καινός and παλαιός, νόμος and λόγος he sees as the remains of primitive catechesis. As examples of a common theological tradition he notes the soteriological scheme σῶμα-πνεῦμα,

---

[8] Mohrmann "Pascha"

[9] Irenaeus *Adversus Haereses* 4.20.1, Justin *Dialogue* 40

[10] *IP*11 and 49

[11] Daniélou "Traversée" 404 with reference to *Quis Rerum Div. Heres* 193

[12] Mohrmann "Pascha, Passio Transitus" 38 n4

[13] Quoted by Hanson *Allegory and Event* 37. See also *SVF* Vol. 1, fr. 549 for another example of Cleanthes' etymology. For the extent to which Melito was himself aware of and influenced by stoic exegetical methods see 3.1.6 above and references ad loc.

the use of the term σφραγίς to describe the effect of the blood of the lamb on the doorposts and the statement that Christ died in the evening. The point of all this is to clarify that *Peri Pascha* is not an entirely original production; even though it maintains a high standard of artistry it is formulated out of a tradition, and out of traditional elements, and part of the tradition is the remembrance of Christ's suffering at pascha.

However, the commemoration of the first Passover is the content of the first part of the work only, the *diegema*. In the second, the *kataskeue*, the vista opens further and the fall of Adam and the exaltation of the human race in Christ become the subject, through the passion and through the triumphant resurrection, the disgrace and the glory. In this respect *Peri Pascha* may be said to have been typical of the Quartodeciman liturgy since in this it follows the Jewish haggadah lying behind the Quartodeciman tradition, as does *In Sanctum Pascha*. The Quartodeciman observance was not then simply the observance of Christ's passion and death, but of the whole of redemption, the events of Good Friday being seen as inseparable from the resurrection: they are parts of the one movement. This much is self-evident from a reading of *Peri Pascha*, beginning as it does with the slaughter of the Passover lamb and concluding in the presence of the risen Christ. Why then is it necessary to state the self-evident?

We have earlier alluded to Bonner's description of *Peri Pascha* as a "Good Friday sermon",[15] and have dealt fairly thoroughly with the second part of this assertion. We must now turn to the first part. This would already appear to be of dubious value in the light of the statements just made concerning the place that the resurrection holds in *Peri Pascha*. Lying behind Bonner's statement is an assumption that the subject of Quartodeciman commemoration was simply the passion and death of Christ and that the fourteenth of Nisan was therefore the Quartodeciman equivalent of the catholic Good Friday. This assumption, together with, or perhaps boosted by, the assumption that *Peri Pascha* was a homily on *Exodus* 12, predetermined Bonner's reading of the text. We must ask whence this assumption derived, and what grounds there are for holding it.

Although issues surrounding the Quartodecimans were discussed from as early as the seventeenth century, the evidence on which the discussion was based was somewhat sketchy, being chiefly that of Eusebius. Schmidt, however, was in a position to discuss the issues

---

[14] Cantalamessa *Omelia* 59
[15] Bonner *Homily* 19

surrounding the Quartodecimans whilst in possession of *Epistula Apostolorum*, a document deriving from a Quartodeciman milieu.[16]

Whereas it had earlier been suggested that the purpose of the Quartodeciman keeping of 14th Nisan was to remember the death of Jesus, Schmidt was able to point to hard evidence in the *Epistula Apostolorum* which indicated that such was the case. There the risen Christ tells the disciples that they are to remember his death at the Pascha.[17] From this Schmidt deduced that the Quartodecimans kept the fourteenth of Nisan as a commemoration of the death of the Lord, following the Johannine chronology, as the death of Jesus coincides with the slaughter of the lambs on the fourteenth, and that it is on the basis of John's Gospel that the observation of this date was established. Herein, according to Schmidt, lay the difference between the Quartodeciman and the Roman practice, namely it was a difference of emphasis. Whereas the Romans concentrated on the resurrection of the Lord the Quartodecimans concentrated on his death. Schmidt summed this up in a much quoted phrase, "dort Passah, hier Ostern."[18]

The first to attempt to counter this view was Brightman.[19] Suggesting that not too much could be read into the statement in this part of the *Epistula Apostolorum*, he cites further evidence to suggest that the 14th Nisan was effectively the Quartodeciman equivalent to the Roman Easter. We do not follow his arguments in detail since the discovery of *Peri Pascha* has made them redundant. In essence he suggests that since the Quartodecimans were forbidden to celebrate the resurrection on any day apart from Sunday, then it must be the resurrection that they are celebrating (irregularly) on the fourteenth.

With the benefit of *Peri Pascha* we may see clearly that the resurrection is indeed celebrated by Melito. This is precisely the direction in which Brightman's evidence points, that the Quartodeciman celebration included a celebration of the resurrection. Does this however mean that there is no distinction at all between the Roman Easter and the Quartodeciman Pascha? That, as Brightman held, Pascha is more or less exclusively focused on the resurrection.

Such a momentous point is not to be gathered from the evidence which he cites. There is a difference between a celebration which

---

[16] Schmidt *Gespräche Jesu*. Excursus on the Quartodeciman celebration 576-725. His arguments concerning the Asian and Quartodeciman origin of the *Epistula* have been disputed but are defended and amplified by Stewart-Sykes "Asian Origin"; see on this 1.2.2 above

[17] *Epistula Apostolorum* 26- tazkara moteya gebaru

[18] Schmidt *Gespräche Jesu* 579. Substantially the same point is made on 611

[19] Brightman "Quartodeciman Question"

takes the resurrection into its scope, such is indicated by the evidence
at Brightman's disposal and confirmed by *Peri Pascha*, and one which
is centred around the celebration of the resurrection. Such does not
appear to be the celebration at which *Peri Pascha* was delivered any
more than "Good Friday". In comparing the Quartodeciman Pascha
either to Good Friday or to Easter Sunday we are not in a position of
comparing like with like. To talk of Good Friday or of Easter in this
context, even while being deliberately anachronising for the sake of
explanation, is to invite invidious comparisons. It is not Good Friday,
nor Easter, but simply Pascha. There is no evidence in the second
century of any other kind of celebration apart from one single celebration of the entire event of redemption.[20]

However, if the Quartodeciman celebration was a celebration of
redemption, that does not exclude the possibility that it had a primary focus in salvation history. This primary focus, it seems, was the
passion. This is indicated by the fact that Theodoret refers to a commemoration of the passion,[21] that Apollinaris in his description of the
Pascha concludes it with the placing of the stone on the grave,[22] by
Melito's derivation of πάσχα from πάσχειν, as well as by the statement
in the *Epistula Apostolorum* concerning the commemoration of Jesus'
death. These all tend to indicate that the celebration is focused primarily on the events of the passion.[23] That said, it is not an exclusive
focus but one which presupposes the joyful outcome of the resurrection and celebrates that also. The choice of the date of 14th of Nisan
however surely indicates that it is not the resurrection which is at the
centre of the frame, whatever else may be.

Apart from the passion and the resurrection, it was argued by
Lohse that the focus of the Quartodeciman celebration was originally
the expectation of the Messiah's coming on Passover night.[24] This
depends on his view that the keeping of Passover by Christians derived directly from the maintenance of Jewish tradition, a view which
will be criticised below. However, we may note that Lohse himself
admits that by the second century the celebration had become fo-

---

[20] Casel "Art und Sinn" 7 points this out with great force and is followed by Botte
"La Question Pascale" and "Pascha"

[21] Theodoret *Haer. Fab. Comp.* 3.4

[22] *Chronicon Paschale* (PG92) Col. 79. This is pointed out by Schmidt *Gespräche Jesu*
627-8

[23] That there had been such a primary focus within the overall celebration of
redemption was argued by Casel "Art und Sinn" followed by van der Veken "De
Primordiis", Hansen *Sitz im Leben* 158-9 and 170, Huber *Passa und Ostern* 16-21, and
Rouwhorst "Quartodeciman Passover" 165

[24] Lohse *Passafest* 81-84

cused on the events of the passion.[25] Although a joyful celebration based around the passion may seem strange to us, it did not seem strange to those in the second century who so celebrated;[26] a church which was able to rejoice in the deaths of its martyrs likewise rejoiced in the cause of their salvation.[27]

There is not the evidence to say whether the same twin focus was to be found in the primitive Roman celebration, or indeed to say with certainty that during the second century there was a "hier" as opposed to "dort",[28] but there is no doubt concerning the basis of Quartodeciman celebration in Asia. *Peri Pascha* gives us a complete picture of the scope of this celebration, and it is one which accords with and makes sense of all the other available evidence.

Schmidt having been proved at least partially correct, though not to the extent which either he or Bonner believed, we must turn to the other part of his theory, that in keeping the Pascha as the commemoration of the death of Jesus the Quartodecimans were following Johannine chronology.

4.1.2 *The Significance of the Fourteenth*

Having established that the Quartodeciman celebration is first and foremost a commemoration of Christ's passion and death, it would seem that the other part of Schmidt's theory, that the Quartodecimans kept the fourteenth in accordance with Johannine passion chronology, must inevitably follow.

There is however another possibility, one which is weakened by the evidence of a celebration focused on the passion but not altogether impossible. That in accordance with the synoptic chronology the Quartodecimans remembered the Last Supper and re-enacted it. This would make sense of a celebration in which the whole of redemption is embraced and give a salvation-historical basis to such a celebration. Indeed Richardson claims that only a celebration based on the Last Supper makes sense of a festival of resurrection not held

---

[25] Lohse *Passafest* 120

[26] Nor indeed did it seem strange to Syrian Christians in the fourth century. see Rouwhorst *Hymnes* 113; see further on links between the Quartodecimans and Syriac Christianity 4.2.5 below

[27] So van Goudoever *Biblical Calendars* 188-189 Kretschmar "Christliches Passa" and Hall "Origins" each indicate the importance of martyrdom for contemporary understandings of the Pascha.

[28] For further discussion of this point with references see footnote 288 below.

on the Sunday.[29] Although we have seen that Pascha is not precisely
a festival of resurrection, a synoptic basis to the celebration would
indeed make sense of an act of commemoration which holds both the
passion and the resurrection in its view.

We may start with what seems to be a strong implication by Melito
himself that he believed the crucifixion to have taken place on the
fifteenth of Nisan, and thus that he followed the synoptic chronology,
one that Huber uses to support his contention that Melito was not a
Quartodeciman[30] and Perler uses to argue that he kept the festival
according to the synoptic chronology.[31]

At PP79 Melito states of the Jews that they killed the Lord ἐν τῇ
μεγάλῃ ἑορτῇ, a statement repeated at PP92; at PP93 he goes on to
say "therefore bitter for you is the feast of unleavened bread." The
most natural reading of these phrases would be to take them as referring to the feast of unleavened bread following Passover, beginning
on the 15th of Nisan. On this basis Melito would be following a
synoptic chronology.

However, although the feast of unleavened bread and the Passover
were originally entirely distinct celebrations, Casel[32] and Heawood[33]
point out that the two were frequently conflated, and so Hansen is
able to argue that since at the time of Melito there was great confusion between them and little distinction made it is not possible to read
into PP79 the implications that Perler would see there.[34] Although
Perler suggests that Melito ought to know better in his context than to
make this confusion,[35] the conflation of the celebrations is to be found
in Jewish sources and so Melito is no different from his contemporaries. By the first century the feasts were run together, so Philo states
that they are each feasts and that they are connected.[36] The conflation caused extensive confusion, evidence of which may be found in
the New Testament (Luke 22:1 refers to the feast of unleavened bread
ἡ λεγομένη πάσχα) in Josephus (who similarly, at AJ 14.21 refers to the
feast of unleavened bread ἣν πάσχα λέγομεν) and in even in Mishnah
Pesahim, which begins with preparations for the celebration of the
feast of unleavened bread and states that the pasch is eaten for seven

---

[29] Richardson "Quartodecimans" notably at 182-183. Richardson subsequently
revised his position.
[30] Huber Passa und Ostern 43-44
[31] Perler Méliton de Sardes: Sur la Pâque 181-183
[32] Casel "Art und Sinn" 3
[33] Heawood "Time"
[34] Hansen Sitz 132-133
[35] Perler Sur la Pâque 182
[36] Spec. Leg. II 28

days,[37] and the *Mishnah Ta'anith* which states that the paschal prayer for rain continues through the days of unleavened bread.[38] Similarly Philo refers to the διαβατήρια δημοφανὴς ἑορτή.[39] One cannot assume that Melito is being precise when he refers to the great feast in this liturgical context when nobody else sought exactitude of expression.

However we shall note below that there were some Quartodecimans who appealed to a synoptic passion chronology for their practice, and argued that they were keeping the Pascha as the Lord had. Whereas it is possible that Melito was one of those who defended Quartodeciman practice by justifying it with a synoptic chronology it would be difficult to argue this solely on these passing references to the great feast. Additional support is found by Perler in the reference to Clement's writing ἐξ αἰτίας Melito's work; since Clement defended the Johannine chronology Perler deduces that Melito must have supported the synoptic chronology. But we have already seen that there is no certainty that Clement and Melito were engaged in a polemic, and we may moreover suggest that just because modern scholarship is interested in chronology that this interest was necessarily shared by the ancients.[40]

Apart from the arguments against seeing the great feast as the first day of unleavened bread there are positive reasons for seeing it as the Passover, and concluding therefore that Melito is celebrating Pascha on the fourteenth. In particular we must note his description at PP80 of the Jewish festivities, the great feast, which co-incided with the sufferings of Christ. Hall points out that the phrase εὐφραινόμενος, used already in *Peri Pascha* of the Passover, the reclining, the dancing all point to a Passover celebration.[41] Although Melito goes on to mention the feast of unleavened bread at PP93, immediately he speaks of the bitter herbs, which are peculiar to the Passover celebration. In this passage the unleavened bread he has in mind is not that of the feast, but the unleavened bread with which, together with bitter herbs, the Passover lamb is to be eaten according to Exodus 12. Insofar as unleavened bread is eaten on the following days Melito is seeing that as punishment, for whereas the Jewish festivities are con-

---

[37] MPes 9.5

[38] MTa'anith 1.2

[39] *Vita Mosis* 2.224

[40] Again we may remind ourselves of Hall's assertion that Melito was not a "liturgiologist anxious to indicate to later generations an interesting aspect of Quartodeciman practice". (Hall "Melito *Peri Pascha* 1 and 2" 247)

[41] Hall *Melito of Sardis* 43. On the dancing see van Unnik "Note" and our comments at 3.2.3 above.

cluded, we shall note below that the Quartodeciman celebration is
only just beginning.[42]

It would therefore seem that the feast referred to is the Passover
itself, a great feast for Christians as well as Jews, and that Melito is
therefore a follower of the Johannine passion chronology. All this is
only what would be expected in view of the extensive links with
Johannine theology which Melito displays and which have already
been uncovered.

As implied above, Richardson's main arguments are theological,
centring on the difficulty of a celebration of the resurrection on the
occasion of the passion.[43] However, we must state again that the
distinction in the manner of remembering Christ's death and resurrection is a late one, and that it would not occur to those in the
second century to make such a distinction. It is moreover the case
that the dispute between Rome and Asia might well have concerned
the occasion on which Pascha should be kept, rather than whether to
keep Pascha or the feast of the Resurrection.[44] Likewise Lohse produces circumstantial arguments[45] which gain an adequate and detailed response from Huber which need not be repeated.[46] Theologically it makes most sense to see Melito as a Johannine follower, since
for him Jesus is present in the paschal lamb; Jesus would not therefore
have eaten it himself.[47] On the same basis Mara sees the chronology
of the *Evangelium Petri* as Johannine; Jesus is the lamb, and therefore
does not himself partake of the Passover.[48] Given the close relationship obtaining between Melito and the *Evangelium Petri* one might
expect them each to have the same passion chronology. There is
however further significant primary evidence with which we must
reckon, and which makes the issue more complex.

There is a fragment of Apollinaris of Hierapolis to be found in the
Chronicon Paschale[49], in which he rebuts the claim of those who would
claim the support of *Matthew* for their view that Christ ate the Passover and suffered on the day of unleavened bread. Lohse reads Apollinaris' opponents as being Quartodecimans who claimed the support

---

[42] A similar use of the idea of the days of unleavened bread as punishment is found
in the Syriac Didascalia.

[43] Richardson "Quartodecimans"

[44] As is pointed out by Dugmore "Note" 412

[45] Lohse *Passafest* 136-137

[46] Huber *Passa und Ostern* 23-25

[47] cf the comments of Visonà "Pasqua Quartodecimana" 281-286 on the two
Quartodeciman theologies of the Pascha

[48] Mara *Évangile* 82

[49] *Chronicon Paschale* PG92 Col. 79

of *Matthew* for their practice of keeping the fourteenth, and concludes from this that the Quartodeciman practice was based on synoptic chronology.[50] However, it would seem unlikely that Apollinaris, coming from Hierapolis, was not himself Quartodeciman. It is true that he does not merit a mention in the letter of Polycrates, and Richardson and Grant thereby deduce that he had abandoned Quartodeciman practice.[51] This, however, is a dangerous argument from silence, there is no guarantee that Apollinaris was dead at the time of Polycrates' letter, nor any evidence that he was a kinsman of Polycrates. Why in any case would he abandon Quartodeciman practice? There is moreover a further fragment extant in which Apollinaris states that the fourteenth is the true Pascha of the Saviour, the day on which he was offered in place of the lamb. This reads as a classic statement of Quartodeciman theology.

This is complicated further due to the preservation of a fragment from Hippolytus, likewise in the *Chronicon Paschale*, which would indicate a Quartodeciman defence on the basis of synoptic chronology.[52] There an opponent argues that Christ ate the Passover and so therefore should he. It would seem that this opponent is a Quartodeciman. Against this must be set the constant appeal of the Quartodecimans to the Johannine tradition made by Polycarp[53] and Polycrates[54], and recorded by Theodoret[55], and indeed the extensive links between *John* and *Peri Pascha* which we have noted throughout this work. This surely would imply a Johannine basis to the Quartodeciman Pascha, and is the basis on which Schürmann, Dugmore, Cadman, and Hansen (among others) all claim that the Johannine passion chronology lies behind the practice of the Quartodecimans.[56] Their opponents can find little with which to answer them. The evidence then seems to be highly contradictory.

One way of resolving the contradictions would be to see with Lohse the Quartodeciman practice deriving directly from the Jewish practice, without reference to the events of the Gospel.[57] However, as Huber points out, it is hard to imagine this situation pertaining for long in view of the indelible association of the events of the passion

---

[50] Lohse *Passafest* 136
[51] Richardson "Quartodecimans" 182 and Grant *Greek Apologists* 89-90
[52] *Chronicon Paschale* PG92 Col. 79
[53] According to Irenaeus, quoted by Eusebius in *HE* 5.24
[54] Quoted by Eusebius in *HE* 5.24
[55] Theodoret *Haer. Fab. Comp* 3.4
[56] Schürmann "Anfänge"; Dugmore "Note"; Cadman "Christian Pascha"; Hansen *Sitz im Leben* 143-147
[57] Lohse *Passafest* passim

with Passover, and hard moreover to see such a festival taking root in gentile Asia.[58] Certainly the Quartodeciman Passover derived directly from the Jewish model and was celebrated by Jewish Christians in continuity with their pre-Christian brethren but, as Richardson states, "with a new meaning and a new haggadah".[59] Of course we have an example of just such a new haggadah in *Peri Pascha*. The new meaning was bound up to the redemption worked by Christ. The future eschatological import of the festival did not disappear but was bound up to the past events of the work of Christ.[60] Thus, although it cannot be accepted in its most simple form, this is nonetheless a step towards a solution, in that it cuts the observance free from any strict adherence to the chronology of any given written Gospel. One of the problems with the argument for the Johannine chronology is that the fourth Gospel states explicitly that Christ died in the afternoon, and yet the Quartodeciman celebration appears to have taken place in the evening.[61] But according to Melito Christ dies in the evening, and indeed contemporaneously with the Passover meal.[62]

The best explanation for this is that he kept the day on the basis of a tradition which stated that Christ died on the evening of the four-teenth, a tradition similar to that lying behind the production of the fourth Gospel. This tradition was held by ps-Hippolytus as well, and indeed by Irenaeus,[63] and is to be found in the *Evangelium Petri*; it is therefore quite possibly one which is common to the Quartodeci-mans. The celebration took place on the basis solely of the liturgically inherited tradition and without actual reference to the written Gos-pel. This would accord with the fact noted above that for all the reference to the fourth Gospel there is nothing like a direct citation.[64] We may call this chronological tradition the "Johannine". Likewise Huber puts this word in inverted commas, noting that there might be a chronological tradition independent of the Gospel.[65] We must then cut the Johannine mission tradition free from any direct dependence on the written Gospel, and accept that the Quartodeciman paschal practice derived from Jewish practice rather than out of any con-scious attempt to follow a particular chronological scheme. When

---

[58] Huber *Passa und Ostern* 25

[59] Richardson "New Solution" 80

[60] This is the view of Strobel *Ursprung* 29-36. We shall return to the question of eschatology at 4.2.3 below

[61] This is seen as a problem by Strobel *Ursprung* 18

[62] PP71, 80

[63] See *Adversus Haereses* 4.10, quoted by Casel "Art und Sinn" 14

[64] As concluded at 1.2.2 above

[65] Huber *Passa und Ostern* 21-23

Polycrates states that the Quartodecimans keep Pascha according to the Gospel, again it is unnecessary to read into this any reference to a written Gospel, rather to see the word in the sense that Melito uses it;[66] they celebrate the liberation that Jesus has brought about by his taking the place of the paschal lamb. This is the Pascha according to the Gospel, as opposed to that according to the law. Not long after Polycrates we find a polemical implication that the Quartodecimans are Judaizers, which could provide the basis of the Roman opposition to the practice.[67] The phrase "according to the Gospel" undoes any such accusation.

There is more yet to be said on this matter. For although we may uphold the "Johannine" tradition of the *Evangelium Petri*, this Gospel includes incidents drawn from the synoptic accounts. The situation appears to be one where a theological tradition which is "Johannine" in origin receives a (written) synoptic-type account, or accounts, of the Passion, which are incorporated without affecting the chronological frame in which the incidents are set.[68] As Mara put it: "notre auteur suit, pour le récit des épisodes, les Évangiles synoptiques; pour la théologie, l'évangile de Jean et l'Apocalypse."[69] We may add that chronology here is wedded to theology. It is entirely reasonable to suggest that. Melito, like the author of *Evangelium Petri*, could easily combine a belief that Jesus died on the fourteenth of Nisan with details which are essentially those of the synoptic Gospels. Whether like his earlier Asian contemporary Papias he gives the (liturgically grounded) oral tradition of which he is heir greater credence than written documents,[70] or has never sought to explore the contradictions within his accounts, or attempts to harmonize the accounts,[71] the basis of confusion is implicit in a situation where a written Gospel is in use which differs from the tradition in the important respect of

---

[66] So Schmidt *Gespräche Jesu* 584 and Dugmore "Note" 415. cf Strobel *Ursprung* 22. It is equally unnecessary to read this as "according to the Lord's example" (Lohse *Passafest* 93). If a written document is intended *Evangelium Petri* is as likely a candidate as any

[67] So Hansen *Sitz im Leben* 165. The polemical implication is to be found in the fragment of Hippolytus already discussed. See our comments in 4.1.3 below

[68] That the author of *Evangelium Petri* worked with a documentary source is the majority view. If one were to accept the suggestion of Brown *Death* 1332-1336 that the influence of the canonical Gospels came about orally the same situation would apply. There is little to commend the view that *Evangelium Petri* precedes the canonical Gospels, on which views see Brown *Death* 1332-1333.

[69] Mara *Évangile* 214

[70] Quoted by Eusebius at *HE* 3.39

[71] As suggested by Hengel *Johannine Question* 141

chronology. A similar situation of Johannine tradition combined with
the fundamental use of Matthew as a written Gospel is mirrored in
Epistula Apostolorum. Schmidt demonstrates the extensive use of Matthew by the redactor of the *Epistula*,[72] and yet there is a strong Johannine flavour to its theology of the *Epistula*, going beyond its chronology of the passion.[73]

But although Melito is able to incorporate a "Johannine" chronology with a "synoptic" account of the passion, this need not be true of
all Quartodecimans. We must postulate the existence of two Quartodeciman parties. The existence of two Quartodeciman parties would
clarify a number of problems. It explains the fragment of Apollinaris,
whom we may now see as a Quartodeciman defending the Johannine
tradition against those Quartodecimans who refer to *Matthew*, and the
fragment of Hippolytus, whose opponent we may now likewise see as
one of those whom Apollinaris likewise opposed, albeit on different
grounds, namely a Quartodeciman defending his action by reference
to *Matthew*. It likewise explains how it is that Polycarp, ignorant of the
fourth Gospel, may nonetheless defend his position by reference to
the Johannine tradition.[74]

The postulation of the existence of two groups of Quartodecimans
is not new, since Perler appears to reckon on the existence of two
such groups,[75] as do Richardson and Strobel.[76] The appeal to different Gospel chronologies would go some way to explain how it is that
such a situation should arise. There are those who employ a written
synoptic Gospel, justifying their keeping of the fourteenth on this
basis, and those who give greater credence to the Johannine oral
tradition. Perler and Strobel both see Melito as one of the "synoptic"
party, principally on the basis of PP92, but since this line has been
shown to indicate a "Johannine" chronology, this is hard to sustain.

We have not sought to enquire into how it is that there are two
chronological traditions within the Gospels;[77] that is not relevant.
What we have done is to reconcile the evidence of two chronological
traditions among the Quartodecimans. Different Quartodeciman
groups employed different scriptural justifications for the same liturgical activity. These justifications however came after the liturgical

---

[72] Schmidt *Gespräche Jesu* 218
[73] Hills *Tradition and Composition* 161 speaks of the "marked, if not pervasive, Johannine character of much of the author's language and theology"
[74] Seen as problematic by Richardson "New Solution" 79
[75] Perler *Sur la Pâque* 182
[76] Richardson "New Solution" 80; Strobel *Ursprung* 19-22
[77] See Hansen *Sitz im Leben* 139-144 and Strand "John as Quartodeciman"

practice was already well established and were not the basis on which the practice came about. Rather the practice came about due to a continuation of the Jewish paschal practice which was bound up to a memory of Christ's passion and death.

In origin then the Quartodecimans kept Passover in memory of Christ's passion, in accordance with a tradition stemming from a "Johannine" source that Christ had died on that occasion. This is the basis on which Polycarp celebrated, as did Polycrates, Apollinaris, and the several authors of the *Epistula Apostolorum*, *In Sanctum Pascha*, and *Evangelium Petri*. This is the basis moreover of Melito's celebration. Others however, originally of the same tradition, subsequently come to defend their actions by reference to *Matthew*; we may speculate that in doing so there is some shift in the focus of the celebration, away from the Passion and onto the Last Supper, since there is a similar shift of understanding exhibited in the Syriac paschal celebrations. For Melito, however, as a "Johannine" type Quartodeciman, the focus of the celebration is firmly on the Passion, and the fourteenth day is kept in accordance with the Johannine passion chronology.

Some Quartodecimans defended their actions with reference to *Matthew*. However, this action was presumably defended only once having been in some way called into question. We must seek to discover the circumstances of that questioning, and whether it would have affected Melito and the manner in which Pascha was kept at Sardis in his time.

4.1.3 *Peri Pascha and the Paschal Disputes*

During the second century there were in fact three "paschal disputes" of which we know. In the 140s Polycarp visited Anicetus at Rome, the Pascha being at issue,[78] and in the later part of that century Victor called into question the whole practice of the Quartodecimans.[79]

The first of these disputes did not, it seems, have any effect on the church in Asia Minor, and the second, whilst major, took place while Melito lay in Sardis awaiting the resurrection. For these reasons we do not concern ourselves with these two "paschal disputes."[80] The

---

[78] Eusebius *HE* 5.24, cf 4.14
[79] Eusebius *HE* 5.23
[80] There is a nest of issues related to these disputes. For discussion and bibliography see especially Richard "Question Pascale"; Mohrmann "Conflit Pascale"; Hall "Origins of Easter" and Visonà "Pasqua Quartodecimana"

third, however, may well have affected Melito in some way. This was the ζήτησις πολλή in Laodicea which, according to Eusebius' source, called forth the publication of *Peri Pascha*.

The first issue surrounding this dispute is the date.[81] Eusebius' source states that the dispute took place when Servillius Paulus was proconsul of Asia. No such character is known in the second century. However, Rufinus' Latin translation of Eusebius attests Sergius Paulus. Sergius Paulus was consul for the second time in 168, and before the second consulate was prefect of Rome. These offices would be consonant with his having held the proconsulate of Asia.

However, it is possible that Rufinus has assimilated Servillius Paulus to the Sergius Paulus of *Acts* 13:7. With this in mind Perler suggests a reading of Servillius Pudens, who was consul in 166, and might thereafter have taken up the proconsulate of Asia.[82] Perler's suggestion is orthographically and historically possible, but does not really help us solve the problem of date. We do not have anything like a complete list of the proconsuls, and for those whose names are known, precise dates are difficult to assign.[83] A date of around 150 has been assigned to the first consulship of Sergius Paulus and there are a number of dates in the later 150s where he could have become proconsul, apart from a time more immediately prior to his second consulate.[84] Likewise Servillius Pudens could have been proconsul around 169. Although certain dates can be ruled out,[85] there is no certainty on this matter. Commentators have tended to prefer a later date, but, as Hall says, this is little more than guesswork.[86]

Another possibility, which alas likewise does not assist us with dating the ζήτησις, may be canvassed here, and that is that the possibility that there is an error in the office which is assigned to Sergius Paulus; the Paulli held family estates in Laodicea and the cognomen is common in the area.[87] Eusebius' source may be thinking of yet another Sergius Paulus, in perhaps a local magistracy.

We may conclude on balance that the dispute took place at some time in the mid to late 160s, but since the connection of *Peri Pascha*

---

[81] See discussions in Perler *Sur la Pâque* 23-24, and Hall *Melito of Sardis* xxi-xxii
[82] Perler *Sur la Pâque* 24
[83] See the divergences between the proconsular lists for the mid second-century in Magie *Roman Rule* 1584-1585 (based on all sources) and Iplikçioglu *Repräsentanten* 289-290 based entirely on inscriptions. For Roman consuls see Degrassi *Fasti*
[84] Westermaier "Sergius Paullus"
[85] eg 166, offered by Hansen *Sitz im Leben* 72
[86] Hall *Melito of Sardis* xxi
[87] See Mitchell *Anatolia* 149-152

with the dispute is possibly indirect *Peri Pascha* could have been produced at any time in the previous fifteen or so years.

The other point of dispute is the subject of this quarrel. The only
direct evidence for this quarrel is the witness of Eusebius. However, it
is quite likely that not only were Melito and Clement involved but,
given the proximity of Hierapolis to Laodicea, that the fragment of
Apollinaris derives from this situation.

Virtually every author who has considered the subject of the
Laodicene strife has a different view of the cause of this dispute. Out
of the welter of suggestions we may discern five possible general approaches, which we may consider in turn.

The first approach is to claim that it is an argument as to whether
Pascha is to be kept on a Sunday or on the fourteenth regardless of
day, especially since the fragment of Apollinaris would imply that the
argument concerned Gospel chronology.[88] However, it most certainly
was not was a dispute between Quartodecimans and Sunday keepers
on the basis of Gospel chronology, the Quartodecimans supporting
the Johannine chronology, the Sunday keepers synoptic. Clement is
not a Quartodeciman, nor is Hippolytus, yet both support the Johannine chronology. This confusion of the Laodicene dispute and that
between Rome and Asia can lead only to further confusion. Nor is it
a local version of that same argument, for although there were certainly Asian Quartodecimans at Rome, it is not likely that there were
a significant number of Sunday-keepers in Laodicea.

Given that only Quartodecimans are involved the dispute at
Laodicea was almost certainly a local argument. Clement's involvement is taken by Richardson to imply that the argument was not
local,[89] but this involvement may well have been later, and uncon-
nected with the immediate cause of the dispute. Eusebius simply
states that Clement had responded to Melito's book. This, as we have
seen, may have been a response to Melito's treatment of the Old
Testament.[90] However, although local, this argument was certainly
one of major significance for the church in Asia, given the involvement of Melito and of Apollinaris.

The second approach is to see the dispute as literary or exegetical,
concerning either the date of Christ's death or the nature of the Last
Supper.[91] The major significance of the argument in the Asian

---

[88] eg Richard "Question"
[89] Richardson "New Solution" 78-79
[90] 3.2.2 above
[91] e.g. Brightman "Quartodeciman Question"; Casel "Art und Sinn" 9

church would imply that the argument is not however simply about exegesis, or about any point of history. In a situation of persecution this would hardly be occupying the major figures of the Asian church. Although the fragment of Apollinaris clearly implies that exegesis is involved, it is involved as the means, not the substance of the argument. As stated above, the appeal to different chronologies are differing defences of the same Quartodeciman position.

The third approach is that of Visonà, who seeks to argue that the dispute is theological in import.[92] He sees two parties, those who keep Pascha κατὰ νόμον, keeping the Passover according with the law, claiming support for this from the synoptic Gospels, and those who in its stead propose a typological understanding of Pascha, claiming with John that Christ suffered (ἔπαθεν) rather than ate (ἔφαγεν), that he took the place of the lamb. But the only evidence that any party of Quartodecimans kept Passover κατὰ νόμον is the fragment of Hippolytus. The Quartodecimans always claim to keep Pascha according to the Gospel, as opposed to the Jews. The statement of Hippolytus is polemical and aimed against Quartodecimans generally by implicitly accusing them of Judaizing. Indeed there is a similar implication in Apollinaris' claim that the "synoptic" party's practices are ἀσυμφώνος ...νόμῳ.

The distinction between ἔπαθεν and ἔφαγεν may well derive from Apollinaris, but these catchwords, characterising the parties and stressing the emphasis on "suffering" within the Johannine tradition, are not of the essence of the dispute. It would seem that Quartodecimans had since the earliest times been concerned to distinguish themselves from Jews and we have seen something of this in the fourth Gospel. The development of a typology may well have been an element in this, but it is difficult to see this as the subject of the dispute. Like the Gospel chronologies to which the typological approaches are bound up, it may have been a weapon in the dispute, as one party accused the other of Judaizing, acquitting itself from this charge by the use of typology such as that of Melito and Apollinaris; the implication of Judaizing may have added spice to the situation but of itself this could hardly have been the cause. In time the accusation of Judaizing may well have affected the approach of the Roman church towards Quartodecimans, and may thus have led to the dispute between Victor and Polycrates, but this theological argument was not itself the dispute at Laodicea.

---

[92] Visonà "Pasqua Quartodecimana"

A fourth suggestion is that of Hansen, who concludes that the question was one of whether a Jewish festival should be kept at all.[93] He believes that the martyrdom of Sagaris gave opportunity to those who did not believe that a Jewish festival should be kept to express their point of view. Along similar lines Talley seems to think that there was tension about whether Pascha should be kept in a church largely made up of Jewish convers, and cites as evidence the question of the disciples at *Epistula Apostolorum* 15 about whether the Lord has definitively eaten the Pascha, and whether the disciples should therefore continue the practice.[94] This is a question which reflects the same exegetical confusion as the Laodicene dispute and which answers the assertion that the Lord had eaten the Pascha (or here drunk) with the instruction that they are to continue the remembrance until his return in a manner which emphasizes his suffering, thus reflecting the ἔπαθεν-ἔφαγεν distinction). In this light we may see that the motivation of the question is not whether the festival should be kept but the reason for keeping it given that a synoptic type chronology would appear to lie behind the phrasing of the question.

Thus far then we have established that the argument is local and conducted on an exegetical basis, although neither exegesis, nor indeed a typological hermeneutic, is its cause; paschal theology is likewise not at issue, although exegetical, hermeneutical and theological considerations are second order issues in the dispute. Chronology seems to be involved, but the argument is between Quartodecimans, and not between Quartodecimans and others.

The final set of possible causes are such liturgical issues as the relative significance of Sunday or the fourteenth, or an issue relating to the breaking of the paschal fast.[95]

The relative significance of Sunday and the fourteenth of Nisan might well be at issue were the two to coincide. This however does not explain how it is that Gospel chronology comes to be involved. On the other hand a dispute concerning the length of the paschal fast, or more particularly the point at which it is to be broken, could certainly be related to Gospel chronology, since slightly differing practices would call forth different scriptural justifications. In time then we must seek to discover what the differing practices were and how it is that they came about. Hopefully we will then be able to say which practice was that of Melito. This, however, must be the substance of a different section.

---

[93] Hansen *Sitz im Leben* 167
[94] Talley *Origins* 7
[95] See eg Hall "Origins of Easter"

For the moment, however, we may reach the conclusion that the argument at Laodicea was local and principally liturgical, that it concerned the time at which the fast was broken and thus the point at which the celebration of Pascha begun, that different parties in this dispute appealed to different traditions, and that Melito was one of those who appealed to the tradition of John to support his practice. In accordance with this Johannine tradition he kept Pascha in memory of the death of the Lord. This is the focus of the celebration, and it is kept on the occasion of the Lord's death. Before beginning to explore the content of that celebration it is necessary further to examine the setting, the time, the date and the nature of the fast.

4.1.4 *The Quartodeciman Paschal Fast*

Since the Quartodeciman paschal practice derived from that of the Jews, the development of a fast was inevitable. The Jews fasted before the Passover meal, according to the *Mishnah* from the time of the afternoon offering, simply in order to be better prepared to eat the paschal repast. Just as the Christians followed this practice, so we may expect them to make slight adjustments, and moreover to adopt a differing justification for their actions.

However Lohse denies that the Jewish fasting has anything to do with that of the Quartodecimans, because the Jewish fast is not a fast in the strict sense of the word, and because the rationales are entirely different.[96] However, the situation is one in which a custom (fasting) precedes the basis on which it is justified. The earliest Christians fasted before Passover because they had always done so, and subsequently justified this by reference to some aspect of the new celebration. This took place just as the celebration of Passover itself was taken from its Jewish background and given a new significance.

In enquiring into the new justification which was given to the old practice of a paschal fast the obvious answer would be to state that it is in memory of the sufferings of the Lord. This is the opinion of Schmidt, who bases it on his theory of a Johannine basis to the Quartodeciman Pascha and for this reason argued that the fast concluded at 3pm.[97] In view of the fact that we now know that the Quartodecimans believed that Christ died in the evening, this latter part of the thesis is untenable, but unnecessary. Nonetheless the possibility that the Quartodecimans fasted in memory of the Lord's suf-

---

[96] Lohse *Passafest* 73-74
[97] Schmidt *Gespräche Jesu* 603

ferings remains a reasonable one. Something of the sort would seem to be implied by Melito at PP80, where he contrasts the sufferings of the Lord with the celebrations of the Jews at the Passover meal. Although there is no explicit indication that Melito is fasting at this point, as Hansen remarks, the passage reflects Melito's own existential situation.[98] It would certainly be incongruous were Melito's congregation to be doing the same as the Jews at this point.

This justification for the fast is supported by Cadman and Cantalamessa partly with reference to Tertullian, and better with reference to *Evangelium Petri*,[99] and by Rouwhorst with reference to *Didascalia* 21[100] but denied by Lohse on the grounds that the fast does not square with the Johannine timing of the passion, the basis of a fast of this nature which was proposed by Schmidt.[101] We now see that it is unnecessary to deny that the fast might have been in memory of the Lord's sufferings for this reason, and that to see the Quartodecimans keeping a festival on the fourteenth of Nisan principally in memory of the sufferings of the Lord does not tie them to the text of the canonical *John*.

However, Irenaeus indicates that there was a degree of variety among Quartodecimans as to the form ($\varepsilon\tilde{\iota}\delta o\varsigma$) of the fast,[102] and Dugmore suggests that this in turn may point to a variety of justifications.[103] In view of the fact that the justifications came into being after the custom of fasting was established this is entirely reasonable. Indeed it does indeed appear that a reason was given for the paschal fast which was distinct from any memory of the sufferings of the Lord; that the fast took place as a vicarious fast for the Jews. This justification is to be found in the Syriac *Didascalia* and in the *Apostolic Constitutions*, and is hinted at by Epiphanius.[104] On this basis it would certainly seem that this justification was held by some Quartodecimans at some time. This does not therefore mean that it is the only justification ever offered. Lohse does consider this to have been the only basis for the fast, and apart from the sources mentioned above professes to find it at PP80.[105] That Melito contrasts the sufferings of

---

[98] Hansen *Sitz im Leben* 161
[99] Cadman "Christian Pascha" 11; Cantalamessa *Pasqua della Salvezza* 148-150. As noted in 1.2.2 above Peter responds to the death of Jesus with a fast, mirroring the practice of the Asian church
[100] Rouwhorst "Quartodeciman Passover" 161; but cf n108 below
[101] Lohse *Passafest* 62
[102] Quoted by Eusebius *HE* 5.24
[103] Dugmore "Note" 416
[104] See Lohse *Passafest* 62-65 for details of the literature
[105] Lohse *Passafest* 65

Christ with the rejoicing of the Jews because he is undergoing a vicarious fast for them is a possible reading of the passage, but that proposed above is equally likely; because Lohse had ruled out a priori the possibility that the fast commemorated the sufferings of Christ on the grounds that it did not fit with the synoptic chronology he was unable to see it here. He goes on to state that this tradition of vicarious fasting for the Jews could only have originated in Palestine,[106] but it is equally likely to have come about in Asia Minor or in Syria, given the significant and numerous Jewish populations of these places.

Another justification for the fast is hinted at by ps-Hippolytus where there is an indication that the fasting is to be undertaken in preparation for the paschal eucharist.[107] This, being so close to the original Jewish motivation, may, in fact, be the original basis for the Quartodeciman paschal fast. It is not, however, a justification demonstrable from *Peri Pascha*.

There were then a variety of practices, and a variety of justifications given. In *Apostolic Constitutions* both fasting in memory of the Lord's sufferings and fasting on behalf of the Jews appear and the Syriac *Didascalia* is obviously aware of fasting in memory of the passion, since the revised *Didascalia* is concerned to combat this practice.[108] On the other hand we may note with Huber the fact that fasting for the Lord and fasting for the Jews are bound up in each other, and that fasting for the Jews may have developed out of fasting for the Lord,[109] particularly considered as fasting instead of the Jews. Rouwhorst similarly suggests that the primary motivation was as an act of mourning for the death of Jesus but suggests that it had an anti-Jewish bent, that Quartodecimans fasted while the Jews feasted in order to distinguish themselves from the Jews.[110] It was later that this anti-Jewish fast was transmuted into a vicarious fast for the conversion of the Jews; this may well have been a development which took place in Syria.

For Melito and the Christians at Sardis we can say that the fast concentrated on the sufferings of the Lord, just as it was broken in his risen presence, but may also read PP80 as indicating that in view of the sufferings of the Lord a deliberate practice of fasting during the Jewish festivities had already come about; given the nature of rela-

---

[106] Lohse *Passafest* 74
[107] *In Sanctum Pascha* c32
[108] Cadman "Christian Pascha" 11 with reference to *Didascalia* c21
[109] Huber *Passa und Ostern* 19
[110] Rouwhorst "Quartodeciman Passover" 161-162

tionships between Christians and Jews at Sardis and the need for
Quartodecimans to define themselves over and against the Jews, both
of which led to the notable anti-Judaism of Melito, this is quite probable.

One question regarding the Quartodeciman fast is the point at
which it began. Dugmore suggests the time of the evening sacrifice on
Sabbath, in accordance with the Jewish custom and with a (canonical) Johannine chronology of Christ's death.[111] This may be ruled out
by virtue of the fact that the "Johannine" source of the Quartodecimans is not the same as the canonical *John*, although given that the
Quartodeciman fast almost certainly originated in the Jewish custom
of pre-Passover fasting, this may well have been the original time at
which the fast began. Moreover it does not square with Irenaeus'
account of a variety of times of fast; he mentions one day or more but
never less. The beginning of the fast would originally have been set
by the Jewish timetable, but obviously this might change with the
years as the basis for the fast changes. Polycrates states that one day
is kept, and this would indicate that the Quartodeciman fast is begun
with 14th Nisan.[112] This said, there is no decisive evidence concerning the point at which the fast begins. The only definite evidence
points to a time of fasting while the Jews celebrate, and so both Lohse
and Rouwhorst suggest that the fast is restricted to the time while the
Jews are celebrating.[113] Whereas this might indicate a fast taking
place on the evening of Pascha only, that is whilst the Jews celebrate,
or perhaps beginning on the afternoon of the fourteenth in conformity with Jewish custom, we have seen this to have been virtually
contradicted by Irenaeus. There is then nothing in the evidence suggesting a precise time for the fast to begin. The statement in the
Didascalia that the Christians should begin fasting at the time the Jews
begin their celebration could perhaps be a reference to a time of
gathering for the paschal vigil, which would be a public continuation
of the fast which had covered at least the whole of the 14th Nisan.
Such a public fast, beginning at sunset, might have given rise to the
Quartodeciman assertion found in *Peri Pascha* and in *Evangelium Petri*

---

[111] Dugmore "Note" 418

[112] Polycrates, quoted by Eusebius, *HE* 5.24; Strobel *Ursprung* 330-331 believes that
this is the earliest practice, and notes that a single day is the first option given by
Irenaeus. He also deduces this practice from Aphraahat *Dem.* 12.8.13; that Hippolytus *Apostolic Tradition* 33 sets a single day as the minimum is further evidence that this
is the original practice.

[113] Lohse *Passafest* 48-50; Rouwhorst "Quartodeciman Passover" 160 (though he
also suggests that this might be put back a few hours.)

that the Lord died in the evening, since the commencement of a public fast at sunset in memory of the sufferings of the Lord might lead to the identification of the hour of public fasting with the hour of the Lord's death.

There may well have been some leeway among Quartodecimans as to the time of beginning of the fast, just as there was variety as to the justifications offered for the practice, but these would not of itself provoke a quarrel like that at Laodicea. What is more likely to cause dissent is the point at which the fast is concluded, for this would in turn signal the time at which the celebration began.

That there was variety and differentiation among Quartodecimans is clear, but we must see how far this was tolerated, since there would clearly be limits. Differences in the time of the conclusion of the fast might even go so far as to affect the date of the festival, as well as its time, and this would clearly cause difficulties. We must therefore examine the questions concerning the date of the Quartodeciman celebration to see whether this might have been the case.

4.1.5 *The Date and Time of the Quartodeciman Celebration*

Whilst we have stated that the Quartodecimans kept Pascha on the 14th Nisan, this according to their own statements.[114] This is of course patient of two understandings, either that the day was marked by the paschal fast and concluded in the evening, at around the time that the Jews kept the Passover, or that the day was marked by celebration, the fast being concluded at the beginning of that day.

This latter view is that adopted by Brightman, followed by Cantalamessa.[115] His principal argument derives from the language of Eusebius. Where Eusebius states that the fasting is to be brought to an end on the fourteenth, this would usually imply that there is to be no fasting at all on that day. He uses the same language about the Catholic Easter, which was of course a feast throughout. Brightman suggests that, unless a time is clearly implied or specified, it is usual when we say that something is to be discontinued on a certain day to understand that it is to be discontinued from the beginning of that day. Therefore, Eusebius should be understood to mean that the fourteenth was spent in celebration, and that the day was preceded by a vigil on the night of the thirteenth, at which the fast was brought to

---

[114] Polycrates at *HE* 5.24
[115] Brightman "Quartodeciman Question"; Cantalamessa *Pasqua della Salvezza* 150-154

an end.[116] His other objection to a day of fasting on the fourteenth of Nisan to be broken that evening is that a day ending with a night vigil or fast would be a strange day, in that a vigil more normally begins a celebration. Brightman considered this conclusive proof that the occasion of the celebration of the Quartodecimans was in fact the night of the thirteenth.[117] Cantalamessa adds the additional arguments that by the time the vigil came to an end, at a time after midnight, it would be the fifteenth, and no longer the fourteenth of Nisan, and that the last supper is situated by John on the evening of the thirteenth.[118] To this latter argument one may reply that the canonical *John* is effectively irrelevant, as we have already seen. With regard to the former argument we may state that since the vigil began before midnight the whole event could be considered to take place on the fourteenth. We go further into this question of times and dates below.

Another basis for situating the Quartodeciman celebration on the night of the thirteenth is suggested by Hall, who lists the various options.[119] The tendency during the second century was for festivals to be transferred to the early morning and so Pascha could thus have been transferred to before the dawn of the fourteenth, what would have been effectively the night of the thirteenth. He suggests that this might be the basis of the argument at Laodicea, in that there would thus be genuine uncertainty among Quartodecimans about which day was the Pascha. Much the same is suggested by Cantalamessa.[120]

To the idea of a celebration on the night of the thirteenth there are however a number of strong objections. In the first instance it would not accord with Jewish practice. Polycrates states that they keep "the day on which the people put away the leaven",[121] thus demonstrating that Quartodecimans in the second century continued to relate their festival to that of the Jews, and fixed it to accord with the time of the Jewish Passover. To keep the night of the thirteenth would break this continued link with Judaism, and moreover would make nonsense of the directions to fast during the Jewish celebrations as Melito would appear to do.[122] The night of Pascha was never in origin that of the thirteenth, and it is impossible to think that it became such anywhere, at any time. Secondly, to keep Pascha on the night of the thirteenth,

---

[116] Brightman "Quartodeciman Question" 260-261
[117] Brightman "Quartodeciman Question" 261-262
[118] Cantalamessa *Pasqua della Salvezza* 151-152
[119] Hall "Origins of Easter"
[120] Cantalamessa *Pasqua della Salvezza* 152-153
[121] Polycrates, quoted by Eusebius, *HE* 5.24
[122] PP80: see also the evidence presented by Lohse *Passafest* 48-50

even at a time approaching the dawn of the fourteenth, would be to anticipate the events that the Quartodeciman celebration intended to commemorate.[123] To keep the memory of the passion fifteen or so hours before the time the passion was believed to have taken place would be nonsensical under these circumstances. Even if a synoptic chronology lies behind the Quartodeciman Pascha this argument holds; the dawn of the fourteenth coincides with absolutely nothing.

To turn more explicitly to the arguments of Brightman, Lohse points out that the language that Eusebius employs is that of the Quartodecimans themselves, who did not compare themselves in the language that they used with the Sunday keepers, and moreover that the language is that of the Old Testament.[124] The fact that Eusebius employs similar language about Sunday-keepers is irrelevant, for he clearly understood that the fast was broken in the course of the day, and his recognition of the Old Testament language is the basis of this obvious implication. One may add that even if it were the case that Eusebius believed the Quartodecimans to have kept the fourteenth as a festival throughout, Eusebius without his primary sources is of himself hardly a reliable witness for the practice of the Quartodecimans. Moreover, to end the fasting during the course of the day is not as unusual as Brightman would have us believe. Lohse cites several Old Testament examples of fasting until the evening,[125] and these are clear Jewish precursors of the Quartodeciman practice.

On these grounds the day of Pascha is not, as Brightman characterised it, a day of celebration ending with a vigil, but a festival of one day's duration, days being "neither added or removed",[126] the day being a day of fasting and preparation and the celebration concluding the day. To see the vigil as the preliminary act of a festival to be kept on the following day is to violate the evidence. The fact that a day of this shape is unique is no argument against this reconstruction, especially given the strong positive evidence in favour. Pascha was itself an unique event.

Brightman was replying to Schmidt, who had based his reconstruction on the *Epistula Apostolorum*. The picture the *Epistula Apostolorum* presents is one which would accord with what we would expect: a meeting for a vigil, concluding with a celebration, more specifically an act of commemoration. It does not explicitly cite a date for Pas-

---

[123] As is pointed out by Cadman "Christian Pascha" 12
[124] Lohse *Passafest* 41-42
[125] Lohse *Passafest* 45
[126] So Polycrates, quoted by Eusebius *HE* 5.24

cha,[127] but for this to be thought to be anything but the fourteenth would be the height of perversity.

We have seen that the paschal fast was broken on the evening of the fourteenth, and that this would be as true for Melito and his church as for any other Quartodecimans. The matter of date does not therefore explain the dissent among Quartodecimans which was so apparent at Laodicea. We must turn ourselves therefore to the matter of the precise time of the evening celebration.

In suggesting that the Quartodeciman celebration might have been transferred to the dawn of the fourteenth, Hall suggested as an alternative that the celebration might have been pushed back later in the evening of the fourteenth, indeed over midnight.[128] Whilst this was strictly the fifteenth, if the worship began before midnight and continued over that hour into the small hours of the next day, this could charitably be considered still to be celebration on the fourteenth, since it would be on that day that the assembly had gathered. Of course, according to Jewish reckoning the fifteenth would begin with sunset in any case.[129] In this case the Jews did not in fact keep the fourteenth of Nisan at all: the term "Quartodeciman" comes from a Christian provenance, and it is even possible that this is a reference not to the fourteenth of Nisan, but to the fourteenth of Xanthikos, the Hellenistic month which in the second century would have run parallel to Nisan.[130] Whereas the evening of the fourteenth/fifteenth would be considered the fifteenth by Jews, the official Roman day ran from midnight to midnight,[131] and so among Christians removed from this Palestinian-Jewish method of calculation time before midnight was still the fourteenth. Pliny says that in common parlance days run from dawn to dawn;[132] if this is the case then any time before dawn on the 15th Nisan/Xanthikos would be considered the fourteenth.

That the celebration as such was preceded by a vigil continuing the fast is indicated strongly by the *Epistula Apostolorum*; a similar practice is hinted at by the Syriac evidence, and in particular the Quartodeciman strand in the *Didascalia*. Schmidt sees the fast and the vigil as separate and distinct,[133] but this is an unnecessary complication. A

---

[127] As Lietzmann "*Epistula Apostolorum*" 175 is quick to point out

[128] Hall "Origins of Easter" 563

[129] A position upheld by Zeitlin "Beginning"

[130] Finegan *Handbook* 73. Certainly Josephus *AJ* II 211 makes the connection between the Jewish and Greek months.

[131] So Pliny *Naturalis Historia* 2.79.188

[132] Pliny *Naturalis Historia* 2.79.188

[133] Schmidt *Gespräche Jesu* 699-700. In fact he sees this disjunction as being a difference between the Quartodecimans and the rest of the church

natural reading of the *Epistula Apostolorum* would imply a vigil spent
fasting followed immediately by the paschal celebration. Schmidt suggests an earlier breaking of the fast because he is still under the spell
of the canonical *John* and feels the need to conform the Quartodeciman celebration to John's timing of the death of Jesus at 3pm. We
have seen that this is unnecessary. It is likewise unnecessary to insert
an interval between the breaking of the fast and the commemorative
celebration with which Pascha was completed, even in a situation like
that envisaged by the *Epistula Apostolorum* where, by being put back
into the night, the commemoration has effectively been transferred
until the following day. Even if this was considered to be a separate
day, which in the light of Pliny's evidence cited above is dubious, the
language of breaking the fast on the fourteenth is traditional and
would therefore be retained.

A transference into the night of the fourteenth would not meet the
same strong objections as the idea of a transference to the previous
night, and would in any case be a comparatively minor adjustment.
There are two possible motivations for such an act. Firstly there is the
reason proposed by Richardson. He discusses the difficulties which
were faced by the Christian agape and suggests that they extended
equally to the annual celebration of Pascha.[134] Principal among these
difficulties was the persecution which would be called forth by an
evening celebration involving a common meal, due to the *lex Julia de
collegiis*. We have already seen that Asia did not escape this persecution, and so this could well have been the grounds on which a celebration taking place in the evening, contemporaneously with the
Jews, was moved to a time later in the evening, perhaps after midnight, the time at which the Jewish celebration concluded. A meeting
of this kind could be kept with greater secrecy.

But whereas this is possible it is unnecessarily speculative. Given
that fasting for the suffering of the Lord might be given an anti-Jewish
bent then this would imply the possibility that the paschal celebration
was deliberately put back in order that it might not co-incide with the
celebrations of Judaism. The *Mishnah* states that the paschal meal is
not to continue beyond midnight, and so in order to differentiate
themselves from the Jews-Rouwhorst suggests that Quartodecimans,
having gathered earlier for a fasting vigil, began their celebrations at
midnight, as the Jews concluded theirs.[135]

---

[134] Richardson "New Solution" 80-81
[135] Rouwhorst "Quartodeciman Passover" 164

This would appear to have been the time at which Melito kept Pascha. He believes that the Lord died whilst the Passover was still being celebrated and so contrasts the sufferings of the Lord with the rejoicing of the Jews,[136] and when the Lord's sufferings have come to an end with the Jewish celebrations he celebrates. On the basis that the Quartodeciman celebration is to be distinguished by the time of the celebration from that of the Jews, and because midnight had both messianic significance and a significance for the mystery religions, Hansen and Strobel both suggest midnight as the time of the Quartodeciman celebration.[137]

However, Richardson suggests that this movement of the celebration into the night did not take place universally, and that this is the basis of the quarrel at Laodicea.[138] Thus there are two groups of Quartodecimans, those who extend the vigil and keep the celebration at night, and those who stand by the original practice of an evening celebration, whatever the dangers. The Lord had kept Pascha and exposed himself to danger, and the disciple must do likewise. The situation becomes fraught at Laodicea because of the implicit danger, instanced by the martyrdom at this time of Sagaris.[139] This is what is meant when the martyrdom is said to be κατὰ καιρόν, it is opportune at the time of Pascha when the death of Christ is remembered.[140] The fact that martyrdom, potential and actual, is involved, is what gives the dispute its bite.

Although we do not need to follow Richardson's explanation of the rationale for postponing or not postponing the paschal vigil, having preferred that of Rouwhorst, we may nonetheless follow him in postulating the existence of two distinct Quartodeciman parties. This is what we have come to expect.[141] We may moreover add that the martyrdom of Sagaris may conceivably have been read in an anti-Jewish light, given the involvement of Jews in the persecution of Christians, and given that Sagaris was himself Jewish.[142]

That Quartodecimans should be divided in this way would accord with the appeal to different Gospel chronologies and justifications. Thus those who retain an evening celebration appeal to *Matthew* and

---

[136] PP80
[137] Hansen *Sitz im Leben* 154; Strobel *Ursprung* 35-36
[138] Richardson "New Solution" 79-84
[139] Richardson "New Solution" 82
[140] So Hall "Origins of Easter" 561
[141] See 4.1.3 above
[142] That Sagaris was Jewish may be deduced from his appearance among the στοιχεῖα of whom Polycrates speaks. On Jewish involvement in persecution see Trebilco *Jewish Communities* 29 with reference to *Martyrium Polycarpi* 12 and 13

to Jesus' example, whereas those who keep the midnight celebration appeal behind the written Gospels to the Johannine tradition, the basis on which they had always kept Pascha. The dispute at Laodicea is then a dispute between the evening keepers and the night keepers. It concerns the point at which the fast is to be concluded and the celebration to take place and is fought with exegetical weapons, the evening keepers being the synoptic party and the "Johannine" party those who kept Pascha at night.

The explanation of the dispute propounded here is in essence that of Richardson.[143] It succeeds in explaining the division among Quartodecimans, and takes account of all the evidence, whilst painting a picture that is entirely reasonable in itself. The tendency for festivals to be transferred until the morning is common enough, and yet it would be improbable were this to take place universally and simultaneously. We have, however, made several refinements, apart from suggesting a·different reason from that of Richardson for the movement of the time. Richardson sees the evening keepers as conservative Quartodecimans. However, they had admitted a new element into Quartodeciman theology in their appeal to the example of the Lord and to the synoptic chronology, and in their effective abandonment of any act of commemoration. Richardson sees the synoptic chronology of the passion as that which was traditional among the Quartodecimans, but this ill accords with the evidence of a Johannine tradition which we have already collected. So it is that Strobel refers to the synoptic party as "historicizing".[144] A defence of keeping the night by reference to *John* is in any case a clumsy defence, given that according to the fourth Gospel the Lord died in the afternoon, and would surely only have come about on the basis that this was the established tradition. It is those who retained the older Jewish custom, and justified it secondarily with reference to the synoptic tradition, against whom Apollinaris and Hippolytus, in their various ways, are ranged. Melito and Apollinaris, as indeed the author of the *Epistula Apostolorum* are, on the other hand, representatives of mainstream Quartodecimanism.

It would be as a representative of mainstream Quartodecimanism that Melito came to be associated with the Laodicene strife by the scribe who prefixed the chronological note to *Peri Pascha*. Melito's emphasis on typology would be an effective argument against the evening keepers since the Lord, being himself the true paschal lamb,

---

[143] Richardson "New Solution" 80-81
[144] Strobel *Ursprung* 21

would not have eaten of it. Even without a polemical intention, *Peri Pascha* might have been received as such at Laodicea. It is this same typological note which appears to have called forth Clement's response.

The mainstream Quartodecimans needed to distinguish themselves from the Jews, and found this easier with a celebration of Pascha at night; their extended paschal fast might then be observed as a deliberate act of fasting in contradistinction to Jewish practice. On the other hand the evening keepers opened themselves to charges of Judaizing, and it is precisely this charge which is levelled against them by Hippolytus, who thinks of them as typifying all Quartodecimans.[145]

We have suggested midnight of the fourteenth/fifteenth as the time of Melito's celebration of Pascha. However, for this to have been considered the fourteenth it would be surely on that evening that the community gathered. The *Epistula Apostolorum* indeed indicates that a vigil preceded the celebration. This vigil would continue the fasting, as the memorial of Christ's passion, the fast being broken at midnight in celebration of the completed work of salvation.

This reconstruction would thus gain support from the *Epistula Apostolorum*. Although Schmidt is followed by Lohse in suggesting that the vigil was extended until dawn of the fifteenth,[146] this is a misreading of the *Epistula Apostolorum*, exacerbated by a misunderstanding of a comment in the *Didascalia* about the breaking of the fast at the third hour.[147] But the *Epistula Apostolorum* is speaking of the conclusion not simply of the vigil, but of the whole celebration. Although the *Epistula Apostolorum* does not specify a time at which the fast should be broken and the celebration begun its evidence is entirely in keeping with our reconstruction. The celebration may follow the vigil, beginning at around midnight, and continuing on until the dawn of the following day.

---

[145] Hippolytus in *Chronicon Paschale*. See also Visonà "Pasqua Quartodecimana" and our comments in 4.1.3 above

[146] Schmidt *Gespräche Jesu* 703; Lohse *Passafest* 84-85. In following Lohse Richardson "New Solution" 82 suggests that Pascha here is being conformed to the shape of a martyr's festival, a vigil followed by a dawn eucharist, and sees this as part of the move to night keeping, the *Epistula* being a propagandist document in this struggle. This is unnecessary and springs from misunderstanding concerning both the cause of the different times of the Quartodeciman celebration and concerning the evidence of *Epistula Apostolorum*.

[147] Rouwhorst "Quartodeciman Passover" 164 points out that the third hour by the reckoning of the *Didascalia* is nine o'clock in the evening; in any case this section is not from the Quartodeciman strand.

We have established that Melito and his community gathered at sunset on the fourteenth of Nisan for a vigil and broke the fast and began the celebration around midnight. The community behind the *Epistula Apostolorum* appears to have done much the same; the celebration here we know was extended until the following dawn, whereas we do not know the extent of that of Melito, but the two groups of Quartodecimans are keeping the same festival in the same way and at the same time. Both moreover are inspired by the Johannine tradition, as opposed to some who continued to keep Pascha at the same time as the Jews, and appealed in doing so to the synoptic chronology. Having established the setting of Melito's paschal celebration we must therefore turn to explore the content of the vigil and of the celebration with which that vigil concluded.

Thus far we have answered the question as to the subject of the dispute at Laodicea. It is a dispute between Quartodecimans concerning the time of the celebration, whether the evening or the late night of the fourteenth of Nisan. More importantly for our purpose we have established that Melito, after keeping the paschal fast in memory of the sufferings of the Lord, breaks the fast and begins to celebrate around midnight, having gathered with his community earlier in the evening. We conclude this on the basis of evidence indicating that the Quartodeciman celebration is distinguished from that of the Jews in the matter of time, and on the basis of the significance of midnight both for Melito's Jewish tradition and for the Hellenistic mystery cults which had exercised their own influence on the mystery of Pascha. Having thus reached conclusions on the setting of Melito's celebration, as well as on its background, we are in a position to proceed to our reconstruction of its content.

4.2 The Quartodeciman Celebration

We have established that the Quartodecimans of Sardis gathered fasting on the evening of the 14th Nisan and kept vigil. Subsequently, at around midnight the fast was broken. It is now our task to fill in the content of this commemoration in its two parts.

4.2.1 *The Reading of Exodus*

That the account of the first Passover was read from *Exodus* 12 is clear from the beginning of *Peri Pascha* and from the opening lines in particular.

ἡ μὲν γραφὴ τῆς Ἑβραϊκῆς Ἐξόδου ἀνέγνωσται
καὶ τὰ ῥήματα τοῦ μυστηρίου διασεσάφηται

We may reasonably suppose this reading to have taken place during the vigil, since it is as part of the vigil that Scripture was read in the paschal rites of the Syrian churches.[148] It remains to ask what language this was read in, and whether anything can be shown to have intervened between the reading and the delivery of *Peri Pascha*.

The question as to whether the reading from *Exodus* might have been read in Hebrew has already been given some consideration. Zuntz had suggested that the opening lines indicated a targum intervening between a reading from *Exodus* in Hebrew and the delivery of *Peri Pascha* and was followed in this by Lohse and Cross.[149] However, we concluded earlier that whereas there may have been some Christian targumic tradition, and that Hebrew may have been used in the synagogue at Sardis, it was nonetheless improbable that the reading had been in Hebrew. This conclusion was reached on the basis of Melito's language in the opening line, for whereas there are no parallel uses to the expression Ἑβραϊκῆς Ἐξόδου which would indicate a meaning "Exodus in Hebrew", parallels exist which would indicate the meaning "Hebraic Exodus".[150] διασαφεῖν may mean "interpret" or "translate" and so an intervening targum might thus be indicated by the second line, but since this is not the usual meaning of the word, and given the difficulty of demonstrating a reading in Hebrew which would require translation, any other possible interpretation is to be preferred. We may therefore conclude against Zuntz that there was no targum delivered between the reading and *Peri Pascha*. Zuntz had followed Bonner in understanding the second line as describing a process distinct from the reading,[151] and the fact that his theory of an intervening targum is not acceptable does not rule out the possibility that an interpretative process of sorts, albeit not a targum, did intervene between the reading and *Peri Pascha*, this process being described in the second line,

Bonner felt that to read the two lines as describing a different procedure from the reading was the most natural way to treat them, in that with ῥήματα, "explain" would be the most natural meaning of διασαφεῖν. The intervening procedure would in that event be a preliminary exegesis, following the reading and preceding the sermon proper. He is not unaware of the difficulty in finding parallels to any

---

[148] See *Didascalia* c21 and *Testamentum Domini* II 18; this is argued by Schmidt *Gespräche Jesu* 704

[149] Zuntz "Opening Sentence"; followed by Lohse *Passafest* 75 and Cross *Early Christian Writers* 105-107

[150] For these parallels see Hall "Melito *Peri Pascha* 1+2" 247

[151] Bonner "Two Problems" and *Homily on the Passion* 30-36

such tripartite procedure, and our realisation that *Peri Pascha* is not a sermon as such does not ease the difficulty. For since the first part of *Peri Pascha* is a midrashic treatment of *Exodus* 12 one would naturally expect it to follow the reading. Bonner indeed suggests that the habit of listening to an explanation in the place where in the synagogue a targum would have followed might have survived,[152] and we have seen that this is a strong possibility, but that this role is already filled by the first part of *Peri Pascha*.[153]

As well as considering the practice of the synagogue, Bonner argues for a process of preliminary interpretation from the practice of the schools, where *enarratio*, the clearing up of difficulties and obscurities in a text, was one of the set exercises.[154] Bonner. also considered that an explanation for a tripartite procedure might be found in the fairly wide functions of the reader in the early church, given which a procedure of explanation bound up to the reading might be common.[155] He finds examples in Origen, where a summary of the text precedes the allegorical interpretation, and Chrysostom, where an ἠθικόν is appended to an explanatory homily. However, in both these cases, the preliminary explanation is given by the preacher, and not by some separate functionary. In the same way a summary explanation is given to us by Melito himself in the first part of his work. The fact that Melito himself summarises the work in his *diegema* is itself the greatest difficulty standing in the way of any interpretation of the opening of Melito's work which would involve understanding the second line as referring to a preliminary work of interpretation. If this process was simply one of the elucidation of the obscure the difficulty is reduced, but against this must be held the evidence of *In Sanctum Pascha*. Such an approach seems to be that adopted by ps-Hippolytus in *his* treatment of *Exodus* 12, and yet the shape of his work is the same as that of *Peri Pascha*. It would seem that there were different procedures for *enarratio*. Ps-Hippolytus uses the opportunity to break down the text, whereas Melito is freer with his approach, giving *enarratio* a much more general sense, διήγημα rather than ἐξήγησις. According to Dionysius Thrax the process of explanation follows that of reading,[156] and so the evidence of the schools, like that of the synagogue, would lead us to expect the *diegema* to follow the reading directly, with nothing intervening.

---

[152] Bonner "Two Problems" 177
[153] See above 3.1.7
[154] Bonner *Homily on the Passion* 33
[155] Bonner "Two Problems" 177-180
[156] Dionysius Thrax *Ars Grammatica* c1

Nonetheless the possibility remains an attractive one and Gärtner, Cantalamessa and Perler attempt to restate Bonner's thesis.[157] These all begin with the suggestion of Wood that the reading of *Exodus* 12 was followed by a passion narrative.[158] This had been the practice described by Etheria in Jerusalem, where *Exodus* 12 was followed by the Johannine passion. In this context Wood notes the strongly Johannine character of Melito's work. Thus Gärtner suggests that Gospel material was read between the lection and the delivery of *Peri Pascha*.[159] Perler goes further and reads the two opening lines as themselves being a statement of Melito's typological system, the ἀνάγνωσις of the law being followed by its natural διασάφησις, the Gospel.[160] But again we come up against the problem that this typological διασάφησις is given us by Melito himself.

The alternative way of understanding the second line is that proposed by Testuz and Hall,[161] that is to see the two lines as simple parallelism adding nothing to the sense. This is given additional support by the fact that "explain" is not the most common meaning of διασαφεῖν, but that "state plainly" or "declare" is far more common. But what, in this case, could διασαφεῖν τὰ ῥήματα mean? At first sight this would appear meaningless, or at best vacuous. It is this difficulty which led Bonner to find the reference to a separate activity of explanation more natural. However, Hall is able to point to examples where the word is used in solemn statements or injunctions.[162] Most interesting there are a number of examples in the Maccabean writings where it refers to a solemn statement of the law. ῥῆμα is the usual word employed to refer to Scripture, and so this line makes sense as a reference to the solemn pronouncement of the word of God in the context of the paschal vigil. The second line in that case does not refer to a separate process, but on the other hand is not entirely redundant, in that it alludes to the solemnity surrounding the reading to which the first line has referred. Far from being a weak opening, it begins *Peri Pascha* with a note of proper resonance.

In setting out this interpretation Hall finds additional support by emending the text of Codex Chester-Beatty on the basis of the Georgian version and on the Latin epitome.[163] In the second paragraph

---

[157] Gärtner *John 6* 33-36; Cantalamessa *Omelia* 435-436; Perler *Sur la Pâque* 131-132
[158] Wood (Review)
[159] Gärtner *John 6* 35
[160] Perler *Sur la Pâque* 132
[161] Testuz *Papyrus Bodmer XIII* 18-19; Hall "Peri Pascha 1 & 2"
[162] Hall "Peri Pascha 1 & 2" 242-246
[163] Hall "Peri Pascha 1 and 2"

Chester-Beatty reads ξύνετε...οὕτως ἐστὶν καινὸν καὶ παλαιὸν, ἀΐδιον καὶ πρόσκαιρον, φθαρτὸν καὶ ἄφθαρτον, θνητὸν καὶ ἀθάνατον τὸν τοῦ πάσχα μυστήριον. This paragraph would most naturally be read as looking back to a typological interpretation which had already taken place. However, if οὕτως is amended to πῶς, or ὅπως, as would be implied by the Georgian and the Latin (the page is wanting in Codex Bodmer), then the natural reading of this paragraph would be that the interpretation is one which is here being introduced. This is consonant with the rest of *Peri Pascha*, since it is precisely such an typological understanding which is subsequently introduced.

If there is no treatment of the reading apart from that in *Peri Pascha* then this means that our information on the paschal vigil is somewhat scanty, unless the treatment of *Exodus* which comprises the first part of *Peri Pascha* was itself delivered as part of the vigil, falling before midnight. Given its close connection with the preceding reading this is a strong possibility. Of course this does not imply that the whole of *Peri Pascha* was delivered before midnight, but that the pre-midnight vigil contained a reading and an explanatory *diegema* is a picture that is quite conceivable. It is possible that further Old Testament readings were added as commemorations of the type, but this cannot be said with certainty.[164] The first part of *Peri Pascha* commemorates the type of the Passover, being delivered on what is still that day, whereas the true Passover is the subject of the second part. In this light we may doubt the suggestion of Wood and Rouwhorst that a reading of the Passion narrative might take place within the vigil, since this concerns the fulfillment of the paschal hope.[165]

Thus far we have seen the paschal vigil to consist of the reading and of related activity, while the fasting continued. We might, however, hope to make our picture of the vigil more complete, before turning to the celebration with which the vigil concluded.

4.2.2 *The Question of Baptism*

In later times the administration of baptism at the Easter vigil became universal, the first definite evidence of this practice dating from the end of the second century, albeit not from Asia.[166] It is possible to

---

[164] Rouwhorst "Quartodeciman Passover" 163 suggests that this may be the case due to the length of the vigil, and because later Easter vigils contained a large number of readings.

[165] Though it is conceivable that such a reading might take place after midnight as part of the celebration of the fulfillment of the type.

[166] The evidence is to be found in Tertullian and in Hippolytus. For the evidence see Wainwright "The Baptismal Eucharist" 10-11

read the foot-washing at the last Supper as a Johannine allusion to paschal baptism.[167] λούμενος, used in Jesus' words to Peter, is a word used throughout the New Testament to refer to the cleansing effect of baptism, and so it is possible to see foot-washing as a baptismal rite in the Johannine community in lieu of the eucharistic celebration at Pascha. So, when Irenaeus treats the foot-washing he implies it has sacramental effect, and according to Beatrice the "spontaneous and natural" association that he makes between baptism and the washing of feet implies that the rite is still practised in Irenaeus' church, as part of a mimetic rite of Johannine Passover.[168] Moreover the Syriac paschal rites included baptism.[169] If, in addition to this, we consider that the whole act of redemption, understood in a Quartodeciman manner, would appropriately be celebrated in baptism, and that the mystery religions practised nocturnal initiation,[170] the possibility that baptism formed part of the Quartodeciman vigil becomes one which presses for investigation.

This was suggested by Schmidt,[171] and prima facie evidence that this is the case is offered by the hymn to the Pascha towards the conclusion of *In Sanctum Pascha*. Ὦ πάσχα, καινῆς λαμπαδουχίας τὸ φώτισμα, παρθενικῆς δᾳδουχίας ἀγλάϊσμα δι' ὃν οὐκέτι σβέννυνται τῶν ψυχῶν αἱ λαμπάδες, ἐνθέως δὴ καὶ πνευματικῶς ἐν πᾶσι τῆς χάριτος δᾳδουχεῖται τὸ πῦρ, σώματι καὶ πνεύματι καὶ ἐλαίῳ Χριστοῦ χορηγούμενον.[172]

That this would appear to indicate a context of baptism derives from the stress on illumination, from the reference to the parable of the wise and foolish virgins, which, as Perler shows, often has a baptismal reference, from the language borrowed from the mysteries, but

---

[167] This suggestion, and the accompanying arguments, are those of Beatrice *Lavanda dei Piedi*. See also Thomas *Footwashing in John 13* who is apparently unaware of Beatrice's work. Thomas likewise suggests that foot-washing as a sacrament continues in the Johannine community, but does not explore that community in the time after John, nor seeks to make any connection with Pascha.

[168] Beatrice *Lavanda dei Piedi* 45-57. We have seen that there is a mimetic element in the Quartodeciman Pascha, but this is not the kind of *mimesis* Beatrice has in mind. Our reconstruction of the Quartodeciman rite, to be undertaken in the following chapter will show that there is not place for such a Johannine Last Supper

[169] So see Aphraahat *Demonstratio* 12. See further on the Syriac paschal rites at 4.2.6 below

[170] Richardson "New Solution" note on 82

[171] Schmidt *Gespräche Jesu* 704

[172] *In Sanctum Pascha* c62. The punctuation here is that of Visonà *Pseudo Ippolyto* 150; cf Nautin *Homélie* 190 who would read the passage "...the fire shines in all, spirit and body, fed with the oil of Christ"

most of all from the reference to the oil of Christ,[173] which would seem at first glance to be a reference to baptismal anointing. However, in the context of this sentence, bound up to the mention of nourishment by the spirit and the body of Christ, this is not the case. Rather Visonà shows that the oil is a reference to the blood of Christ,[174] as the visible manner in which the invisible gift of Christ's spirit is transmitted. This theory is bound up to stoic physics, the influence of which is noticeable elsewhere in the homily. In other words the reference is eucharistic. In the same way the sign of the blood in *Exodus* is held to typify the blood of Christ.[175] Thus references to sealing and anointing with the blood of the lamb in *In Sanctum Pascha* would thus not appear to be references to any initiatory rite, baptismal or otherwise, but references to the effect of Christ's blood as it is received by believers, whose reception of the spirit of Christ is the mystery which is being celebrated.

Although Cantalamessa had considered that these references were initiatory,[176] we must add to Visonà's positive arguments for seeing the references differently the negative argument that in spite of these apparent references to unction there is no reference to the accompanying baptism. A rite of unction without baptism is unthinkable in the second century, although Cantalamessa canvasses the possibility. In spite of seeing initiatory references in *In Sanctum Pascha*, he concludes that it is impossible to determine whether the rite of baptism itself was actually administered. In the absence of these references it would appear that this was not the case.

Turning to *Peri Pascha* the situation would appear to be similar. There are similar references to sealing with the blood of the lamb, and the doorposts are "anointed". Additionally the shed blood "illuminates" Israel. Commentators have therefore read into this vocabulary references to baptism.[177] However, once again we must note the absence of any reference to the water of baptism.[178] Even if we cannot build up a case like that of Visonà with regard to *Peri Pascha*, it would seem probable that the background of this imagery is the same

---

[173] Perler *Hymnus* 37-52

[174] Visonà *Pseudo-Ippolyto* 149-157

[175] *In Sanctum Pascha* c2

[176] Cantalamessa *Omelia* 282-328

[177] e.g. Perler *Sur la Pâque* 204 cf *Hymnus* 66; Blank *Meliton* 92-93

[178] So Hawthorne "Christian Baptism". Although Codex Bodmer reads λουτρόν at PP103 (Chester Beatty is damaged) λύτρον is preferred (though Blank *Meliton* 93 reads λουτρόν) in accordance with the Latin and Georgian, and on the grounds of sense. Melito's silence on the subject of baptism is also noted by Beatrice *Lavanda dei Piedi* 36, but the voice of Irenaeus is louder in his ears and so the silence is discounted

as that of *In Sanctum Pascha*, given that Melito, like ps-Hippolytus, has a christology of σῶμα-πνεῦμα and a similar stoic background. The blood of the lamb at these points in the text is therefore a type of the blood of Christ, conveying his spirit to the believer. It is interesting to note that Apollinaris likewise shares this stoic belief in the blood conveying the spirit; it would thus seem that this is a Quartodeciman commonplace.[179] One may also note that Apollinaris associates the water from the side of Christ with the word of God. Were baptism part of the Quartodeciman paschal rite, one would surely expect a reference to baptism here.

Apart from these references, baptism has been seen by to be implied in the christological titles which Melito applies, which have a soteriological impact,[180] and in the concluding invitation to receive forgiveness. There is however, no necessary reference here to baptism. The reference throughout is to Christ, who is present in all things.

This does not mean to say that there is no sacramental mediation of Christ. Whilst correct in denying any reference to baptism in the concluding section of *Peri Pascha*, Hawthorne uses language of personal encounter and in doing so makes Melito sound like a modern evangelical.[181] Christ is encountered in being commemorated in the liturgical act lying behind *Peri Pascha*, and his spirit received in receiving the blood which bears his spirit.

On this evidence it would seem that there was no baptism at the Quartodeciman paschal vigil at Sardis. There is however further evidence than *Peri Pascha*. This is fragment 17, six lines appearing overleaf from *Peri Pascha* in Papyrus Bodmer. Perler has argued that they are by Melito, are the second book of which Eusebius speaks, and that they derive from a Quartodeciman liturgy.[182]

That they may be the second book of which Eusebius speaks is quite possible. We have had to reject Hall's explanation of this passage, on the grounds that it does not seem that the extant *Peri Pascha* was at any time divided into books at its central point, and so Perler's is the only theory so far suggested left in play. This does not, however, mean that the fragment is necessarily by Melito, only that it was

---

[179] Apollinaris interprets the blood and water which flowed from the side of Jesus as ὕδωρ καὶ αἷμα, λόγον καὶ πνεῦμα. It would seem that this idea ran deep in the Johannine tradition. *I John* 5:6-8 would imply a similar association

[180] So G. Racle "A Propos du Christ-Père" who believes that the rite is baptismal and interprets the statement that Christ is the Father (PP9) in that light

[181] Hawthorne "Christian Baptism" 245

[182] Perler *Hymnus* passim; note especially 25-32 on the question of the two books

thought to be so. The fact that this fragment follows *Peri Pascha* in the
manuscript, that it is in the same hand, and that it ends the collection,
implies that it may have been connected with *Peri Pascha* early in its
history; Eusebius' source might likewise have believed this work to be
part of *Peri Pascha*, but this belief implies neither Melito's authorship
nor a Quartodeciman background. There is a further unidentified
fragment in Codex Crosby-Schøyen, which appears to concern, in
part, the parable of the ten virgins, and is presumably paschal in
character, since it is to be found in what is a collection of paschal
readings.[183] This fragment may be part of the same work, but the
condition of both is too fragmentary to allow of any firm conclusion.

Melito's authorship has been suggested for both works principally
on stylistic grounds. Fragment 17 most certainly betrays the influence
of the second sophistic,[184] but this does not mean that it is necessarily
by Melito. It is too small to enable us to ground any firm conclusions
on these grounds alone. Much the same can be said of the Crosby-
Schøyen fragment.[185] In conclusion, there are no positive reasons to
deny Melito's authorship of fragment 17, but it cannot be held as
established on the limited evidence available. Might it then derive
from the Quartodeciman liturgy, whilst not necessarily being by
Melito himself? If this were the case then that would explain how it
was that the fragment became associated with *Peri Pascha*.

Perler describes the fragment as being part of an opening dialogue
introductory to the agape, its genre αἰνήσις.[186] His description of the
genre would seem to be correct on stylistic grounds, and the reference
to drinking would certainly seem to indicate a table rite. On the other
hand there is no specifically Christian content in the fragment; it
could equally be gnostic, a possibility that Perler considers but rejects.[187] Hall suggests that its source is the gnostic rite of the bride-
chamber.[188] but whereas the ascription of praise to the mother is
certainly sufficient to arouse suspicion Perler explains this as a reference to the church who, as the neophyte is reborn in baptism, becomes as it were the mother of the soul.[189] This is not as fanciful as

---

[183] So Allen Cabaniss "University of Mississippi Coptic Papyrus" 70-72
[184] As Perler *Hymnus* 16-17 shows beyond any doubt
[185] Melito's authorship has been tentatively suggested, but as Goehring *Crosby
Schøyen Codex* 263-265 points out, there is not enough material on which to ground a
decision. It is even possible that this is the second book to which Eusebius refers, but
not only does the fragmentary nature of evidence make a conclusion impossible, the
fragment is separated in Codex Crosby-Schøyen by another work
[186] Perler *Hymnus* 79-81
[187] Perler *Hymnus* 11-13
[188] Hall *Melito of Sardis* xxxviii-xxxix
[189] Perler *Hymnus* 61

first it sounds as Müller produces evidence from second century Asia which indicates that the church is considered as mother to the believer.[190]

This bridal imagery is the basis on which Perler would see baptisms taking place at the paschal vigil. But even supposing that the fragment is Quartodeciman, there is no proof here that any reference to baptism is implied or intended. Perler produces evidence for bridal imagery being used of the soul in baptism, but none of it is Asian or deriving from the second century. The Asian evidence, to be found in ps-Hippolytus, *Epistula Apostolorum* and Irenaeus, uses the parable of the wedding feast and that of the ten bridesmaids to eschatological import. The wedding feast is the messianic banquet, to which the faithful are admitted and from which the ungrateful are banished. The reference is therefore more probably to some kind of table rite of eschatological significance. The reference to drinking may also reflect this setting.

The negative conclusion concerning the practice of baptism derives fundamentally from Melito's silence on the subject. This is not a simple argument from silence, in that we would expect reference to baptism to appear in Melito's work given its fundamentally liturgical character. As such it is a much stronger argument than speculations deriving from the exegesis of either Aphraahat or Irenaeus. For although Aphraahat sees the foot-washing at the Johannine last supper as the formal institution of the rite of baptism this he derives from *John*, not from the tradition of his church; after all he celebrates a eucharist as Pascha, and as such is far from being typically Johannine, rather he is thus concerned to reconcile the Johannine and the synoptic accounts.[191]

Finally we should note that our negative conclusions accord with those of Hall who, after a review of all the evidence, reaches entirely negative conclusions concerning the practice of paschal baptism at the time of the New Testament.[192] Positively however we may state that the encounter with Christ which we have seen to have taken place at the Quartodeciman vigil could have been understood in eschatological terms. The fragment then could be a reflection of that aspect of Quartodeciman paschal practice.

On these grounds we may continue to allow the possibility that the fragment is Quartodeciman. In view of these findings we must further go on to explore the Quartodeciman understanding of eschatology,

---

[190] Müller *Ecclesia-Maria* 56-57
[191] So Duncan *Baptism* 69
[192] Hall "Paschal Baptism"

whether an eschatological understanding of Pascha is reflected in any
other trace of their ritual and in particular whether this can be placed
in the Quartodeciman vigil, and finally to observe the manner in
which Melito reflects this belief.

4.2.3 *The Quartodecimans and Messianic Expectation*

We have already suggested that messianic expectation played a role
in the Jewish Passover.[193] Since the Quartodeciman Pascha was a
continuation of this ancient rite, we might equally expect that this
expectation would continue in a Christianized form.

However, Bokser has disputed whether the messianic aspects of
the Passover played a role before the second century.[194] If this were
the case then messianism would hardly have been contributed to
Christianity. It is true that much of the evidence for this is late in
redaction, and thus the same problems of date that we have already
encountered are met again. Whereas Petuchowski attempts to argue
against Bokser by reference to certain aspects of the Passover ritual,
his evidence suffers in that so much of it is impossible to date.[195]
Much the same can be said of that collected by Strobel.[196] However
a notable exception to this late evidence is the poem of the four nights
found in the targum *Neofiti* at *Exodus* 12:42. This sees the parousia as
being the fourth night of redemption, taking place at Passover.[197]
Remembering that on this night the Messiah will come is on this
evidence as much part of the celebration as remembering the liberation from Egypt. In this light we may understand the history of revolt
around Passover time. As Petuchowski says, even if Bokser is techni-
cally correct in his review of the evidence, he is psychologically
wrong.[198] We may lend further precision to this by stating that a
degree of messianic expectation is implicit in the act of remembering
the past liberation of Israel; in being remembered a hope is expressed
that this should be realised again.[199]

The clearest evidence that such an understanding of Pascha was
transmitted to Quartodeciman Christianity is to be found in the *Epistula Apostolorum*. There the risen Lord tells the disciples that the parou-

---

[193] 2.2
[194] Bokser *Origins* 74-78
[195] Petuchowski "Messianische Elemente"
[196] Strobel "Passa-Erwartung"
[197] On this poem see 3.1.8 above and refs. Strobel "Passa-Erwartung" admits that
this is the best evidence.
[198] Petuchowski "Messianische Elemente" 38
[199] So see le Déaut *Nuit Pascale* 279

sia will take place around the time of the Pascha. The text here is corrupt and it is difficult to reconstruct a Greek original. Lohse, for whom eschatological expectation is constitutive of the Quartodeci-man pascha conjectures an extensive emendation,[200] but as Rou-whorst points out, one should be suspicious of this emendation, which makes *Epistula Apostolorum* say what he wants it to say.[201] However Pascha is described elsewhere in the *Epistula* as "a night of keeping watch", the watching being for the coming of the Messiah. These very words reflect Jewish terminology. But the eschatological element within *Epistula Apostolorum* can be exaggerated; for much as there is a futuristic expectation of the coming of the messiah it is held together with a realised eschatology as well.[202]

Other evidence of Quartodeciman expectation at Pascha has been cited, such as the letter of Polycrates and the account of the martyr-dom of James recorded by Eusebius, as well as later Christian evi-dence implying that the eschatological climate of Pascha was trans-ferred to Easter;[203] Huber casts a critical eye on this and shows that none of it can be shown for certain to indicate a belief in the parousia at Pascha.[204] It is certainly true that on its own this evidence would indicate nothing except that the earliest Christians had lively eschato-logical hopes. On the other hand the evidence of *Epistula Apostolorum*, combined with the Jewish evidence, and the resulting likelihood that Jewish messianic expectation would be transferred into its corre-sponding Christian context, means that it is really beyond doubt that the Quartodecimans kept Pascha in expectation of the coming again of Christ at this time.

That the Quartodecimans kept Pascha principally for this reason is the theory of Lohse.[205] Blank takes issue with this and suggests the ritual commemoration of the events of the passion as the basis.[206] We have already argued extensively for the view espoused by Blank, Pas-cha would be meaningless without any reference to the events be-lieved to have taken place at that time, but this does not exclude an element of eschatological waiting; the argument between Lohse and Blank is an artificial one. The Jews commemorated their liberation,

---

[200] See Lohse *Passafest* 78-79
[201] Rouwhorst "Quartodeciman Passover" 167 n75. The texts read variously that the Lord will come "in the days of the Pentecost and Passover" or "between the Pentecost and the Passover". Lohse excises the reference to Pentecost.
[202] So Stewart-Sykes "Asian Context"
[203] Notably by Lohse *Passafest* 79-84 and Strobel *Ursprung* 35-36
[204] Huber *Passa und Ostern* 209-212, 215-218
[205] Lohse *Passafest passim*
[206] Blank *Meliton* 38-40

and this concrete memorial had a future aspect as they looked for these promises to be fulfilled again. Surely the Christians would likewise remember Christ and in doing so look for the fulfilment of their hopes in him. The *Epistula Apostolorum* clearly looks forward to the coming of the Messiah on Passover night, but equally clearly sees Pascha as the commemoration of Christ. Commemoration, for Jews and Quartodecimans alike, looks forward as well as backward.

With this in mind we should ask why it is that there is nothing of this obviously indicated by Melito. We may recall that this lack of eschatological tone was the basis on which Huber denied the Quartodeciman provenance of *Peri Pascha*.[207] Although we should not expect anything so explicit as is found in *Epistula Apostolorum*, since we are not dealing with a treatise. nonetheless we should expect to find something which would at least imply an messianic viewpoint. Lohse professes to see this at the end of *Peri Pascha*, where an eschatological element in Melito's thought is clearly present,[208] but not, apparently, one regulated by the idea of the Messiah's imminent return. Hall characterises this as a futuristic eschatology;[209] the vision is one of a future time in which the victory which has already been won by Christ shall be worked out. But the reference is not directly to a future time of parousia, the future tenses in this final passages of *Peri Pascha* are related to the results of responding to the promises that Christ makes. Christ here speaks in the present tense as in the first person. In fact the eschatological note is not at all futuristic, and for this reason there is no reference to an imminent parousia, indeed there is no mention of any future eschatological event except in the vaguest terms.[210] This is not to suggest that there is a deliberate de-eschatologizing tendency in Melito's work,[211] rather that there is a distinct eschatological dimension, but that it is not an eschatology orientated towards the future.

Is the eschatology therefore a realised eschatology? And if so, on what basis? A realised eschatology may be perceived in *Peri Pascha* in that in the highly charged passages at the end of the document Christ speaks through Melito in the first person and in the present tense. This use of *ethopoiia* is surely meant to indicate that Christ is present. This presence in which he is encountered is the result of the act of commemoration, since in being remembered liturgically he comes to

---

[207] Huber *Passa und Ostern* 41-45. See also 1.1.1
[208] Lohse *Passafest* 81
[209] Hall *Melito of Sardis* xliv-xlv
[210] So Vignolo "Storia della salvezza"
[211] As does Racle "Perspectives Christologiques" 268-269

be present in the assembly. Thus there is no looking forward to the coming of the Messiah simply because the Messiah is already present, and the eschatological hope of the Quartodecimans is already real-ised in the present of the paschal night. In the act of celebration Christ is encountered.

Visonà comments with regard to *In Sanctum Pascha* that the future eschatological expectation of the Jewish Passover has been turned into a sacramentally realised eschatology.[212] Thus the preparation for the reception of the Messiah is turned by ps-Hippolytus into prepara-tion for the reception of Christ's eucharistic body.[213] However, al-though we have found eucharistic references within *Peri Pascha*, the realised eschatology of Melito is not the same narrowly sacramental realisation of ps-Hippolytus. For Melito Christ is encountered not in the eucharistic gifts but in the entirety of the liturgical action. On this basis Christ speaks through Melito, he is present by virtue of being liturgically remembered, not simply by being identified with what, for Melito, are the agencies by which his spirit is imparted to the believ-er. The spirit of Christ is given in the eucharistic gifts, but he is encountered in himself by participation in the act of commemoration. Cantalamessa refers to this as an "epifania cultuale".[214]

Cantalamessa suggests that a realised eschatology has developed because of the introduction of a historical element into Pascha, neces-sary to combat gnosticism.[215] This, however, is to complicate matters unnecessarily. Commemoration of a historical event, the passion and resurrection of Christ, was always part of the Christian Pascha, just as this commemoration naturally led to an eschatological hope. That in a liturgical context a realisation of the presence of Christ should come about, is likewise natural.

The whole of the vigil and celebration may be seen as a liturgical expression of the act of waiting. Huber notes that in the treatment of the parable of the wise and foolish virgins given in *Epistula Apostolorum*, the wise virgins do not go to sleep at all, and their lamps are never dimmed. He suggests that this reflects a liturgical *Sitz im Leben*, that the night is one of waiting, lamps lit in readiness.[216] A similar under-standing of the night of vigil as eschatological, culminating at mid-night, may be gathered from the Syriac *Testamentum Domini* with its

---

[212] Visonà *Pseudo-Ippolyto* 149
[213] *In Sanctum Pascha* 32
[214] Cantalamessa *Pasqua della Salvezza* 213
[215] Cantalamessa *Pasqua della Salvezza* 212
[216] Huber *Passa und Ostern* 212. We should also note the presence of δᾳδοῦχοι in the mystery religions. See Anderson *Second Sophistic* 61

instructions that children should be prevented from going to sleep.[217] On the basis of our observation of the liturgical realisation of this eschatological hope we may go beyond characterising the vigil as eschatological, and state that the watch of the paschal night was fulfilled in the presence of the risen Christ.

We may therefore see that the Quartodecimans' understanding of their own eschatological beliefs varied, but that some belief of this kind was never absent, and that it was always bound up to the principal act of remembering Christ. In the assembly gathering before midnight, the lamps being necessary in any case because of the darkness, they heard the word of God and recalled the events of the first Passover. And then as the celebration climaxed they recalled the suffering and resurrection of Christ, and in doing so encountered him.

The content of fragment 17 is not inimical to this reconstruction, although it is not yet clear where it may have fitted into the structure of the rite. However, our examination of the celebration is not yet complete, in that we have yet to deal in any detail with the celebration itself, the breaking of the fast. We have an outline of the vigil, but not of the conclusion of the night of waiting. To this we must turn.

4.2.4 *The Celebration of Pascha*

In *Epistula Apostolorum* the risen Christ instructs his apostles that the disciple who has been released from prison in order to keep Pascha will be returned when the agape and "commemoration" (Coptic: the commemoration which is for me and my agape) are complete.

Questions emerge from this. What are the agape and the commemoration, and in what way are they connected? Are two separate rites being described, or one combined rite? The agape is surely a reflection of the table rite which, as we have argued above, the Quartodecimans continued to keep in accordance with Jewish tradition[218] and may thus be understood as being a reference to the seder of the Quartodecimans. What then is the act of commemoration? The Ethiopic word *tazkar* is that which is used in the Ethiopic version of *Exodus* to render זכרון. On this basis the word standing in the Greek may well have been μνημόσυνον; alternatively, in view of the Coptic rendition, ἀνάμνησις may have stood in this place.[219] In either event this

---

[217] For the eschatological explanation of this instruction see Strobel "Bösen Buben"
[218] 2.1.4
[219] As Lietzmann (Review) suggested

has universally been assumed to be a reference to the eucharist.[220] There are however grounds to question this assumption.

The Coptic translator evidently thought that a eucharist was being referred to, and brings this out in his translation. Not only is the commemoration qualified as being in memory of Christ, thereby conforming it to *I Corinthians* 11, he reverses the order from that reflected in the Ethiopic, in order to conform with what was more common in Egypt, a eucharist followed by the agape.[221] However, this evidence is hardly reliable, the fact remains that the Greek appears to be referring to something else. If the eucharist is meant we should demand reasons for the circumlocution so evident in the Coptic. *Tazkar* simply does not mean εὐχαριστία but ἀνάμνησις or μνημόσυνον (the words are interchangeable). On the other hand, if no eucharist were celebrated this would be strange, especially in view of the eucharistic references which we have found within *Peri Pascha*. There are no explicit references apart from the image of the marking with the blood, although others have been seen,[222] but even this oblique reference makes the absence of a eucharist unlikely. Schmidt and Cantalamessa both claim that the paschal eucharist was constitutive of the Quartodeciman celebration;[223] Pascha without eucharist would certainly be incongruous.

Although the ἀνάμνησις/μνημόσυνον was apparently something other than the eucharist, it may nonetheless be possible to see it functioning as such. Unleavened bread would probably have been used at the seder in keeping with the ancient tradition,[224] and wine, of course, was drunk. Interestingly the taking of bread and wine are marks of the Jewish Passover that Melito describes;[225] he singles these aspects out for comment and groups them together in a way which is not natural for an observer of the Jewish rite. In this way he makes the Jewish Passover sound like a eucharist; it would seem that what Melito is really describing here is a Quartodeciman celebration of Pascha projected onto Jews, and so bread and wine are clearly consti-

---

[220] Firstly by Schmidt *Gespräche Jesu* 700-701 and subsequently by Lohse *Passafest* 84-85, Perler *Hymnus* 65-66, Cantalamessa *Pasqua della Salvezza* 150, Rouwhorst "Quartodeciman Passover" 163

[221] Lohse *Passafest* 79-80

[222] Hansen *Sitz im Leben* 163 sees a eucharistic reference in Melito's assertion that the mystery of the Pascha was accomplished in the body of the Lord, but this is a Christological, not sacramental, statement

[223] Schmidt *Gespräche Jesu* 697-701; Cantalamessa *Pasqua della Salvezza* 220-222

[224] Lohse *Passafest* 87

[225] PP80

tutive of Pascha as they are of the eucharist. However, since the whole of the seder was intended as a commemorative liturgy it is to be asked whether there is reference here to a separate event at all, or whether the commemoration was simply part of the agape. Lohse notes that the two are mentioned in one breath (as indeed they are) and concludes that they are therefore one and the same celebration.[226] He sees this as an ancient rite, similar to that reflected by the *Didache*, in which the agape and eucharist are not separated, as they are in Justin. However, Huber responds by showing that even as early as the time of Paul the eucharist and agape were at least in principle separate events,[227] and that, even if kept together, they could be separated out and distinguished from one another. This may be so, but it remains a fact that the agape and commemoration are mentioned together here, and would therefore appear to refer to the same thing. Just because the Pauline communities were capable of distinguishing two parts to their table rite does not mean that other communities could do the same.

Thus it would seem that a combined rite is intended, a commemoration within the agape. From the order of events and the manner in which they are mentioned together described it would seem that the commemoration overarched the agape and continued beyond it, rather as the Greek symposium followed the meal and was yet a constituent part of it, and the declaration of the haggadah at the seder would extend beyond the consumption of the paschal lamb. Since the function of the seder was itself one of commemoration, we would expect a close relationship between these two parts of the rite, closer than that obtaining between the Pauline agape and eucharist, such that one would not be possible without the other. On this basis we may suggest that the μνημόσυνον, extending beyond the agape, fulfilled the commemorative effect of the seder and focused it. If the μνημόσυνον related to the seder in the same way that the eucharist would normally relate to the agape, we may see that as the seder came to be seen as an agape, so the μνημόσυνον might come to be seen in the light of the eucharist.

On this basis we may see the μνημόσυνον functioning as a eucharist, but undivided from the preceding seder. As a rite bound up to the seder in this way it would have had considerable antiquity even at the time of Melito, and was therefore probably an annual rite pecu-

---

[226] Lohse *Passafest* 86
[227] Huber *Passa und Ostern* 25-27

liar to Passover, quasi-eucharistic, but distinct from the Sunday celebration.[228]

The *Epistula Apostolorum* implies that the rite is to conclude with cockcrow, and on this basis Lohse put the agape at 3am.[229] However, we have seen already that there is some misunderstanding of this passage, and so we may perhaps place this agape at a time after midnight. This was late enough to distinguish the celebration from that of the Jews, since the Jews were forbidden to continue their festivities beyond that time. This occasion of breaking the fast was essentially a joyful one, undertaken in memory of the Christ who was raised, and concluded in his presence. The mood changed as the people are brought from disgrace into glory, "from slavery to liberty, from darkness to light, from death to life..." We have already seen Melito's statement that the Jewish Passover was marked by music and dancing, and may suggest that this, like the prominent reference to bread and wine, reflects the setting of the Quartodeciman Pascha as much as that of the Jews.

Thus the vigil of reading and waiting would climax in the breaking of the fast with a joyous table rite. This table rite is the context in which Perler saw the use of fragment 17, but this rather depended on a view of *Peri Pascha* as purely a homily on *Exodus* 12. However, since we have identified *Peri Pascha* as itself liturgical, and have been able to see the first part only being delivered before midnight, this would tend to cast doubt on Perler's thesis. We should in any case examine the place of *Peri Pascha* in the celebration. This may enable us to see the rite in more detail and understand it more deeply.

We have moved towards a picture of the paschal liturgy of the Quartodecimans in which the fasting community assembles before midnight, in an atmosphere of eschatological expectation. They hear a reading of *Exodus* 12, and remember and celebrate the events of the first Passover, and those of the last under the old dispensation. At the climax of the occasion comes a joyous table rite, at which they believed the Lord to be present. This table rite was unique to Passover, being a continuation of the ancient seder, but with eucharistic overtones. It was called a μνημόσυνον (or perhaps ἀνάμνησις), and had the principal intention of calling Christ to mind, in such a way that he might be present to and in the worshipping community. As such it was bound up closely to the action of the seder, and indeed was seen as an extension of the seder.

---

[228] cf van der Veken "De Primordiis Liturgiae Paschalis" 492-493 who suggests that the Sunday eucharist and the paschal eucharist were little different

[229] Lohse *Passafest* 89

This in outline is the Quartodeciman Pascha. However, we have not yet been able to account for the function of *Peri Pascha* within the ritual. In order to complete our picture of the Pascha at Sardis, we should attempt to do so now. We have sought to show that Peri Pascha is itself liturgical, and so we must seek to see how this liturgy held its place in the rite which we have described here.

4.2.5 *The Place of Peri Pascha*

As we have seen, the first editor of *Peri Pascha* characterised it as a homily.[230] Not only has that description stuck, but since then it has determined the issue of the place of *Peri Pascha* in the Quartodeciman celebration; it was the homily, delivered after the reading. This was the opinion of Lohse,[231] based on Bonner's assumption, and he is followed in this by Perler and Cantalamessa.[232] Given our challenge to Bonner's generic classification of *Peri Pascha* we are now in a position to challenge his identification of its role in the Quartodeciman liturgy.

We have shown that a homiletic position does indeed approximate to the place of the first part of the document, following on from the reading, and comprising a midrashic treatment of *Exodus*; we have also argued that this was delivered before midnight, comprising the chief liturgical content of the vigil.[233] This "homily" was thus liturgical to a much higher degree than has heretofore been realised, in that like the haggadah itself it had a function of remembrance, in this case of the type.[234] Even in the darkness of the vigil the light of redemption was implicitly present, as the midrashic treatment of the *Exodus* lection functioned, as did the seder, to commemorative effect. However, *Peri Pascha* falls into two halves, and these parts cannot both be the homily.

We have further shown that the second half of the document is essentially a liturgy, and distinct in form and function from the first half. All we know of the Quartodeciman celebration after the conclusion of the vigil is that it consisted of the seder, described as an agape, and the μνημόσυνον. We need to determine the place of *Peri Pascha* in this context.

---

[230] Bonner *Homily* 19
[231] Lohse *Passafest* 75
[232] Perler *Sur la Pâque* 24-29, with some reservations; Cantalamessa *Pasqua della Salvezza* 154
[233] 4.2.4
[234] 3.2.3

Whilst it is possible that there was some other rite intervening between the preliminary midrash and the haggadah, or indeed taking place after the seder, to which *Peri Pascha* corresponds, there is a simpler solution at hand. Given that the second half was delivered in the same position in the agape as was the haggadah in the Jewish seder, we may see this part of *Peri Pascha* being likewise delivered at the table. Moreover, since its function, like that of the Passover haggadah on which it was modelled, is commemorative, we may see this part of *Peri Pascha* as comprising the liturgy for the μνημόσυνον, by virtue of being the haggadah and by virtue of its liturgically commemorative function by which the presence of Christ is brought to the hearers. In other words, Melito gives us the actual text of the liturgy he used, including the quasi-eucharistic liturgy to which we referred above. These may well seem a surprising conclusion, but given that the function of *Peri Pascha* was commemoration, and that it is essentially liturgical in form, then that it was itself the μνημόσυνον, that is to say the commemorative liturgy, is the simplest conclusion to any question about its place in the rite.

It may seem odd for there to be a eucharistic liturgy without reference to the Last Supper, but as such this is far from unique, and this concern need not detain us for long. We may mention in this regard the liturgy of the *Didache*, and that of the *Acta Johannis* as examples of this. The latter is roughly contemporaneous with Melito, whereas the former, although considerably earlier, may well be of a similar age to the tradition which Melito preserves, given that the custom practised by Melito was already ancient in the middle of the second century. Later in time we have *Addai and Mari* and, more controversially, it is possible that the liturgy described by Cyril of Jerusalem did not mention the Last Supper, despite being a paschal eucharist.[235] Finally we may note that in the *Apostolic Tradition* of Hippolytus, although commemoration of the Last Supper is made, it appears only as part of the recitation of God's mighty acts, in a subordinate clause.[236] It is thus not in any way the climax or determining feature of the rite.

Despite this evidence Wainwright suggests that the Last Supper must have been mentioned at the early paschal eucharists, and that it was necessary as a charter, a haggadah he says.[237] Similarly Felmy, noting the absence of any words of institution from the rite of the *Didache* suggests that their function in the primitive eucharist was that

---

[235] So, with literature, Fenwick *Techniques* 13-15
[236] As Mazza "Omelie Pasquali" 445 points out
[237] Wainwright "Baptismal Eucharist" 30-31

of the haggadah, a charter for the rite.[238] Finally along similar lines
Rouwhorst, who is prepared to accept that a large number of rites do
not make reference to the last supper, suggests that the appearance of
these words in so many eucharistic prayers was something which
originated in the paschal eucharist, the direct commemoration of the
events which the Last Supper precipitated, and that the appearance
of the words derived from their role as substituting for the haggadah.[239] All of this is unnecessary since the commemoration of the acts
of God goes beyond the Last Supper. In the case of *Peri Pascha* we
have already perceived that the second half of the work is itself the
haggadah, and it is able to function as such because although not
relating to the last supper it is nonetheless a commemoration in form
and function of the passion of Christ. Were Melito to tie this commemoration to the Last Supper that would indicate that he was following the synoptic chronology of the passion. We have already presented ample evidence that this is not the case, and so no mention of
the Last Supper is to be expected.

Although the absence of any mention of the Last Supper is not in
itself problematic, it is worthwhile looking at the rite contained in *Peri
Pascha* to see whether there are any other traces of it to be found. The
absence of a mention of the Last Supper is not a trait that the euchologia mentioned hold in common, and that the absence of any such
mention should be noticed is a modern perception; no incongruity
would have appeared to Melito or to his contemporaries. Rather
these liturgies are different rites, of different origins and roots; the
inclusion of the Last Supper in the eucharistic prayer must have come
from another source again, the origins of the eucharist being multiple
and complex.

Of the extant rites mentioned above both *Addai and Mari* and *Apostolic Tradition* have certain similarities with *Peri Pascha*. Obviously *Addai
and Mari* is a much more developed rite than that reflected by *Peri
Pascha*, it is after all considerably later, but it is perhaps possible to go
behind the extant rite and to find something more primitive. It is of
course a Syrian rite, and therefore one which could well have been
influenced by the same tradition which lay behind the Quartodecimans; for this reason it is worth investigating any potential similarity.

The first attempt to find a more primitive rite behind *Addai
and Mari* was that of Ratcliff.[240] He excised the both the private

---

[238] Felmy "Was unterscheidet"
[239] Rouwhorst "Célébration" 108-111
[240] Ratcliff "Original Form"

(ܐܪܙܐ) and the public (ܐܢܘܡܐ) intercessions and various other items which he saw as accretions such as the sanctus and the epiklesis, to reveal a basic shape in which praise is given to the creator, thanks given for the acts of Christ for humanity, and the death and resurrection commemorated. Although Ratcliff's work has been questioned, and further material has become available, the prevailing tendency has been to assent to the principle of simplifying the rite. It would seem that the intercessions should be retained, but that a two-fold scheme emerges, in which praise and thanksgiving is given for creation and redemption, and prayers of intercession are offered.[241]

The similarity with *Peri Pascha* lies principally in the fact that, beginning with creation and going on to encompass the work of Christ, *Addai and Mari* contains a rehearsal of sacred history. Ratcliff refers to this as a εὐχαριστία, his own term, but it might equally be called an μνημόσυνον, since this is effectively a commemoration of what God has done through Christ. There is no literary relationship, but this is not to be expected, since *Peri Pascha* is the prayer of one particular congregation and the hand of Melito is moreover heavy upon it. Likewise *Addai and Mari* has undergone some development, and has its own structure. Nonetheless Gelston does pick up some similarities with *Peri Pascha* in the references to the work of Christ at the heart of the anaphora.[242] These are, however, somewhat imprecise and stem from the fact that the subject matter is the same. But this similarity of subject matter is more significant than any verbal parallel since it indicates that the commemorative intent of the rites is the same, even though there is no literary relationship.

There have been several attempts to link *Addai and Mari* to various prayers from the synagogue service, notably the *yoser* and the *ahabah*,[243] as well as to the Jewish meal blessings known as the *birkat hamazon*.[244] Whereas these may go some way to explaining the structure of this prayer as thanksgiving and the concluding intercession, the detail in which salvation history is repeated must derive from

---

[241] See for discussion and bibliography Spinks *Addai and Mari* and Gelston *Eucharistic Prayer*. Gelston offers his own reconstruction at 118-123 which accords to this twofold shape

[242] Gelston *Eucharistic Prayer* 92 and 94

[243] For criticism and references see Spinks *Addai and Mari* 11-12 with references and Gelston *Eucharistic Prayer* 70-71

[244] Gelston *Eucharistic Prayer* 7-11; cf Rouwhorst "Jewish Liturgical Traditions" 79-80; for a text and discussion of these blessings note Finkelstein "Birkat ha-Mazon" though this should be treated with some caution as Bradshaw *Search* 24-26 makes clear

elsewhere. Perhaps it is here that one might discern the influence of Passover keeping on the eucharist, and that of the haggadah on the eucharistic rite, in that a basic blessing for the work of God has been expanded to treat of God's history of salvation in more detail.[245]

A similar process would appear to lie behind the construction of Hippolytus' *Apostolic Tradition*. Mazza finds a series of parallels between the rehearsal of God's acts in Hippolytus and the paschal "homilies" (as he calls them) of Melito and of ps-Hippolytus. He is led to suggest that the genre of the paschal "homily", which had in turn developed from the haggadah, has contributed to Hippolytus' anaphora.[246] Not all of Mazza's parallels are equally convincing, but the number and weight of the parallels are striking. The question which is then posed is the nature of the relationship between the paschal "homilies" and Hippolytus' anaphora. Given the eastern origin of Hippolytus the probability is that the paschal tradition has been mediated to Hippolytus through the Asian church rather than directly through Judaism. It is quite possible that Hippolytus' community had a Quartodeciman past.[247]

A degree of literary relationship was earlier discerned between *Peri Pascha* and the liturgy of *Apostolic Constitutions* 8.[248] We do not suggest that this liturgy is a direct descendant of *Peri Pascha*, but nonetheless the similarities would indicate that some source is held in common; this source is probably ultimately Jewish. The preface, in which the parallels with *Peri Pascha* are to be found, would appear to be an independent product, to which the compiler has added other elements, in particular using the prayer of Hippolytus' *Apostolic Tradition*, itself, as we have seen, related to the paschal celebration of primitive Christianity. The ultimate source of this preface may be something analogous to the haggadah, a statement of God's acts in creation and redemption, originating in Judaism, although having undergone further development in its Christian context.[249] Pitt goes so far as to suggest that this was a eucharist of the Jerusalem type;[250] in support

---

[245] Felmy "Was unterscheidet" suggests that the original table rites were simple blessings (εὐλογίαι), but sees the influence of the haggadah differently, as explained above

[246] Mazza "Omelie Pasquali" 412-438

[247] See Brent *Hippolytus* 63-68

[248] 3.2.3 above

[249] That there has been Christian development of this prayer cannot be overstressed. We are not claiming that the compiler of *Apostolic Constitutions* lifted a Jewish prayer. See on this Fiensy *Prayers Alleged to be Jewish* notably at 154

[250] Pitt "Anamnesis"

of this unprovable claim we may note that the eucharist described by Cyril, which would appear to omit mention of the Last Supper, was the paschal eucharist. Although the phrases which this prayer holds in common with *Peri Pascha* may seem to be isolated fragments, it is significant that they are all to be found in the same part of the liturgy, as they are in *Peri Pascha*. This would indicate that they had been related whilst still Jewish property, and that the Christian tendency has been to expand them.

It is particularly interesting that as in the *dayyenu* the rehearsal of Old Testament salvation history ends with the occupation of the land, and has no mention of conquest. From here the liturgy passes to the acts of salvation of the New Testament, the establishment of the new temple in Christ's body, where the *dayyenu* describes the building of the temple. The same point of conclusion to Old Testament history may be discerned in the analogous passages of *Peri Pascha*. There would seem to be something here of a common source.[251]

If this preface is a product independent of the rest of the anaphora, it is not an isolated incident of such an occurrence. The same has been claimed for the preface in the *Liturgy of the Twelve Apostles*, that it is a prayer complete in itself, encompassing creation, redemption and parousia, an independent product which a compiler has employed.[252] This has also been suggested with regard to the preface of the liturgy of St. Mark, now found independently in the Strasbourg Manuscript.[253] The history of salvation from creation to redemption (seen as a future event) was a basic theme in Jewish prayer at the time of the parting of the Jewish and Christian ways,[254] and so such a theme was almost bound to enter into Christian prayer. We see something of this in Peter's prayer in *Acts* 4. However, whatever the Jewish-Christian origin of these independent euchologia, we must enquire into the manner by which they became incorporated into the table rites of primitive Christianity.

Primary among these table rites was the Passover. Our suggestion is that the haggadah was the basis on which the commemoration of salvation history became part of the normative eucharistic prayer, since this was the model with which Christians were presented at the

---

[251] For the date of the *dayyenu* see Finkelstein "Pre-Maccabean Documents" and our discussion in 3.1.2 above

[252] Engberding "Syrische Anaphora"

[253] Ligier "Origins"; also note Cuming "Anaphora" and Wegman "Anaphore incomplete?"

[254] According to Heinemann, cited by Jasper and Cuming *Prayers of the Eucharist* 8

agape/seder of Pascha.[255] This commemoration of saving history could be bound up to intercession (as it is in Addai and Mari and in the Strasbourg prayer) as a result of the paschal embolism in the birkat ha mazon which seek to make remembrance before God on behalf of God's people.[256] The paschal haggadah and its surrounding ritual was not the only source of the eucharistic prayer, any more than Passover was the only source of the practice of the eucharist, but it was nonetheless an element in the whole, and most particularly the means by which the recitation of the themes of salvation history might become part of the table rite.

What we have sought to show here is that a liturgical recitation of the acts of God, such as *Peri Pascha*, was not unusual as a table rite, and indeed that it was normal at Pascha. There were probably a whole series of prayers of this kind which in time were attracted into the eucharist, and of which some traces survive in later liturgies. *Peri Pascha* is unusual in that it is so clearly a literary product (which in turn ensured its survival) and in the complexity of its structure; however it was on the model of such commemorations as this that blessings for the redemptive act of God became commemorations of his past mercies recited over the table of God in the hope of their communication to the believer and participant.

We have argued that the second half of *Peri Pascha* is a table liturgy on the grounds that its function is liturgical and commemorative, on the grounds that there are formal contacts with other liturgical texts, on the grounds that the attribution of such a function to *Peri Pascha* enables us to see the manner in which it might fit into the Quartodeciman seder, and on the grounds that the similarities between these later rites and elements of *Peri Pascha* indicate the possibility of a common tradition stemming from a series of table rites. We may also note that epideictic speech in the Hellenistic world might function liturgically. But if this thesis is to be further sustained we should

---

[255] It is on a similar basis that Fuller "Double Origin" suggests that the act of commemoration became bound up to the table-fellowship of the early Christians; it is also possible that in some communities, though not that of Melito, that this commemoration included mention of the Last Supper and that this is the means through which this enters the eucharistic prayer, as Rouwhorst "Célébration" suggests. Given the emphasis on the Last Supper in the Syriac rites (on which see Rouwhorst "Quartodeciman Passover" 165-166) it quite possible that this was marked in Syriac speaking regions.

[256] As Cuming "Anaphora" suggests at 120; in adopting this suggestion we need not conclude with Wegman "Anaphore Incomplete?" 437-438 that these blessings are the sole source of the Christian eucharist

attempt to see how it functioned as such. The complex structure could assist us in this.

The second half of *Peri Pascha* is divided into two subsections by a doxology at PP65. Each subsection forms a separate disgrace-glory pattern, the whole adding up to the haggadah. Doxologies mark the major sections of this text, as we have already seen, and so this subdivision must therefore have some significance. Hall suggests that the second half could have been divided differently,[257] but given the tight organisation of *Peri Pascha* we should assume that the division at this point is a significant one, and seek to discover its rationale.

Interestingly it is immediately after this doxology that the word ἀφικόμενος is introduced, and from this point on the style becomes yet more hymnic; perhaps this reflects the hymnic conclusion to the Jewish seder. This is significant in view of Hall's suggestion that the word ἀφικόμενος here reflects the *aphikomen* of the Jewish rite.[258] This is a piece of unleavened bread which is broken off and put aside at the beginning of the seder, only to be revealed and reunited with its loaf at the end of the meal. Daube had argued that its significance was messianic and that the Hebrew word was derived from the Greek ἀφικόμενος, the very word which we meet in *Peri Pascha*.[259] This is the basis for Hall's suggestion, in that the context in *Peri Pascha* is a strong statement of Jesus' messiahship. Daube went on to argue that it was the *aphikomen* that Jesus had taken at the Last Supper and identified with himself.

Daube's etymology of *aphikomen* is better than any other which has been offered, given that the word is almost certainly Greek. Other offered interpretations, such as ἐπὶ κομμόν and ἐπὶ κῶμον have been forced in the extreme.[260] It is the derivation of *aphikomen* from ἀφικό-μενος which forms the basis for Daube's suggestion that the *aphikomen* had a messianic significance. Again, this is preferable to any other explanation which is offered, such as that it is a ploy to keep children awake during the night.[261] Further to these negative arguments we must note the untranslatable nature of the instruction concerning the *aphikomen* in the *Mishnah*, which would indicate that the communication of the arcane is intended since in the context of the seder it is the

---

257 Hall *Melito of Sardis* xxii. He makes reference here to other attempted divisions of the second half
258 Hall *Melito of Sardis* xxvii and 35
259 Daube *He that Cometh*
260 For the suggested alternatives see Carmichael "David Daube on the Eucharist"
261 For these alternative explanations see Carmichael "David Daube on the Eucharist"

summary of the meaning of Passover offered to the wise disciple. On this basis it cannot simply be a children's game; that the coming of the Messiah is intended is far more probable in the Passover context. If it is an element of the seder which Christians had taken up then this provides a further reason to obscure its messianic meaning, since to the compilers of the *Mishnah* the rite might well have had Christian overtones. Finally in support of this interpretation of ἀφικόμενος and its derivation from *aphikomen* understood in the messianic sense we should note that ἀφικόμενος is used with a clearly messianic intention elsewhere in *Peri Pascha*.

Given the absence of a benediction of the loaf of the *aphikomen* it is suggested that, like the sandwich of Hillel which likewise lacks a blessing, it is originally the practice of a sectarian group. The employment of a Greek word may indicate that this sectarian group was based within a circle of Hellenistic influence, whether within Palestine or without. We do not follow Daube's suggestion that herein lies the origin of Jesus' action with the bread at the Last Supper for this is unnecessary for our purpose. What we are claiming is that Melito understood the messianic significance of the ἀφικόμενος, and that this ritual was part of his paschal tradition. After he has delivered the first substructure of the haggadah over the meal, and the meal is eaten, he begins the second substructure by revealing the Messiah.

Whether the *aphikomen* represents the Messiah as it does in the Jewish rite, or is identified with the Messiah as in the eucharist of the greater church is unclear; either meaning is possible from Melito's words. What he does do is deliver a panegyric of the Christ who is come and is present in the seder. οὗτος ἀφικόμενος ἐξ οὐρανῶν ἐπὶ τὴν γῆν... We can assume that the *aphikomen* is shared out among the company at the triumphant conclusion of Melito's rite as it was in the Jewish ritual. It is the bread of life, the messianic bread of which *John* 6 speaks; it is by virtue of the rite of *aphikomen* that the bread of life becomes a subject of pre-Passover teaching in the Johannine church. This ritual forms the first part of the μνημόσυνον, the summary of the haggadah and of the commemorative intent of the seder. In this act Christ is present.

However, there is also the wine to be shared. We picked up allusions to the blood of Christ in the words concerning the blood of the lamb on the lintels, and argued that this was the means by which Christ's spirit was imparted to the believer.[262] This would imply a ritual with the wine. However, there is no trace of this in *Peri Pascha* as there is of the *aphikomen* indicating a bread-rite. This absence of

---

[262] See 4.2.3 above

focus would fit in with evidence that the wine was of lesser significance in the primitive eucharist than the bread. For instance in *Acts*
there is reference to the breaking of bread. This does not necessarily
imply that there was no rite of taking wine, simply that it was of
secondary significance. In the same way the order of bread and wine
varies in the accounts of the Last Supper, and there is greater consist-
ency in the reporting of the words over the bread. Daube suggests
that this comes about due to the secondary significance of wine in the
seder.[263] Wine is not unique to Passover, is not interpreted by
Gamaliel, and is not expounded as is the unleavened bread. Since it
is not expounded in this context we may suggest that this is the reason
for the failure of Melito to make significant mention of wine.

Thus the same relative insignificance of wine in the Jewish Pesah
would appear to be mirrored in that Quartodeciman Pascha. The
wine is of different, and lesser, significance. Whereas the ἀφικόμενος is
the messianic guest, in whose presence the Messianic age is inaugurated, the wine has the function of conveying the spirit of the present
Messiah to the believer. But in accounting for the manner in which
this took place some speculation is inevitable.

However, we noted above some possibility of flexibility in the
number of cups of wine taken at the seder.[264] We may thus suggest
that at the Quartodeciman seder, after the μνημόσυνον was complete,
an additional cup was taken, perhaps passed round,[265] to represent
the blood of the lamb whose spirit was thus conveyed to protect the
believer, and that in this way the rite was completed. Some indication
of this may be found in fragment 17. The fragment mentions drinking, and it may well be that this drinking is the way in which the
brides are to be united to Christ their bridegroom. It was suggested
above that this fragment is pregnant with eschatological import, but
also that it reflected the locus of a table rite.[266] Both insights may be
true, as the eschatological realisation may be the result of the table
ritual in just the same way that the messiah is met in the rite of the
aphikomen.

Having argued that Melito's eschatology was liturgically and sacramentally realised, and having now seen that the *aphikomen* was the
basis of the Quartodeciman paschal liturgy we can see that this came

---

[263] Daube *Wine* 14-17

[264] 2.1.4

[265] That this, apart from the usual tradition of individual cups, might take place is
a suggestion of Daube *Wine* 18, based on the reports of the Last Supper of Matthew
and Mark. On the basis of a rabbinic midrash concerning the Messianic banquet he
suggests that this action might have some messianic significance

[266] 4.2.2

to be the case because the *aphikomen* was the means by which the Lord
bestowed his presence to the believers.

However we have further argued that the wine had a different
function, that of conveying to the believer the spirit of Christ. But
given that Quartodeciman eschatology was realised in the sacramental presence of the Lord it is quite possible that the functions merged
into one another. Fragment 17 is a hymn of praise to the Christ who
has united his spirit to that of the believer. Its reference to drinking
may indicate that a cup rite is its *Sitz im Leben*, and yet its language is
eschatological. It would seem that the twin functions of eschatological
fulfilment and personal communion have been merged here. On this
basis we are able to see the fragment as a fragment of a cup rite
which followed on from the rite of the *aphikomen*,[267] a rite which has
been theologically assimilated to the *aphikomen*. But whereas the existence of this fragment points to the existence of such a rite the differing theology lying behind the fragment indicates that the fragment
was not employed in the ritual at the time of Melito, and that the
fragment is not therefore from his hand.

Peri Pascha is complete on its own, but as the functions of the bread
and wine converged a congregation must have felt the need to supply
a liturgy to accompany the sharing of the cup. Fragment 17 is a
survival of this liturgy, not by Melito or from his time, but from Asia
nonetheless and from a Quartodeciman liturgical setting. By virtue of
this identical setting it is then associated with *Peri Pascha* and even
thought of as second book.

We thus have a picture of *Peri Pascha* as a commemorative rite, this
commemoration constitutive of the Quartodeciman celebration. The
focus of this μνημόσυνον fell at the end, the position both of Melito's
hymning of the ἀφικόμενος, the rite of *aphikomen* in the Jewish seder,
and the position that would be anticipated in view of the evidence
presented from the *Epistula Apostolorum*. The name of Melito is attached to this and, as we have seen, he has treated the tradition with
great creativity and originality.

Given Melito's authorship of *Peri Pascha* we might reasonably claim
that he delivered it himself at the seder at Sardis. In this case he
would preside over the rite, as does the father in a Jewish family, or
indeed as one might expect a bishop to have done in a Christian
congregation. This picture of Melito, presiding at a rite in the manner
which we would expect of a bishop, lends support to our interpreta-

---

[267] cf Chrestos "ἔργον" who suggests that further liturgical items such as this were
interposed between the four sections of *Peri Pascha* rather than being supplementary
rites

tion of *Peri Pascha* as a liturgical act. However, although Melito presides, this does not necessarily mean that he does so in his capacity of bishop.

The office of teacher was revered in the Johannine community,[268] and given his rhetorical training, and the fact that sophists functioned as teachers, it is possible that it is as teacher that Melito presides. In *Peri Pascha* we see the meeting of the house of midrash with the school of the sophist: an inscription from the synagogue refers to a σοφοδι-δάσκαλος, apparently a fusion of sophist and rabbi,[269] and it would be tempting to apply this title to Melito. This however must remain attractive speculation, since the inscription in question comes from the fourth century! More to the point we may perceive that it is as a sophist that he gives hymnic expression to the liturgy of his community.

Alternatively, given the regard in which prophecy was held among the Quartodecimans and the fact that Melito was himself a prophet,[270] we may perhaps see him as a kind of hierophant, claiming inspiration and speaking in the place of Christ. This too is in keeping with his rhetorical training; we have seen that there were several sophists who were hierophants.[271] We have already suggested that at PP103 when Melito speaks for Christ that he is speaking in a prophetic speech mode.[272] Whereas it may be suggested that this is simply a part of his rhetorical technique, and that he is employing the rhetorical technique of *ethopoiia*, we may respond firstly that there is no necessary contradiction in one who is equally wedded to the worlds of Asian Christianity and the second sophistic, and secondly to suggest that a sophist acting as hierophant and a Christian prophet might equally well claim inspiration.

For Melito to have presided over the seder it would not be necessary for him to be bishop, even though that would probably be more usual. For whereas the paterfamilias was the usual host at the Jewish seder, a distinguished rabbi was permitted to take his place.[273] Furthermore we may note the provisions of the *Didache* permitting a prophet to give thanks at length.[274] Clearly to give thanks at the

---

[268] See e.g. *I John* 2:27, *John* 3:1-2; Polycrates at Eusebius *HE* 5.21 describes John as a teacher. See also Trevett "Other Letters"
[269] cf Kraabel *Judaism* 222
[270] On Melito as prophet see 1.2.2 above and references
[271] 3.2.3 above
[272] 1.2.2
[273] Daube "Earliest Structures" 174
[274] *Didache* 10.7

eucharist was a normal prophetic function in that community. Either
of these provisions may have been in operation at Sardis. Thus it
cannot be said with certainty that Melito presides in his capacity as
Bishop; although he is Bishop he was one well qualified to declare the
haggadah, as prophet and teacher, regardless of his episcopacy, and
this may be the reason for his presidency.[275] In other words Melito's
qualification for delivering the haggadah is charismatic as well as
traditional; it may indeed be on a charismatic basis that he is the
bishop. In his capacity as bishop, appointed to that post on the basis
of his prophetic and rhetorical charism, he brings the memory of
Passover to mind, in type and reality by his rhetorical treatment of
the set themes, and makes present the reality of Christ to the community. It is a role which he takes on as prophet, as bishop and as
teacher; these roles all point to the celebratory and liturgical function
which, we have argued, was fulfilled by *Peri Pascha*.

4.2.6 *The Development of the Quartodeciman Celebration*

We have a picture of the rite of the Quartodecimans at the time of
Melito and of the role of *Peri Pascha* in this. This picture is, however,
difficult to reconcile with the evidence of ps-Hippolytus, who presents
us with a work very close in shape to that of Melito, but one which is
clearly a homily of some kind, albeit with liturgical fragments worked
in. However, in dealing with the problem presented by the evidence
of ps-Hippolytus we may recall that it was earlier suggested that *In
Sanctum Pascha*, being a later work than *Peri Pascha*, had come under
the influence of the written New Testament to a much greater extent,
and had become more forthrightly homiletic under this influence.[276]

It remains to be asked how this came about. How did a liturgy
become a homily, even granted that the liturgy was itself originally
homiletic? Ps-Hippolytus is clearly aware of traditions concerning the
Last Supper as a result of his greater exposure to the written New
Testament, and moreover he sees the Last Supper as being the locus
of the institution of the eucharist.[277] On this basis it would be difficult
for him to have recognised *Peri Pascha* as a liturgy which was quasi-
eucharistic in intent. We do not know what Melito's congregation did

---

[275] cf Cross *Early Christian Writers* 109 who sees evidence here that the functions of
presidency at Passover had passed to the Bishop by virtue of his office. Burtchaell
From Synagogue to Church 330-332 points out the interplay of charism and office in the
earliest church.
[276] 3.2.2
[277] *In Sanctum Pascha* c26

on Sundays,[278] but it may even be that the difficulty was already felt. What is suggested is that given this difficulty, and moreover given that the sharing of the elements took place at the end of the rite, a eucharistic liturgy making mention of the Last Supper was added on to the rite. This meant that the haggadah, already partly homiletic in intent, was free to become a homily in its entirety. The division between the two parts likewise became blurred as the whole of the celebration is transferred to a time after midnight in accordance with the general tendency of the late second century. The whole haggadah would thus follow on directly from the reading of Scripture without interruption, and would thus become a homily in this setting. Since *In Sanctum Pascha* concludes with a reference to the singing of the song of Moses it is possible that further ritual yet was added after the homily and before the eucharist.

On the other hand *In Sanctum Pascha* does preserve the liturgical tradition of a hymnic conclusion; the singing of the song of Moses, bound up to Passover in Jewish circles,[279] may be a piece of local tradition which has survived. Indeed, in the homiletic form of *In Sanctum Pascha* certain elements of the liturgy are preserved; not only should we note the hymnic conclusion but the opening hymn as well, with reference to the Pascha as πανήγυρις, to the διήγημα of the glory of God, to the feast as a μνημόσυνον and to Christ as the one σωμα-τικῶς ἀφικνούμενον.[280]

The fact that the rite developed in this way does not cast any doubt on the recognition of *Peri Pascha* as a liturgy. Not only would the degree of flexibility which is anticipated in liturgical keeping of Pascha/Pesah[281] lead to variations of this kind in the way the rite developed, but in the survival of the rite of Sardis, we have an insight into a very pure and primitive form of the Quartodeciman celebration.

Different developments of the Quartodeciman rite took place in the Syriac speaking churches, as a result of the significant Jewish presence in these areas and later as a result of the move to Sunday keeping which derived from submission to Nicene orthodoxy.[282] We alluded earlier to the Quartodeciman past of Syriac Christianity which was apparent from the evidence of the *Didascalia*. Apart from

---

[278] That they made eucharist is a reasonable assumption. cf Geraty "Pascha" who suggests that Sunday came to be kept as an extension of the Pascha, implying that eucharist was originally an annual event only

[279] Manns "Traces" 292 collects this evidence

[280] *IP* 1-3

[281] Daube "Earliest Structures" 174-187

[282] So Rouwhorst "Date of Easter" 1376

this specific instance, parallels between the Syriac Pascha and that of the Quartodecimans are noted by Rouwhorst,[283] the primary focus on the passion in the Syriac celebration and the fact that it is an unitary celebration embracing both passion and resurrection, the widespread use of the typology of the immolation of the paschal lamb, the blame attached to the Jews for the passion and the consequent fast during the time of the Jewish festivities. To these we may add the fact that baptism appears not to have been part of the Syriac rite until comparatively late (for which reason it receives little comment)[284] and the secondary role played by wine in the eucharistic celebration.[285] Although Pascha was no longer celebrated in Syria on the fourteenth of Nisan, the Quartodeciman past of these congregations had clearly left its mark on their celebration.

The outline of Pascha celebrated by Aphraahat may indeed be reconstructed since he describes it briefly.[286] He mentions fasting and prayer, praise and psalm-singing, unction and baptism, and finally the eucharist. The unction and baptism are additions to the rite, and for this reason there is little comment about these aspects; with these taken out we may see that the basic outline of a fasting gathering culminating in a joyful eucharist has been preserved. However, there would have been keenly felt difficulties about recognising the μνημόσυνον as a eucharist since, as a result of the harmonisation of the Gospel accounts, the Last Supper is recognised in the Syrian churches as being the true fulfilment of the Pascha, and claimed as such in their rites.[287] We may thus anticipate that the commemoration would in some way be altered to take account of this.

We may perceive the remains of the haggadah in the word ܐܬܫܒܘܚܬܐ, translated above as "praise". This is the word used at *Exodus* 15:1, and may therefore be taken to in this context to refer to hymn-singing. Its root, ܫܒܚ, translates such Greek words as ὕμνω, αἰνῶ and εὐχαριστῶ. Thus the haggadah survives, understood as a prose hymn or panegyric in the Syriac rites. The first part likewise becomes a hymn, the *madrasha*. The hymnic tendency comes here to the fore just as the homiletic tendency is most present in *In Sanctum Pascha*.

We may thus see that the Quartodeciman liturgy varied, as indeed did the Jewish ritual on which it was based. Further variations came about as the ritual spread from Palestine and was received in different

---

[283] Rouwhorst *Hymnes* 128
[284] Rouwhorst *Hymnes* 201
[285] Rouwhorst *Hymnes* 90-91
[286] *Demonstratio* 12.13
[287] Rouwhorst *Hymnes* 89-92; Cantalamessa *Pasqua della Salvezza* 221-223

communities. The Quartodecimans have so often been treated as though they were a denomination with a denominational degree of uniformity, but whereas their paschal rites would presumably have much in common, we must recognise the possibility of change in local custom and manner of celebration as well as throughout history.

However, although we may say that there was no such thing as "the" Quartodeciman liturgy, we may perceive a basic outline of table celebration with haggadah, preceded by a vigil. This outline is preserved in all evidence of the primitive paschal celebration. This evidence is all Syrian or Asian, but we may suggest that it is this pattern also which was once known at Rome,[288] in view of its deriva-

---

[288] The question of the original Roman practice turns on *HE* 5.24, where Irenaeus reports that Anicetus and Polycarp were in agreement even though one was "keeping" and one was not, and that bishops of Rome before the time of Soter did not "keep". The question is therefore one of the object of τηρεῖν. Richard "Question Pascale" revives an old suggestion that the object is πάσχα, and reads this passage as stating that Rome did not keep an annual festival at this time. Mohrmann "Conflit" responds by demonstrating that τηρεῖν is never used with a festival as its object, but that the object is "the fourteenth day", in other words that Rome had always kept Pascha, and on Sunday, rather than on the fourteenth. Rouwhorst "Quartodeciman Passover" 158-159 would appear to assent to this reconstruction, whereas Talley *Origins* 23-4 appears to agree with Richard; however when he brings into play the question the *Epistula Apostolorum* 15 raises about the propriety of keeping Pascha he is confusing a dispute in Rome with one which was specifically Asian. It is even possible, however, that Rome was Quartodeciman from the beginning, as Hall "Origins of Easter" suggests. He notes that the context of Irenaeus' report is a discussion concerning fasting practice, rather than the day on which to celebrate. From this he deduces that since there was disagreement about the fast, there must have been agreement about the day. Campenhausen "Ostertermin oder Osterfasten?" agrees with Hall that the fast is intended, but cannot accept that Rome was ever Quartodeciman; rather he believes that disagreement about the nature of the fast derived from disagreement over the day. The only answer to this nest of problems is to cut through them. In fact a variety of practices were probably in effect from the beginning of Roman Christianity, and continued at least to the time of Victor. This may have involved the keeping of an annual festival in some Roman communities but not in others, and may have involved different methods of computing the Pascha among those who kept (on which different methods see Talley *Origins* 7-12 and references;) Victor seeks some conformity across the oikumene because of the variety of practices at Rome brought in by immigrants, especially from the eastern Empire. When, as would appear to have been the majority Roman practice, Pascha is kept on a Sunday regardless of the day it is simple for confusion to arise between the (normal) Sunday eucharist and the paschal commemoration. Evidence of Asian Quartodeciman practice at Rome may perhaps be found in the paschal tables of the statue found on the Via Tiburtina. On this see Brent *Hippolytus* 63-68. Beyond Rome, Rouwhorst "Quartodeciman Passover" 158-159 suggests that Quartodeciman practice might have been further extended and that this is the reason for the letters sent to Victor from synods in Palestine, Gaul, Pontus and Palestine (*HE* 5.23). Although there can be no certainty on this, given the wide distribution of Asians throughout the empire this is a possibility. In any event, as Rouwhorst points out, there is little theological distinction been Pascha and Easter.

tion from the pattern of the Passover of the Jews,[289] and which continued to be kept by Asians in Rome.

4.2.7 *Conclusion: Peri Pascha and the Quartodeciman Paschal Liturgy*

Having investigated the development of the Quartodeciman Pascha in the time after that of Melito we reach the end of our investigation. From our review of the evidence, and in particular from our reading of *Peri Pascha* we may see that the Quartodecimans at Sardis gathered, fasting in memory of the sufferings of the Lord, before midnight of the fourteenth Nisan/Xanthikos. They heard a reading from *Exodus* 12 with a *diegema*, and kept watch with their lamps lit. Around midnight they broke their fast and joined in a joyous table rite, with music and dancing, as they realised the presence of the risen Lord among them and received his spirit. He became present to them through the medium of the *aphikomen* and of the cup, and most importantly through the liturgy by which they remembered the acts of their salvation.

Peri Pascha is that liturgy. It is a complex work, containing in itself a number of forms, and a number of functions, as well as simultaneously being a product of Hebrew tradition and Hellenistic culture. Overall it is a commemoration of the sufferings and triumph of the now exalted saviour-lamb; but as part of this we find teaching, deriving from its function in the vigil, the realisation of eschatological fulfilment as the climax of the rite and the hymn with which the rite concluded as celebration of the completed work of Christ. All of these are bound into the haggadah which was the ultimate basis of this ritual commemoration. Through this rite and its accompanying actions the benefits of Pascha are mediated to the believer.

All these aspects are present in various ways in the relics of the paschal celebration of other communities, but in the commemorative rite which is *Peri Pascha* they may be found gathered together in what may now be recognised as the most ancient Christian liturgy known to us in its completeness.

---

[289] This is not a reversion to the idea of a united form of Judaism, since we have learnt to accept a degree of variety in Passover rites. But nonetheless, for Jews as for Quartodecimans, despite a variety of practice in detail, there was a basic pattern held in common in the first century.

BIBLIOGRAPHY

Note: This Bibliography contains only works to which direct reference is made in the course of the work. Further bibliography on Melito may be found at R.M. Mainka "Melito von Sardes, eine Bibliographische Übersicht" *Claretianum* 5 (1965) 225-255 and Hubertus Drobner "15 Jahre Forschung zu Meliton von Sardes (1965-1980): eine kritische Bibliographie" *VigChr* 36 (1982) 313-333

Graham Anderson *The Second Sophistic: a Cultural Phenomenon in the Roman Empire* (London: RKP, 1993)
D.E. Aune *The New Testament in its Literary Environment* (Cambridge: Clarke, 1987)
W. Bacher *Die Proömien in der alten Jüdischen Homilie* (Leipzig: Hinrichs, 1913)
Gordon J. Bahr "The Seder of Passover and the Eucharistic Words" *NovT* 12 (1970) 181-202
D.L. Balch "Two Apologetic Encomia: Dionysius on Rome and Josephus on the Jews" *JSJ* 13 (1982) 102-22
Gustav Bardy (review of Schmidt *Gespräche Jesu*) *RB* 30 (1921) 110-134
L.W. Barnard *Athenagoras* (Paris: Beauchesne, 1972)
C.K. Barrett *The Gospel of John and Judaism* (London: SPCK, 1975)
Richard Bauckham "Papias and Polycrates on the Origin of the Fourth Gospel" *JTS* (ns) 44 (1993) 24-69
W. Bauer *Orthodoxy and Heresy in Earliest Christianity* (ETr) (Philadelphia: Fortress, 1971)
P.F. Beatrice *La Lavanda dei Piedi* (Rome: BEL Subsidia 28, 1983)
C. Bigg *Epistles of St. Peter and St. Jude*[2] ICC (Edinburgh: Clark, 1902)
Per Bilde *Flavius Josephus: between Jerusalem and Rome* (Sheffield: JSOT, 1988)
Matthew Black *The Scrolls and Christian Origins* (New York: Scribners, 1961)
Matthew Black *An Aramaic Approach to the Gospels and Acts*[3] (Oxford: Clarendon, 1967)
J. Blank *Meliton von Sardes "Vom Passa"* (Freiburg im Breisgau: Sophia, 3 1963)
Baruch M. Bokser *The Origins of the Seder: The Passover Rite and Early Rabbinic Judaism* (Berkeley: University of California, 1984)
P.A.H. de Boer *Gedenken und Gedächtnis in der Welt der Alten Testaments* (Stuttgart: Kohlhammer, 1960)
Campbell Bonner "Two Problems in Melito's Homily on the Passion" *HThR* 31 (1938) 175-182
Campbell Bonner *The Homily on the Passion by Melito Bishop of Sardis and some fragments of the apocryphal Ezekiel* (London: Studies and Documents 12, 1940)
Campbell Bonner "A Supplementary Note on the Opening of Melito's Homily" *HThR* 36 (1943) 317-319
Campbell Bonner "The Text of Melito's Homily" *VigChr* 3 (1949) 184-185
M.E. Boring "The Influence of Christian Prophecy on the Johannine Portrayal of the Paraclete and Jesus" *NTS* 25 (1979) 113-123

Peder Borgen *Bread from Heaven: an Exegetical Study of the Concept of Manna in the Gospel of John and the Writings of Philo* (Leiden: Brill, 1965)

Peder Borgen "Observations on the Targumic Character of the Prologue of John" *NTS* 16 (1969-1970) 288-295

H. Botermann "Die Synagoge von Sardis: eine Synagoge aus dem 4 Jahrhundert" *ZNW* 81 (1990) 103-121

B. Botte "La Question Pascale" *Maison Dieu* 41 (1955) 84-95

B. Botte "Pascha" *OrSyr* 8 (1963) 213-226

André Boulanger *Aelius Aristide et la Sophistique dans la Province d'Asie au Deuxième Siècle de nôtre Ère* (Paris: Bibliotheque des Écoles Françaises d'Athènes et de Rome 126, 1923)

G.W. Bowersock *Greek Sophists in the Roman Empire* (Oxford: Clarendon, 1969)

J.W. Bowker "Speeches in Acts: a Study in proem and yelammadenu form" *NTS* 14 (1967-1968) 96-111

J.W. Bowker *The Targums and Rabbinic Literature* (Cambridge: CUP, 1969)

Paul Bradshaw *The Search for the Origins of Christian Worship* (London: SPCK, 1992)

Allen Brent *Hippolytus and the Roman Church in the Third Century* (Leiden: Brill, 1995)

F.E. Brightman "The Quartodeciman Question" *JTS* 25 (1924) 254-270

Sebastian P. Brock "Syriac and Greek Hymnography: Problems of Origin" *StPatr* 16 (Berlin: TU 129, 1985) 77-81

M. Brocke "On the Jewish Origin of the Improperia" *Immanuel* 7 (1977) 44-51

R.E. Brown *The Death of the Messiah* (London: Geoffrey Chapman, 1994)

Felix Buffière *Heraclitus Allegories d'Homère* (Paris: Belles Lettres, 1962)

James Tunstead Burtchaell *From Synagogue to Church* (Cambridge: CUP, 1992)

Allen Cabaniss "The University of Mississippi Coptic Papyrus Manuscript: a Paschal Lectionary?" *NTS* 8 (1961-1962) 70-72

W.H. Cadman "The Christian Pascha and the Day of the Crucifixion: Nisan 14 or 15" *StPatr* 5 (Berlin: TU 80, 1962) 8-16

Hans Freiherr von Campenhausen "Ostertermin oder Osterfasten? Zum Verstandnis des Irenäusbriefs an Viktor" *VigChr* 28 (1974) 114-138

R. Cantalamessa "Meliton de Sardes: une Christologie antignostique du IIe Siècle" *RevSR* 37 (1963) 1-26

R. Cantalamessa *L'Omelia 'In S. Pascha' dello ps-Ippolyto di Roma* (Milan: Vita e Pensiero, 1967)

R. Cantalamessa "Questioni Melitoniane: Melitone e i latini; Melitone e i quartodecimani" *RSLR* 6 (1970) 245-267

R. Cantalamessa *La Pasqua della Salvezza* (Turin: Marietti, 1971)

Deborah Bleicher Carmichael "David Daube on the Eucharist and the Passover Seder" *JSNT* 42 (1991) 45-67

Odo Casel "Art und Sinn der ältesten christlichen Osterfeier" *JLW* 14 (1938) 1-78

Sofia Cavaletti "Le Fonti del "Seder" Pasquale" *Bibbia e Oriente* 7 (1965) 153-160

Bruce Chilton *A Feast of Meanings: Eucharistic Theologies from Jesus through Johannine Circles* (Leiden: Brill, 1994)

Fritz Chenderlin *Do This as My Memorial* (Rome: AnBib 99, 1982)

Panagiotos Chrestos "Τὸ ἔργον τοῦ Μελίτωνος Περὶ Πάσχα καὶ ἡ Ἀκολουθία τοῦ Πάθους" *Kleronomia* 1 (1969) 65-78

M.L. Clarke *The Roman Mind* (London: Cohen and West, 1956)

Lynne Cohick "Melito of Sardis *Peri Pascha* and its Israel" forthcoming *HThR*

Leopold Cohn "An apocryphal work ascribed to Philo of Alexandria" *JQR* 10 (1898) 277-332

R.H. Connolly *Didascalia Apostolorum* (Oxford: Clarendon, 1929)

F.M. Cross (Review) *JTS* (ns) 11 (1960) 162-163

F.M. Cross *Early Christian Fathers* (London: Duckworth, 1960) 103-109

O. Cullmann *The Johannine Circle* (ETr) (London: SCM, 1976)

G. Cuming "The Anaphora of St. Mark: a study in development" *Le Muséon* 95 (1982) 115-129

N.A. Dahl "Anamnesis" *STh* 1 (1947) 69-95

Robert J. Daley *Christian Sacrifice: The Judaeo-Christian Background before Origen* (Washington: Catholic University of America, 1978)

Jean Daniélou "Figure et Événement chez Meliton de Sardes" *Neotestamentica et Patristica: Freundesgabe Cullmann* (Leiden: NT Supp 6, 1962) 282-292

Jean Daniélou "Traversée de la Mer Rouge et Baptême aux Premiers Siècles" *Rech Sc Rel* 33 (1946) 402-430

Jean Daniélou *The Theology of Jewish Christianity*: (ETr) (London: DLT, 1964)

David Daube "Rabbinic Methods of Interpretation and Hellenistic Rhetoric" *HUCA* 22 (1949) 239-264

David Daube *The New Testament and Rabbinic Judaism* (London: Athlone, 1956)

David Daube "The Earliest Structures of the Gospels" *NTS* 5 (1958-1959) 174-187

David Daube *He That Cometh* (London: Diocese of London, 1966)

David Daube *Wine in the Bible* (London: Diocese of London, 1974)

David Daube "Typology in Josephus" *JJS* 31 (1980) 18-36

W.D. Davies *Paul and Rabbinic Judaism*[3] (London: SPCK, 1970)

Roger le Déaut *La Nuit Pascale* (Rome: AnBib 22, 1963)

Roger le Déaut (Review) *Biblica* 48 (1967) 141-145

Roger le Déaut "A propos d'une definition du Midrash" *Biblica* 50 (1969) 395-413

Attilio Degrassi *I Fasti Consolari dell' Impero Romano* (Rome: Sussidi Eruditi 3, 1952)

C.H. Dodd *The Interpretation of the Fourth Gospel* (Cambridge: CUP, 1953)

F.G. Downing "Ethical Pagan Theism and the Speeches in Acts" *NTS* 27 (1980) 544-563

C. Dugmore "A Note on the Quartodecimans" *StPatr* 4 (Berlin: TU 79, 1961) 411-421

Edward J. Duncan *Baptism in the Demonstrations of Aphraates the Persian Sage* (Washington: Catholic University of America Studies in Christian Antiquity 8, 1945)

J.D.G. Dunn "Prophetic 'I'-sayings and the Jesus Tradition: the Importance of testing Prophetic Utterances within Early Christianity" *NTS* 24 (1978) 175-198

Hieronymus Engberding "Die Syrische Anaphora der zwölf Apostel und ihre Paralleltexte" *OrChr* 34 (1937) 213-247

Eugéne de la Faye *Origéne: sa Vie, son Oevre, sa Pensée* II (Paris: Ernest Leroux, 1927)

Karl Christian Felmy "Was unterscheidet diese Nacht von allen anderen Nächten?" *JLH* 27 (1983) 1-15

Rupert Feneberg *Christliche Passafeier und Abendmahl* (Munich: Kösel, 1971)

John Fenwick *Fourth Century Anaphoral Construction Techniques* (Bramcote: Grove, 1986)

John Fenwick *The Missing Oblation* (Bramcote: Grove, 1989)

David A. Fiensy *Prayers Alleged to be Jewish: an Examination of the Constitutiones Apostolorum* (Chico: Scholars, 1985)

Jack Finegan *Handbook of Biblical Chronology* (Princeton: Princeton UP, 1964)

Lewis Finkelstein "The Birkat ha-Mazon" *JQR* 19 (1928-1929) 210-268

Lewis Finkelstein "The Oldest Midrash: Pre-Rabbinic Ideals and Teachings in the Passover Haggadah" *HThR* 31 (1938) 291-317

Lewis Finkelstein "Pre-Maccabean Documents in the Passover Haggadah" *HThR* 35 (1942) 291-332 and 36 (1943) 1-38

Lewis Finkelstein "The Origin of the Hallel" *HUCA* 23 (pt2) (1950-1951) 319-337

Elisabeth Schüssler Fiorenza "The Quest for the Johannine School: The Book of Revelation and the Fourth Gospel" *The Book of Revelation: Justice and Judgement* (Philadelphia: Fortress, 1985) 85-113

J.A. Fitzmyer *The Genesis Apocryphon of Qumran Cave 1: a Commentary* (Rome: Biblical Institute, 1971)

D. Flusser "Hebrew Improperia" *Immanuel* 4 (1974) 51-54

D. Flusser "Some Notes on Easter and the Passover Haggadah" *Immanuel* 7 (1977) 52-60

Edward Foley *Foundations of Christian Music* (Bramcote: Grove, 1992)

Edwin D. Freed *Old Testament Quotations in the Gospel of John* (Leiden: Brill, 1965)

R.H. Fuller "The Double Origin of the Eucharist" *BibRes* 8 (1963) 60-72

B. Gärtner *John 6 and the Jewish Passover* (Lund: Coniectanea Neotestamentica 17, 1959) 25-29

A. Gelston *The Eucharistic Prayer of Addai and Mari* (Oxford: Clarendon, 1992)

Lawrence T. Geraty "The Pascha and the Origin of Sunday Observance" *AUSS* 3 (1965) 85-96

James E. Goehring *The Crosby Schøyen Codex: MS 193 in the Schøyen Collection* (Louvain: Peeters, 1990)

O. Giordano "Il Millenarismo orientale alla fine del secondo secolo" *Helikon* 3 (1963) 328-352

J. van Goudoever *Biblical Calendars*[2] (Leiden: Brill, 1961)

R.M. Grant "Melito of Sardis on Baptism" *VigChr* 4 (1950) 33-36

R.M. Grant *Greek Apologists of the Second Century* (London: SCM, 1988)

Robert M. Grant "Five Apologists and Marcus Aurelius" *VigChr* 42 (1988) 1-17

A. Grillmeier *Christ in Christian Tradition I* (ETr) (London: Mowbray, 1975)

J. de Matons Grosdidier *Romanos le Mélode et les Origines de la Poesie Religieuse a Byzance* (Paris: Beauchesne, 1977)

H. Gross "Zur Wurzel zkr" *BZ* 4 (1960) 227-237

H. Grotz (Review) *ZKTh* 90 (1968) 494-495

Marie-Joseph le Guillou "La Résurrection dans le *Peri Pascha* de Méliton de Sardes" *Resurrexit: Actes du Symposium International sur la Résurrection de Jesus* Ed. E. Dhanis (Rome: Libreria Editrice Vaticana, 1974) 532-545

S.G. Hall "Melito's Paschal Homily and the *Acts of John*" *JTS* (ns) 17 (1966) 95-98

S.G. Hall "Melito *Peri Pascha* 1 and 2. Text and Interpretation" *Kyriakon: Festschrift Johannes Quasten* ed. Patrick Granfield and Josef A. Jungmann (Münster: Aschendorff, 1970) 236-248

S.G. Hall "Melito in the Light of the Passover Haggadah" *JTS* (ns) 22 (1971) 29-46

S.G. Hall "Paschal Baptism" *StEv* 6 (1973) (Berlin: TU 112, 1973) 239-251

S.G. Hall "The Christology of Melito: a Misrepresentation Exposed" *StPatr* 13 (Berlin: TU 116, 1975) 154-168

S.G. Hall *Melito of Sardis: On Pascha and Fragments* (Oxford: Clarendon, 1979)

S.G. Hall "The Origins of Easter" *StPatr* 15 (Berlin: TU 128, 1984) 554-567

Thomas Halton "Stylistic Device in Melito *Peri Pascha*" in *Kyriakon: Festschrift Johannes Quasten* ed. Patrick Granfield and Josef A. Jungmann (Münster: Aschendorff, 1970) 249-255

G.M.A. Hanfmann, Fikret Yegül, and John S. Crawford "The Roman and Late Antique Period" *Sardis from Prehistoric to Roman Times: Results of the Archaeological Exploration of Sardis 1958-1975* Ed. G.M.A. Hanfmann (Cambridge MA: Harvard UP, 1983) 139-167

G.M.A. Hanfmann and Hans Buchwald "Christianity: Churches and Cemeteries" *Sardis from Prehistoric to Roman Times: Results of the Archaeological Exploration of Sardis 1958-1975* Ed. G.M.A. Hanfmann (Cambridge MA: Harvard UP, 1983) 191-210

A. Hansen *The Sitz im Leben of the Paschal Homily of Melito of Sardis with special reference to the Paschal Festival in Early Christianity* (Diss. Northwestern University, 1968)

R.P.C. Hanson *Allegory and Event* (London: SCM, 1959)

D.J. Harrington Charles Perrot and Pierre-Maurice Bogaert *Pseudo-Philon: les Antiquités Bibliques* II (Paris: Cerf, 1976)

A.E. Harvey "Melito and Jerusalem" *JTS* (ns) 17 (1966) 401-440

Gerald F. Hawthorne "Christian Baptism and the Contribution of Melito of Sardis Reconsidered" *Studies in New Testament and Early Christian Literature* Ed. D.E. Aune (Leiden: Brill, 1972) 241-251

G.F. Hawthorne "Christian Prophets and the Sayings of Jesus: Evidence of and Criteria for" *SBL Seminar Papers* 1975 (Vol. 2) (Missoula: Scholars, 1975) 105-129

P.J. Heawood "The Time of the Last Supper" *JQR* (ns) 42 (1951-1952) 37-44

Joseph Heinemann "The Triennial Lectionary Cycle" *JJS* 19 (1968) 41-48

Joseph Heinemann "The Proem in the Aggadic Midrashim" *Studies in Aggadah and Folk Literature* Ed. Joseph Heinemann and Dov Noy (Jerusalem: Scripta Hierosolymitana 22, 1971) 100-122

C.J. Hemer *The Letters to the Seven Churches of Asia in their Local Setting* (Sheffield: JSNT Supplement 11, 1986)

Martin Hengel *Judaism and Hellenism* (ETr) (London: SCM, 1974)

Martin Hengel *Earliest Christianity* (ETr) (London: SCM, 1986)

Martin Hengel *The Johannine Question* (ETr) (London: SCM, 1989)

Julian Hills *Tradition and Composition in the Epistula Apostolorum* (Minneapolis: Fortress, 1990)

D.A.G. Hinks "Tria Genera Causarum" *CQ* 30 (1936) 170-176

Manfred Hornschuh *Studien zur Epistula Apostolorum* (Berlin: Patristische Texte und Studien 5, 1965)

J.K. Howard "Passover and Eucharist in the Fourth Gospel" *SJT* 20 (1967) 329-337

W. Huber *Passa und Ostern: Untersuchungen zur Osterfeier der alten Kirche* (Berlin: BZNW 35, 1969)

John Hull *Hellenistic Magic and the Synoptic Tradition* (London: SCM, 1974)

Nils Hyldahl "Zum Titel *Peri Pascha* bei Meliton" *STh* 19 (1965) 55-67

Sitki Isa Bülent Iplikçioglu *Die Repräsentanten des senatorishen Reichsdienst in Asia bis Diokletian im Spiegel der ephesishen Inschriften* (Vienna: Verband der Wissenschaftlichen Gesellschaften Österreichs, 1983)

Sheldon R. Isenberg "On the Jewish Palestinian Origins of the Peshitta to the Pentateuch" *JBL* 90 (1971) 69-81

M.R. James *The Biblical Antiquities of Philo* (with prolegomena by Louis H. Feldman) (Repr.) (New York: Ktav, 1971)

R. Jasper and G. Cuming *Prayers of the Eucharist: Early and Reformed* (New York: Pueblo, 1987)

J. Jeremias *The Eucharistic Words of Jesus* (ETr) (London: SCM, 1966)

S.E. Johnson "Laodicaea and its Neighbours" *BA* 13 (1950) 1-18

S.E. Johnson "Early Christianity in Asia Minor" *JBL* 77 (1958) 1-17

S.E. Johnson "Christianity in Sardis" *Early Christian Origins* Ed. Allen Wikgren (Chicago: Quadrangle, 1960) 81-90

S.E. Johnson "Asia Minor and Early Christianity" *Christianity, Judaism and other Greco-Roman Cults II* Ed. J. Neusner (Leiden: Brill, 1975) 74-145

G. Johnston *The Spirit Paraclete in the Gospel of John* (Cambridge: CUP, 1970)

A.H.M. Jones *The Greek City from Alexander to Justinian* (Oxford: Clarendon, 1940)

Douglas Jones "'Ανάμνησις in the LXX and the Interpretation of *I Corinthians* 11:25" *JTS* 6 (ns) (1955) 183-191

B. Jongelin C.J. Labuschagne, A.S. van der Woude *Aramaic Texts from Qumran* (Leiden: Brill, 1976)

P. Kahle "Was Melito's Homily on the Passion Originally Written in Syriac?" *JTS* 44 (1943) 52-56

Stanley Kazan "Isaac of Antioch's Homily against the Jews" *OrChr* 45 (1961) 30-53; 46 (1962) 87-95; 47 (1963) 89-97; 49 (1965) 57-78

F.G. Kenyon *The Chester Beatty Biblical Papyri: Fascicle 8, Enoch and Melito* (London: Emery Walker, 1940)

E.J. Kilmartin "Liturgical Influence on *John* 6" *CBQ* 22 (1960) 183-191

Guido Kisch *Pseudo-Philo's Liber Antiquitatum Biblicarum* (Indiana: University of Notre Dame, 1949)

Helmut Koester "ΓΝΩΜΑΙ ΔΙΑΦΟΡΑΙ: The Origin and Nature of Diversification in the History of Early Christianity" *HThR* 58 (1965) 279-318

Hans Kosmala "Das tut zu meinem Gedächtnis" *NovT* 4 (1960) 81-94

H.B. Kossen "Who were the Greeks of *John* 12:20?" *Studies in John presented to J.N. Sevenster* (Leiden: NovT Supp 24, 1970) 97-110

A.T. Kraabel *Judaism in Asia Minor in the Imperial Period* (Diss. Harvard, 1968)

A.T. Kraabel "ΥΨΙΣΤΟΣ and the Synagogue at Sardis" *GRBS* 10 (1969) 81-93

R.A. Kraft "Barnabas' Isaiah Text and Melito's Paschal Homily" *JBL* 80 (1961) 371-373

R.A. Kraft "In Search of "Jewish Christianity" and its "Theology": Problems of Definition and Methodology" *Judéo-Christianisme* (Paris: Recherches de Sciences Religieuses, 1972) 81-92

R.A. Kraft "The Multiform Jewish Heritage of Early Christianity" *Christianity, Judaism and other Graeco-Roman Cults* Ed. J. Neusner (Leiden: Brill, 1975) 175-199

G. Kretschmar "Christliches Passa im 2 Jahrhundert" *RechSR* 60 (1972) 287-323

D.J. Ladouceur "The Language of Josephus" *JStJ* 14 (1983) 18-38

G.W.H. Lampe and K.J. Woollcombe *Essays on Typology* (London: SCM, 1957)

J.Z. Lauterbach "The Ancient Jewish Allegorists in Talmud and Midrash" *JQR* (ns) 1 (1910-1911) 291-333 and 503-31

H.J. Lawlor and J.E.L. Oulton *Eusebius: The Ecclesiastical History and the Martyrs of Palestine* II (London: SPCK, 1928)

M.R. Lehmann "I Q Genesis Apocryphon in the light of the Targumim and Midrashim" *RQ* 1 (1958-1959) 249-263

Saul Liebermann *Hellenism in Jewish Palestine*² (New York: Jewish Theological Seminary of America, 1962)

H. Lietzmann *"Epistula Apostolorum"* (Review) *ZNW* 20 (1921) 173-176

J. Lieu *Image and Reality: the Jews in the World of the Christians in the Second Century* (Edinburgh: Clark, 1996)

L. Ligier "The Origins of the Eucharistic Prayer" *StLiturg* 9 (1973) 161-185

Barnabas Lindars *Behind the Fourth Gospel* (London: SPCK, 1971)

Barnabas Lindars *The Gospel of John* (Grand Rapids: Eerdmans, 1972)

B. Lohse *Das Passafest der Quartadecimaner* (Gütersloh: Bertelsmann, 1953)

P. Maas "Das Kontakion" *ByZ* 19 (1910) 285-306

Robert S. MacLennan *Early Christian Texts on Jews and Judaism* (Atlanta: Scholars, 1990)

Menahem Macina "Fonction Liturgique et Eschatologique de l'Anamnese Eucharistique" *EL* 102 (1988) 3-25

D. Magie *Roman Rule in Asia Minor* II (Princeton: Princeton UP, 1950)

A. Manis "Melito of Sardis: Hermeneutic and Context" *GOTR* 32 (1987) 387-401

Jacob Mann *The Bible as Read and Preached in the Old Synagogue* (Vol. 1) (Cincinnati: Private Publication, 1940)

Frédéric Manns "Traces d'une Haggadah Chrétienne dans l'Apocalypse de Jean?" *Anton.* 56 (1981) 265-295

M.G. Mara *Évangile de Pierre* (Paris: Cerf, 1973)

A. Marmorstein "The Background of the Haggadah" *HUCA* 6 (1929) 141-204

Henri Marrou *The History of Education in Antiquity* (ETr) (London: Sheed and Ward, 1956)

S. Maybaum *Die ältesten Phasen in der Entwicklung der jüdischen Predigt* (Berlin: Dümmler, 1901)

E. Mazza "Omelie Pasquali e Birkat ha-Mazon: Fonti dell' Anafora di Ippolito?" *EphLit* 27 (1983) 409-481

J.I.H. McDonald "Some Comments on the Form of Melito's Paschal Homily" *StPatr* 12 (Berlin: TU, 115 1975) 104-112

Wayne Meeks "Am I a Jew?" *Christianity, Judaism and other Greco-Roman Cults* Ed. J. Neusner (Leiden: Brill, 1975) 161-185

H. Metzger *St. Paul's Journeys in the Greek Orient* (ETr) (London: SCM, 1955)

Stephen Mitchell *Anatolia: Land Men and Gods in Asia Minor* II (Oxford: Clarendon, 1993)

D.G. Mitten "A New Look at Ancient Sardis" *BA* 29 (1966) 38-68

Christine Mohrmann "Pascha, Passio, Transitus" *EL* 66 (1952)

Christine Mohrmann "Le Conflit Pascale au 2e siècle" *VigChr* 16 (1962) 154-171

George Foote Moore *Judaism in the First Centuries of the Christian Era* (Cambridge MA: Harvard UP, 1927)

Alois Müller *Ecclesia-Maria: die Einheit Marias und der Kirche* (Freiburg: Paradosis 5, 1955)

Robert Murray *Symbols of Church and Kingdom* (Cambridge: CUP, 1975)

P. Nautin "L'Homélie de "Méliton" sur la Passion" *RHE* 44 (1949) 429-438

P. Nautin *Une Homélie Inspirée du Traité sur la Pâque d' Hippolyte* (Paris: Cerf, 1950)

Pierre Nautin *Lettres et Écrivains Chrétiens des IIe et IIIe Siècles* (Paris: Cerf, 1961)

Jacob Neusner *Pesiqta de Rab Kahana: An Analytical Translation* (Vol. 2) (Atlanta: Scholars, 1987)

G.W.E. Nickelsburg *Jewish Literature between the Bible and the Mishnah* (London: SCM, 1981)

De Lacey O'Leary *The Apostolical Constitutions and Cognate Documents* (London: SPCK, 1906)

Othmar Perler *Ein Hymnus zur Ostervigil von Meliton? (Papyrus Bodmer 12)* (Freiburg: Paradosis 15, 1960)

Othmar Perler "L'Évangile de Pierre et Méliton de Sardes" *RB* 71 (1964) 584-59

Othmar Perler *Méliton de Sardes: Sur la Pâque* (Paris: Cerf, 1966)

R.I. Pervo "Johannine Trajectories in the Acts of John" *Apocrypha* 3 (1992) 47-68

J.J. Petuchowski "Do This in Remembrance of Me" *JBL* 76 (1957) 293-298

J.J. Petuchowski "Wirkliche und Vermeintliche Messianische Elemente der Seder" *Judaica* 41 (1985) 37-44

S. Pines "From Darkness into Great Light" *Immanuel* 4 (1974) 47-51

W.E. Pitt "The Anamnesis and Institution Narrative in the Liturgy of the *Apostolic Constitutions* Book 8" *JEH* 9 (1958) 1-7

Gary Porton "Midrash: Palestinian Jews and the Hebrew Bible in the Greco Roman Period" *Aufstieg und Niedergang der Römischen Welt* 2.19.2 Ed. Wolfgang Haase (Berlin: De Gruyter, 1979) 103-138

V.S. Pseftogas Μελίτωνος Σαρδέων Περὶ τοῦ Πάσχα δύο (Thessaloniki: Analecta Vlatadon 8, 1971) (French abstract 244-247)

G. Racle "A Propos du Christ-Père dans l'*Homélie Pascale* de Méliton de Sardes" *RechSR* 50 (1962) 400-408

G. Racle "Perspectives Christologiques de l'Homélie Pascale de Méliton de

Sardes" *StPatr* 9 (Berlin: TU 94 1966) 263-269

Tessa Rajak *Flavius Josephus: Jewish History and the Greek World* (Diss. Oxford, 1974)

W.M. Ramsay *The Historical Geography of Asia Minor* (London: Supplementary Papers of the Royal Geographical Society 4, 1890)

E.C. Ratcliff "The Original Form of the Anaphora of Addai and Mari: a Suggestion" *JTS* 30 (1929) 23-32

Günter Reim *Studien zum Alttestamentlichen Hintergrund des Johannesevangeliums* (Cambridge: CUP, 1974)

M. Richard "La Question Pascale au 2e siècle" *OrSyr* 6 (1961) 179-212

Cyril C. Richardson "The Quartodecimans and the Synoptic Chronology" *HThR* 33 (1940) 177-190

Cyril C. Richardson "A New Solution to the Quartodeciman Riddle" *JTS* (ns) 24 (1973) 74-84

G. Richter "Zur Formgeschichte und literarischen Einheit von *Joh* 6 31-58" *ZNW* 60 (1969) 21-55

G.A.M. Rouwhorst "The date of Easter in the Twelfth Demonstration of Aphraates" *Studia Patristica* 18 Ed E.A. Livingstone (Oxford: Pergamum, 1982) 1374-1380

G.A.M. Rouwhorst *Les Hymnes Pascales d'Ephrem de Nisibe* (2 Vols) (Leiden: Brill 1989)

G.A.M. Rouwhorst "La Célébration de l'eucharistie dans l'Église Primitive" *Questions Liturgiques* 74 (1993) 89-112

G.A.M. Rouwhorst "The Quartodeciman Passover and the Jewish Pesach" *Questions Liturgiques* 77 (1996) 152-173

G.A.M. Rouwhorst "Jewish Liturgical Traditions in Early Syriac Christianity" *VigChr* 51 (1997) 72-93

F. Mendoza Ruiz "Los Hapax Legomena en la Homilia Pascual de Meliton de Sardes" *StPatr* 12 (Berlin: TU 115, 1975) 238-241

D.A. Russell *Plutarch* (London: Duckworth, 1973)

D.A. Russell *Criticism in Antiquity* (London: Duckworth, 1981)

Jorg Christian Salzmann *Lehren und Ermahnen: zur Geschichte des christlichen Wortgottesdienstes in der ersten drei Jahrhunderten* (Tübingen: WUNT 2 Reihe 59, 1994)

Samuel Sandmel "Parallellomania" *JBL* 81 (1962) 1-13

K. Schäferdiek "Herkunft und Interesse der alten Johannesakten" *ZNW* 74 (1983) 247-267

Jefim Schirmann "Hebrew Liturgical Poetry and Christian Hymnology" *JQR* (ns) 44 (1953-1954) 123-161

Carl Schmidt *Gespräche Jesu mit seinen Jüngern nach der Auferstehung* (Leipzig: TU 43, 1919)

R. Schnackenburg *The Gospel according to St. John* III (ETr) (London: Burnes and Oates, 1982)

Udo Schnelle *Antidocetic Christology in the Gospel of John* (ETr) (Minneapolis: Fortress, 1992)

S. Schulz *Komposition und Herkunft der Johanneischen Reden* (Stuttgart: Kohlhammer, 1960)

Heinz Schürmann "Die Anfänge Christlicher Osterfeier" *ThQ* 131 (1951) 414-425

A.R. Seager "The Building History of the Sardis Synagogue" *AJA* 76 (1972) 425-435

J.B. Segal *The Hebrew Passover* (London: OUP, 1963)

E. Selwyn *The First Epistle of Peter* (London: Macmillan, 1946)

Avigdor Shivan "Sermons, Targums and the Reading from Scriptures in the Ancient Synagogue" *The Synagogue in Late Antiquity* ed. Lee I. Levine (Philadelphia: ASOR, 1987) 97-110

R.J.H. Shutt *Studies in Josephus* (London: SPCK, 1961)

J. Smit Sibinga "Melito of Sardis: The Artist and his Text" *VigChr* 24 (1970) 81-104

Stephen Smalley *John: Evangelist and Theologian* (Exeter: Paternoster, 1978)

B.D. Spinks *Addai and Mari- the Anaphora: a Text for Students* (Bramcote: Grove, 1980)

W.R. Stegner *Narrative Theology in Early Jewish Christianity* (Louisville: Westminster John Knox, 1989)

S. Stein "The Influence of Symposia Literature on the Literary Form of the Pesah Haggadah" *JJS* 8 (1957) 13-44

A. Stewart-Sykes "Melito's Anti-Judaism" *JECS* 5 (1997) 271-283

A. Stewart-Sykes "The Asian Origin of *Epistula Apostolorum* and of the new prophecy" *VigChr* 51 (1997) 416-438

Stanley K. Stowers *The Diatribe and Paul's Letter to the Romans* (Atlanta: SBL Dissertation series 57, 1981)

Kenneth A. Strand "John as Quartodeciman: a Re-appraisal" *JBL* 84 (1965) 251-258

August Strobel "Die Passa-Erwartung als Urchristliches Problem in *Lc* 17:20f" *ZNW* 49 (1958) 157-196

A. Strobel "Die Bösen Buben der Syrischen Ostervigil" *ZKG* 7 (1958) 113-114

August Strobel *Ursprung und Geschichte des frühchristlichen Osterkalendars* (Berlin: TU 121, 1977)

J. Suggit "*John* 17:17: ὁ λόγος σος ἀλήθεια ἐστιν" *JTS* (ns) 35 (1984) 104-117

Thomas J. Talley *The Origins of the Liturgical Year* (New York: Pueblo, 1986)

J. Tate "The Beginnings of Greek Allegory" *CR* 41 (1927) 214-215

J. Tate "Plato and Allegorical Interpretation" *CQ* 23 (1929) 142-154; 24 (1930) 1-10

M. Testuz *Papyrus Bodmer XIII, Méliton de Sardes Homélie sur la Pâque* (Geneva: Bodmer, 1960)

H. St.J. Thackeray *Josephus Jewish Antiquities* (London: Heinemann, 1930)

J.C. Thomas *Footwashing in John 13 and the Johannine Community* (Sheffield: JSNT Supp 61, 1991)

Max Thurian *The Eucharistic Memorial: Part One, the Old Testament* (ETr) (London: Lutterworth, 1960)

H. Thyen *Der Stil der Jüdisch-Hellenistischen Homilie* (Göttingen: FRLANT 65 (NF47), 1955)

Paul Trebilco *Jewish Communities in Asia Minor* (Cambridge: SNTSMS 69, 1991)

Christine Trevett "The Other Letters to the Churches of Asia: *Apocalypse* and Ignatius of Antioch" *JSNT* 37 (1988) 117-135

Étienne Trocmé *The Passion as Liturgy* (ETr) (London: SCM, 1983)

B.G. Tsakonas "The Usage of the Scriptures in the Homily of Melito of Sardis On the Passion" *Theologia* 38 (1967) 609-620

E.G. Turner *Greek Manuscripts of the Ancient World*[2] (London: Institute of Classical Studies, 1987)

W.C. van Unnik "A Note on the Dance of Jesus in the *Acts of John*" *VigChr* 18 (1964) 1-5

L. Vaganay *L'Évangile de Pierre* (Paris: Gabalda, 1930)

B.J. van der Veken "De Primordiis Liturgiae Paschalis" *Sacris Eruditi* 13 (1962) 461-501

B.J. van der Veken "De Sensu Paschatis in Saeculo Secundo et Epistula Apostolorum" *Sacris Eruditi* 14 (1963) 5-33

Geza Vermes *Scripture and Tradition in Judaism*[2] (Leiden: Brill, 1970)

R. Vignolo "Storia della salvezza nel *Peri Pascha* di Melitoni di Sardi" *La Scuola Cattolica* 99 (1971) 3-26

Guiseppe Visonà *Pseudo Ippolyto: In Sanctum Pascha. Studio Edizione Commento* (Milan: Studia Patristica Mediolanensia 15, 1988)

Guiseppe Visonà "Pasqua Quartodecimana e Cronologia Evangelica della Passione" *EL* 102 (1988) 259-315

Geoffrey Wainwright "The Baptismal Eucharist before Nicaea" *StLiturg* 4 (1965) 9-36

H. Wegman "Une Anaphore incomplete?" R. van der Brock, M. Vermaseren Ed. *Studies in Gnostic and Hellenistic Religions* (Leiden: Brill, 1981) 432-450

E.J. Wellesz "Melito's Homily on the Passion: an Investigation into the Sources of Byzantine Hymnography" *JTS* 44 (1943) 41-52

Paul Wendland *Die Hellenistisch-Romanische Kultur* (Tübingen: Mohr, 1912)

E. Werner "Melito of Sardes, First Poet of Deicide" *HUCA* 37 (1966) 191-210

E. Westermaier art. "Sergius Paullus" (Berlin: PW Supp VI, 1935)

Richard C. White *Melito of Sardis Sermon on the Passover* (Lexington: Lexington Theological Seminary Library, 1976)

A. Wifstrand "The Homily of Melito on the Passion" *VigChr* 2 (1948) 201-223

Robert L. Wilken "Melito, the Jewish Community at Sardis and the Sacrifice of Isaac" *ThS* 37 (1976) 53-69

L.P. Wilkinson *Golden Latin Artistry* (Cambridge: CUP, 1963)

Valentine Wood (Review) *Blackfriars* 22 (1941) 619-62

Addison G. Wright "The Literary Genre Midrash" *CBQ* 28 (1966) 105-38, 417-457

W.C. Wright *Philostratus and Eunapius: Lives of the Sophists* (London: Heinemann, 1921)

W. Wuellner "Greek Rhetoric and Pauline Argumentation" W.R. Schoedel and R.L. Wilken *Early Christian Literature and the Classical Intellectual Tradition* (Paris: Beauchesne, 1979) 177-188

J. Yahalom "The Piyyut as Poetry" *The Ancient Synagogue* ed. Lee I. Levine (Philadelphia: ASOR, 1987) 111-126

Frances M. Young *Sacrificial Ideas in Greek Christian Writers from the New Testament to John Chrysostom* (Cambridge MA: Philadelphia Patristic Foundation, 1979)

Solomon Zeitlin "The Beginning of the Jewish Day during the Second Commonwealth" *JQR* (ns) 36 (1945-1946) 403-414

Solomon Zeitlin "The Liturgy of the First Night of Passover" *JQR* (ns) 38 (1947-1948) 431-460

Solomon Zeitlin "Midrash: a Historical Study" *JQR* (ns) 44 (1953-1954) 21-36

Solomon Zeitlin "The Hallel" *JQR* (ns) 53 (1962-1963) 22-29

N. Zernov "Eusebius and the paschal controversy at the end of the second century" *CQR* 116 (1933) 24-41

G. Ziener "Johannesevangelium und Urchristliche Passafeier" *BZ* 2 (1958) 263-274

G. Zuntz "On the Opening Sentence of Melito's Paschal Homily" *HThR* 36 (1943) 299-315

G. Zuntz "Melito—Syriac?" *VigChr* 6 (1952) 193-201

INDICES

GENERAL INDEX

INDEX OF REFERENCES

A *Biblical, Christian and Jewish Authors*

B *Index of Classical Authors*

Hermogenes			Pliny		
Progymnasmata	2	74	*Naturalis Historia*		
	5	75		2.79.188	167
Longinus			Plutarch		
De Sub	19.22	82	*De Alexandri Magni Fortuna*		
				326E	80
Maximus of Tyre				327A	80
Dialexis	5	86		327C	80
				328C	80
Philostratus					
Vitae Sophistorum	I.20 413	132	Quintilian		
	I.21.515	130	*Institutio Oratorica*		
	I.25.533	129		2.4.2	90
	II.3.567	84		2.4.18	74
	II.4.586	130		3.7.4	130
	II.5.570	84		3.7.8	136
	II.20.600	130		4.2.50	122
	II.26.613	130		4.3.1	114
	II.27.620	132			
			Tacitus		
Plato			*Annales*	4.55	11
Cratylus	427A	83			

C *Index of Modern Authors*

SUPPLEMENTS TO VIGILIAE CHRISTIANAE

1. TERTULLIANUS. *De idololatria.* Critical Text, Translation and Com-mentary by J.H. WASZINK and J.C.M. VAN WINDEN. Partly based on a Manuscript left behind by P.G. VAN DER NAT. 1987. ISBN 90 04 08105 4
2. SPRINGER, C.P.E. *The Gospel as Epic in Late Antiquity.* The *Paschale Carmen* of Sedulius. 1988. ISBN 90 04 08691 9
3. HOEK, A. VAN DEN. *Clement of Alexandria and His Use of Philo in the* Stromateis. An Early Christian Reshaping of a Jewish Model. 1988. ISBN 90 04 08756 7
4. NEYMEYR, U. *Die christlichen Lehrer im zweiten Jahrhundert.* Ihre Lehrtätigkeit, ihr Selbstverständnis und ihre Geschichte. 1989. ISBN 90 04 08773 7
5. HELLEMO, G. *Adventus Domini.* Eschatological Thought in 4th-century Apses and Catecheses. 1989. ISBN 90 04 08836 9
6. RUFIN VON AQUILEIA. *De ieiunio* I, II. Zwei Predigten über das Fasten nach Basileios von Kaisareia. Ausgabe mit Einleitung, Übersetzung und Anmerkungen von H. MARTI. 1989. ISBN 90 04 08897 0
7. ROUWHORST, G.A.M. *Les hymnes pascales d'Éphrem de Nisibe.* Analyse théologique et recherche sur l'évolution de la fête pascale chrétienne à Nisibe et à Édesse et dans quelques Églises voisines au quatrième siècle. 2 vols: I. Étude; II. Textes. 1989. ISBN 90 04 08839 3
8. RADICE, R. and D.T. RUNIA. *Philo of Alexandria.* An Annotated Bibliog-raphy 1937–1986. In Collaboration with R.A. BITTER, N.G. COHEN, M. MACH, A.P. RUNIA, D. SATRAN and D.R. SCHWARTZ. 1988. repr. 1992. ISBN 90 04 08986 1
9. GORDON, B. *The Economic Problem in Biblical and Patristic Thought.* 1989. ISBN 90 04 09048 7
10. PROSPER OF AQUITAINE. *De Providentia Dei.* Text, Translation and Com-mentary by M. MARCOVICH. 1989. ISBN 90 04 09090 8
11. JEFFORD, C.N. *The Sayings of Jesus in the Teaching of the Twelve Apostles.* 1989. ISBN 90 04 09127 0
12. DROBNER, H.R. and KLOCK, CH. *Studien zu Gregor von Nyssa und der christ-lichen Spätantike.* 1990. ISBN 90 04 09222 6
13. NORRIS, F.W. *Faith Gives Fullness to Reasoning.* The Five Theological Orations of Gregory Nazianzen. Introduction and Commentary by F.W. NORRIS and Translation by LIONEL WICKHAM and FREDERICK WILLIAMS. 1990. ISBN 90 04 09253 6
14. OORT, J. VAN. *Jerusalem and Babylon.* A Study into Augustine's *City of God* and the Sources of his Doctrine of the Two Cities. 1991. ISBN 90 04 09323 0
15. LARDET, P. *L'Apologie de Jérôme contre Rufin.* Un Commentaire. 1993. ISBN 90 04 09457 1
16. RISCH, F.X. *Pseudo-Basilius: Adversus Eunomium IV-V.* Einleitung, Übersetzung und Kommentar. 1992. ISBN 90 04 09558 6

17. KLIJN, A.F.J. *Jewish-Christian Gospel Tradition*. 1992. ISBN 90 04 09453 9
18. ELANSKAYA, A.I. *The Literary Coptic Manuscri pts in the A.S. Pushkin State Fine Arts Museum in Moscow*. ISBN 90 04 09528 4
19. WICKHAM, L.R. and BAMMEL, C.P. (eds.). *Christian Faith and Greek Philosophy in Late Antiquity*. Essays in Tribute to George Christopher Stead. 1993. ISBN 90 04 09605 1
20. ASTERIUS VON KAPPADOKIEN. *Die theologischen Fragmente*. Einleitung, kritischer Text, Übersetzung und Kommentar von MARKUS VINZENT. 1993. ISBN 90 04 09841 0
21. HENNINGS, R. *Der Briefwechsel zwischen Augustinus und Hieronymus und ihr Streit um den Kanon des Alten Testaments und die Auslegung von Gal. 2,11-14*. 1994. ISBN 90 04 09840 2
22. BOEFT, J. DEN & HILHORST, A. (eds.). *Early Christian Poetry*. A Collection of Essays. 1993. ISBN 90 04 09939 5
23. McGUCKIN, J.A. *St. Cyril of Alexandria: The Christological Controversy*. Its History, Theology, and Texts. 1994. ISBN 90 04 09990 5
24. REYNOLDS, Ph.L. *Marriage in the Western Church*. The Christianization of Marriage during the Patristic and Early Medieval Periods. 1994. ISBN 90 04 10022 9
25. PETERSEN, W.L. *Tatian's Diatessaron*. Its Creation, Dissemination, Significance, and History in Scholarship. 1994. ISBN 90 04 09469 5
26. GRÜNBECK, E. *Christologische Schriftargumentation und Bildersprache*. Zum Konflikt zwischen Metapherninterpretation und dogmatischen Schriftbeweis-traditionen in der patristischen Auslegung des 44. (45.) Psalms. 1994. ISBN 90 04 10021 0
27. HAYKIN, M.A.G. *The Spirit of God*. The Exegesis of 1 and 2 Corinthians in the Pneumatomachian Controversy of the Fourth Century. 1994. ISBN 90 04 09947 6
28. BENJAMINS, H.S. *Eingeordnete Freiheit*. Freiheit und Vorsehung bei Origenes. 1994. ISBN 90 04 10117 9
29. SMULDERS s.J., P. (tr. & comm.). *Hilary of Poitiers' Preface to his* Opus historicum. 1995. ISBN 90 04 10191 8
30. KEES, R.J. *Die Lehre von der* Oikonomia Gottes in der Oratio catechetica *Gregors von Nyssa*. 1995. ISBN 90 04 10200 0
31. BRENT, A. *Hippolytus and the Roman Church in the Third Century*. Communities in Tension before the Emergence of a Monarch-Bishop. 1995. ISBN 90 04 10245 0
32. RUNIA, D.T. *Philo and the Church Fathers*. A Collection of Papers. 1995. ISBN 90 04 10355 4
33. DE CONICK, A.D. *Seek to See Him*. Ascent and Vision Mysticism in the Gospel of Thomas. 1996. ISBN 90 04 10401 1
34. CLEMENS ALEXANDRINUS. *Protrepticus*. Edidit M. MARCOVICH. 1995. ISBN 90 04 10449 6
35. BÖHM, T. *Theoria – Unendlichkeit – Aufstieg*. Philosophische Implikationen zu *De vita Moysis* von Gregor von Nyssa. 1996. ISBN 90 04 10560 3
36. VINZENT, M. *Pseudo-Athanasius, Contra Arianos IV*. Eine Schrift gegen

Asterius von Kappadokien, Eusebius von Cäsarea, Markell von Ankyra und Photin von Sirmium. 1996. ISBN 90 04 10686 3

37. KNIPP, P.D.E. *'Christus Medicus' in der frühchristlichen Sarkophagskulptur*. Ikonographische Studien zur Sepulkralkunst des späten vierten Jahrhunderts. *In Preparation.*

38. LÖSSL, J. *Intellectus gratiae*. Die erkenntnistheoretische und hermeneutische Dimension der Gnadenlehre Augustins von Hippo. 1997. ISBN 90 04 10849 1

39. MARKELL VON ANKYRA, *Die Fragmente. Der Brief an Julius von Rom.* Herausgegeben, eingeleitet und übersetzt von Markus Vinzent. 1997. ISBN 90 04 10907 2

40. MERKT, A. *Maximus I. von Turin*. Die Verkündigung eines Bischofs der frühen Reichskirche im zeitgeschichtlichen, gesellschaftlichen und liturgischen Kontext. 1997. ISBN 90 04 10864 5

41. WINDEN, J.C.M. VAN. *Archè*. A Collection of Patristic Studies by J.C.M. van Winden. Edited by J. den Boeft and D.T. Runia. 1997. ISBN 90 04 10834 3

42. STEWART-SYKES, A. *The Lamb's High Feast*. Melito, *Peri Pascha* and the Quartodeciman Paschal Liturgy at Sardis. 1998. ISBN 90 04 11236 7